Glenda Jackson

Glenda Jackson

THE
BIOGRAPHY

CHRIS BRYANT

HarperCollins*Publishers*

HarperCollins*Publishers*
77–85 Fulham Palace Road,
Hammersmith, London w6 8jb

Published by HarperCollins*Publishers* 1999
1 3 5 7 9 8 6 4 2

A catalogue record for this book
is available from the British Library

ISBN 0 00 255911 0

Set in Postscript Linotype Jansen by Rowland Phototypesetting Ltd,
Bury St Edmunds, Suffolk

Printed and bound in Great Britain by
Clays Ltd, St Ives plc

To Alex Craig

Acknowledgements

I am immensely grateful to all those people who responded to my request for help with writing this biography. In particular Glenda herself, Lynne Jackson and Daniel Hodges, Roy Hodges, Andy Phillips and Genista MacIntosh; and everyone who replied to my enquiries, namely Alec McCowen, Anna Welsh, Audrey Jowett, Barry Stanton, Bill Reimbold, Brenda Vaccaro, Brian Spink, Bridget Armstrong, Charles Kay, Charles Marowitz, Chris Smith, Clifford Rose, Clifford Williams, Daniel Jackson, David Dodd, Deborah Findlay, Diana Rigg, Dirk Bogarde, Donald Burton, Dorothy Furniss, Eleanor Bron, Elizabeth Spriggs, Eric Wilson, Frank Windsor, Fred Dowie, George Segal, Georgina Hale, Harriet Walter, Henry Woolf, Hugh Manning, Ian Holm, Ian McKellen, Ian Richardson, Izabella Telezsynska, Jack Shepherd, James Cellan Jones, James Hazeldine, Janet Suzman, Jean Hibbert, Jennie Linden, Joan Matthews (nee Hadwin), John Bowe, John Castle, John Nettleton, John Schlesinger, John Woodvine, Jonathan Burn, Jonathan Pryce, Josie Kidd, Joyce Marlow, Julian Barnes, Juliet Stevenson, Ken Colley, Marcia Ashton, Margery Stone, Mary Allen, Michael Apted, Michael Bryant, Michael Elwyn, Michael Gough, Michael Pennington, Michele Dotrice, Miriam Karlin, Neil Kinnock, Nick Prior, Nigel Hawthorne, Pat Nicholson, Patrick Stewart, Peter Brook, Peter Eyre, Sir Peter Hall, Philip Prowse, Prunella Scales, Richard Fleischer, Richard Griffiths, Robert Aldous, Robert Altman, Roy Dotrice, Sally Dobson, Silvio Narizzano, Stanley Lebor, Sylvia Kay, Tim Walker, Timothy West, Vivian James and Walter Matthau. And the many others who preferred not to be named.

Contents

LIST OF ILLUSTRATIONS viii

INTRODUCTION ix

1 Early Years 1

2 Work, Work, Work 24

3 Brook, Marowitz and Shakespeare 46

4 Making a Name 75

5 Motherhood and Movies 88

6 A Touch of Class 107

7 A Passionate Affair 127

8 Back to the Stage 147

9 Thatcherism and Theatre 163

10 The Celebrity Candidate 188

11 A New Life 213

12 Power at Last 225

Chronology 255
Select Bibliography 269
Notes 271
Index 277

Illustrations

Between pages 116 and 117

Glenda with a school friend
Glenda at ballet school
Glenda in her first stage appearance
An early publicity still of Glenda
Glenda and Roy on their wedding day
Glenda in *Marat/Sade*, © Morris Newcombe
Glenda in New York
Glenda and Jennie Linden, *Women in Love*, © Brandywine Productions/ The Ronald Grant Archive
Baby Daniel with his parents
Glenda in *The Music Lovers*, © United Artists/The Ronald Grant Archive
Glenda in *Sunday Bloody Sunday*, © Vic Productions/The Ronald Grant Archive
The Hodges family
Glenda in *Mary, Queen of Scots*, © United Artists/The Ronald Grant Archive
Glenda with Morecambe and Wise, © BBC Worldwide

Between pages 164 and 165

Glenda with Oscar, © Mander & Mitchenson
Glenda and George Segal, *A Touch of Class*, © Avco Embassy, courtesy of Kobal
Glenda and the cast of *Hedda*
Glenda, Geraldine Page and Anne Jackson, *Nasty Habits*, © Bowden Productions/The Ronald Grant Archive
Glenda and members of Equity with the Czech Foreign Minister, 1976, © Mander & Michenson
Glenda and Walter Matthau, © Universal Pictures/The Ronald Grant Archive
Glenda and Clifford Williams
Glenda and Alan Howard, *Antony and Cleopatra*, © Morris Newcombe
Glenda Jackson and Alan Bates, *Return of the Soldier*, © 20th Century Fox Film Corporation/The Ronald Grant Archive
Glenda in *Mother Courage*, © John Barr
Labour Party leaflet, © The Labour Party
Glenda and Glenys Kinnock, © Frank Martin/*Guardian*
Glenda in Benidorm, © PA News Photolibrary
Hampstead general election candidates, © Nigel Sutton
Glenda launching a charity cycle ride, © PA News Photolibrary
Glenda on Hampstead Heath, © Nigel Turner (Insight)

Introduction

Glenda Jackson has triumphed twice at St Pancras Town Hall, though few people noticed the first occasion, back in November 1956.

Then Glenda was a plump, raw-edged twenty-year-old drama student from the Wirral, just finishing her final year at the Royal Academy of Dramatic Art. As part of a special George Bernard Shaw anniversary celebration the cavernous Edwardian hall had been turned into a theatre for a week's performances of Shaw's comedy of class, *Pygmalion*. Glenda was playing Eliza Doolittle, the cockney florist who is re-created as a polite lady of society by Professor Higgins. It was an ideal part for Glenda, imbued with irony. She had undergone a similar transformation herself at RADA, losing her Northern vowels, learning how to fold her legs neatly beneath her, acquiring at least the semblance of elegance and respectability that the polite theatre of the fifties required. She sparkled with a homely, down-to-earth wit. Her cut-glass rendition of the play's most famous, truculent, line, 'Not bloody likely,' brought the house down, and earned her a standing ovation. Before the night was out Glenda had gained that most precious of theatrical commodities, an agent.

Two Oscars, two Emmies, five *Morecambe and Wise Shows*, one husband, one lover, one son and thirty-six years later Glenda returned to St Pancras. Now she was no longer an actress, but a candidate in the 1992 general election, fighting the marginal constituency of Hampstead and Highgate for the Labour Party. The television news crews, banished to a balcony above the hall, were anticipating a result at one o'clock in the morning, and since all the recent opinion polls indicated victory for Neil Kinnock, they anticipated a triumph for Glenda as well. But as the night wore on the truth began to trickle through. First the BBC exit poll predicted that John Major's Conservatives would form the largest party in the House of Commons. Then real constituency results pointed to a growing Tory majority, and a fourth general election win for them in a row.

Meanwhile Camden Council sorted, checked and counted the Hampstead and Highgate ballot papers at a painfully slow pace. The mood in the hall changed. Tory activists grew wild with excitement as every new, unexpected victory was announced. Labour hearts sank. All did not augur well for Glenda, who needed a bigger swing to Labour than other candidates in marginal constituencies were achieving, if she was to take the long-held Tory seat. As the possibility of a national Labour victory receded, Glenda's campaign team hoped ever more fervently that her result would buck the trend.

Finally, at three o'clock, fully two hours late, the returning officer assembled the candidates and their electoral agents on the stage; the news cameras focused on him as he started to read out the results. Against the odds, and with a swing to Labour that was double the national trend, Glenda Jackson had wrested Hampstead and Highgate from the Conservatives and secured a majority of 1,440 votes.

Glenda's 1992 triumph came, as that of thirty-six years earlier, not at the culmination, but at the start, of a new career. Since then there have been further political successes: another general election; a swift promotion to the Opposition Front Bench; prominent campaigns in the United States and in Benidorm; an appointment as a minister in Labour's first Government for eighteen years. There has been much talk of Glenda as a possible first ever directly elected Mayor for London, and she has proved herself a redoubtable campaigner and an astute politician. She confuses her Conservative opponents, who cannot comprehend why she should choose to renounce a successful film and theatre career in order to answer parliamentary questions on shipping to a virtually empty House of Commons. She confounds those who expect her to be no more than a Labour luvvie, by mastering policy detail and by talking about integrated transport policies. She is passionate and articulate about the ideals of socialism – a word she uses regularly – and yet she is one of the most pragmatic of Blair's ministers, decried by Ken Livingstone as 'the most right-wing minister the Labour Party has ever produced'.

*   *   *

Introduction

Above all she radiates personal candour and integrity, yet, despite two very public careers, she remains an enigmatic and deeply private person. Any biography of such a person, even one in a public role, will always feel like an intrusion. Yet the *person* of Glenda Jackson is infinitely more intriguing even than the *figure* of the double Oscar-winning actress turned Parliamentary-under-Secretary for Transport.

CHAPTER ONE

―――――― ✸ ――――――

Early Years

JOAN JACKSON gave birth to her first child, a daughter, in an upper room in number 151, the seventh house from last on Market Street in Birkenhead, on Saturday 9 May 1936.

It was not a glamorous location. The rooms that Joan and her husband Micky shared with her parents, May and James Pearce, were cramped and spartan. Nearby lay the icy waters of the Mersey and the cranes, capstans and derricks of the main local employer, the shipbuilder Cammel Lairds. And thirties Birkenhead was grimy, noisy and poor, her people well acquainted with the dole queue.

So it was only natural that in looking for a name for her new-born daughter, Joan turned to a more exciting world, one that seemed to have survived the Depression years unscathed. In search of a sprinkling of glamour many thousands of English mothers had named their babies after the stars of the silver screen – Bette Davis, Joan Crawford, Anna Neagle, Barbara Stanwyck, Anne Dvorak, Katharine Hepburn, even Gracie Fields.

Joan's choice of name (and it *was* Joan's choice rather than Micky's) was characteristically out of the ordinary. She was called Glenda after the inimitably ebullient, wisecracking American movie star Glenda Farrell, who had made forty-two movies since 1930, and had played a hard-bitten, witty blonde in every one. May 1936 saw Miss Farrell at the height of her popularity, with recent hits like *The Mystery of the Wax Museum*, *In Caliente*, *Go Into Your Dance*, *Gold Diggers of 1935* (whence the song 'Lullaby on Broadway') and *We're in the Money* to her credit.

For a second name Joan turned to her mother Mabel, who was known to all the world as May. May came from Wales, and she

I

and her husband James, originally a stable-boy from Shropshire, now a labourer, had settled in Birkenhead in search of work. Their rooms in Market Street were more than crowded with the presence of the young Jacksons and their baby. So although Glenda May was born into this confined Birkenhead environment, where occasional labour was the norm, she was to grow up in a very different, although equally poor, world. Within a few months of her birth the young Jackson family moved some nine miles from the grime of Birkenhead, taking their 'oh so solemn-looking baby' to the salubrious coastal village of Hoylake.

The Hoylake they arrived in was still, just, a maritime village. It had at one time derived its livelihood – and its name – from the sea, being the village, or conglomeration of villages, that lay closest to the 'Hoyle-lake', the marine lake in the Dee Estuary that separated the Hyle ('Hoyle' or 'Hill') Sand Banks from the land. There had been work in Hoylake for mariners of every denomination: smack fishermen; pilots who steered ships through the sand banks of Liverpool Bay; customs officers and lighthouse keepers; even shell gatherers. But by the twenties the Hoyle-lake was beginning to silt up, making it impassable except at high tide, the pilot trade had all but disappeared, and the Hoylake fishing fleet was slowly diminishing, its fishermen removing either to Fleetwood or Hull.

Hoylake was also a refined holiday spot with a race course, an exceptional golf course (the Royal Liverpool), several grandiose hotels, an elegant promenade and a splendiferous Town Hall – all the middle classes of Liverpool could desire. In 1899 an official guide to Hoylake bragged:

> the place is entirely free from the abominable nuisance of swing-boats, merry-go-rounds, and such like, with their blatant organs. Such a thing as an epidemic of disease has never been known. The water supply is both plentiful and pure; and lastly, the objectionable and rowdy element of visitors, who inflict their company on most other watering places, is unknown.[1]

The twentieth century saw Hoylake continue to develop as a resort: ornamental gardens were opened in 1909; a bandstand was built in 1912 and an open-air swimming pool the following year.

The Depression had reduced the gentility of the Wirral coast, but Hoylake was still wealthy enough to rebuild the original baths in 1931, its shops still prospered, and large new villas were still being built along the main road into West Kirby. Hoylake continued to think of itself as a cut above the rest. Even in 1955 a guidebook declared:

> local councillors in their wisdom have managed to avoid the vulgarity so often denoted by the word 'popular'. Here you will find no Fun Fair or Pleasure Beach; no souvenir kiosks or questionable postcards; no bathing belles competing for some title and a substantial money prize; no fake auctions to trap the unwary; no touting; no blaring loud-speakers.[2]

So Hoylake turned its back on its maritime past. The narrow streets of its old centre, with their two-up, two-down fishermen's cottages, were no longer, by the mid-thirties, the heart of the village. It was to this traditional fishermen's enclave within Hoylake that the young Jackson family moved from Birkenhead. For Micky this was returning home: the Jacksons were a long-established Hoylake fishing family. Joan and Micky did not stay long in their first Hoylake house, as the rent was too expensive, but when they moved into a smaller two-up, two-down at 21 Lake Place – one of the oldest cottages in Hoylake – they had a large number of close relatives living no more than a couple of hundred yards away. Micky's father, William Jackson, and his second wife Jane (known to her stepfamily as 'Aunt Pop'), lived round the corner at 12 Evans Road, and in number 4 was Micky's sister Esther and her husband, George Garside. William Jackson was one of the local characters and, in Glenda's words, 'Hoylake through and through'. An active fisherman still out on the smacks in his seventies, he wore his blue fisherman's gansey (jersey) every day of his life, and had served on the lifeboat since the 1890s. Several people thought his nickname, 'Father' Jackson, came from some High Church faith, but in fact he acquired this in 1920 when he took his eldest son, another William, out on the lifeboat with him. The first week the secretary of the lifeboat station noted down William Jackson Senior and William Jackson Junior on the time sheets, but the next time a new secretary resolved the duplication by referring to 'Father' Jackson and Bill Jackson. He became 'Father' alongside his lifeboat companions 'Turk' and 'Mackie' Armitage, 'Yonk', 'Long Ted' and 'Twigger' Beck, and 'Scroggie' and 'Little Un' Hughes.

The two Williams were not the only Jacksons to man the prestigious Hoylake lifeboat. Micky's grandfather had served as its coxswain and at various points in the twenties and thirties the boat's register records an Eric, an Edgar, a Tom (Micky's brother), an Arthur and a Harry. So the Jacksons were an integral part of old Hoylake. As Glenda puts it: 'Everyone who lived in Hoylake seemed to be a relative in some way or another.'[3] The family was very tight-knit: apart from Esther and William, Micky's brother Billy lived in Hoylake; Jack was in nearby West Kirby; and the one brother to move away, Tom, had only escaped a few miles up the coast to Blackpool. Even Edith ('Queenie'), Micky's youngest sister, was an essential part of the Jackson clan, despite having been put out to adoption in Fleetwood when William's first wife died giving birth to her.

Glenda's family might have been part of the fishing aristocracy of Hoylake but they were still extremely poor. Her paternal grandparents had survived on a fisherman's minimal earnings, but the silting of the estuary meant that for Micky and his brothers the life of the open sea was not an option. When Micky first appears in the council register, under his formal name of Harry, he is titled a seaman, but within a couple of years he reappears as a labourer. Micky and his brother Jack had both become jobbing builders. Sometimes this meant Micky would lay bricks, but more often he worked as a hod-carrier, heaving bricks up ladders to the more skilled and better-paid bricklayers. Wages for this type of work were always paltry and 21 Lake Place was all the Jacksons could afford. Like all its neighbours it was a simple two-up, two-down, with the toilet in the garden. The only running water came from a cold tap in the kitchen, and a bath meant filling a tin tub with water heated on the fire. It was so cramped that tidiness was paramount – tea had to be cleared, washed and dried before anyone could sit back and enjoy a newspaper or a book, and the bedrooms scarcely accommodated enough mattresses, let alone extensive cupboards. A large extended family meant that there were plenty of hand-me-downs, and Aunt Esther, who had no children of her own, was particularly generous, but thrift was the vital household virtue.

By all accounts Micky, who was twenty-nine when Glenda was born, was a jovial soul who loved a smoke and a drink. One colleague, Eric Wilson, who worked with him in the sixties, recalls that he would whistle and sing throughout the day (mostly Engelbert Humperdinck), only stopping during lunch, when he would sit down to study the racing form in meticulous detail before placing his bet for the day. Micky had also been a caddie at the grand Royal Liverpool Golf Course as a youth, and was a regular player at the municipal golf course, but his greatest claim to fame lay in his regular performances at the local pub, the Lake, where he would accompany himself on the ukulele, singing favourites like 'Who's Sorry Now?' Glenda's younger sister Lynne remembers that 'He used to love to sing and play. Well, when I say play, it was more of a sort of strum. He clearly thought he was George Formby, but I don't think anyone else did. He certainly had a great sense of humour, though.' Indeed, the only occasion on which either Glenda or Lynne can recall him losing his temper was when the youngest of his daughters, Elizabeth, dressed the cat up in doll's clothes and nearly strangled the poor animal. When the cat started to scratch Elizabeth during her attempts to remove the offending clothes Lynne was summoned to calm the cat, but when Micky returned home both Lynne and Elizabeth got it in the neck. Apart from this incident Glenda's memory of Micky is that 'he never once raised his hand or even his voice'.

Joan, by contrast, was a determined, even stubborn, woman, whose word was law at home, but who was rarely forthcoming outside the family circle. Maintaining a family on the tiny income of an occasional labourer was no mean task, so throughout her married life, and with only the briefest of respites for childbirth, Joan worked to supplement the meagre household finances. She charred for half a crown at some of the grander villas in what Glenda called the 'nob streets',[4] worked on the cash desk in the local supermarket, and pulled pints at the Blue Anchor. But her most onerous task was keeping the tiny worker's cottage in Lake Place, and facing, in Glenda's words, the very real worry of quite simply 'balancing the budget'.[5] In this the Jacksons were not unusual in Hoylake. Most families lived on various forms of credit, either paying the 'tallyman' a shilling a week so as to buy major items like clothes and furniture with 'provident cheques' once a year or running up an account at one of the local shops. Pat Nicholson, who ran a local corner shop from 1942, remembers that nearly all her customers would buy everything on credit throughout the week, and then pay off as much as possible at the end of the week. Only occasionally was there 'any daylight from living on tick'. The Second World War brought a new round of privations, but even after its end people led a simple hand-to-mouth existence. Indeed, when an Electrolux representative visited Pat's shop in 1946, trying to persuade her to stock his vacuum cleaners, and offering to show her how well they would clean her carpets, she laughed him out of the shop with 'What carpets, man?'

Glenda was three, and still the only child, when Hitler invaded Poland and the Second World War was declared. Within months Micky was called up to serve on the mine-sweepers, and for the next six years Glenda saw her father only on rare occasions. The war was to take her Uncle Billy's life when his gun exploded in his hands. Glenda's world changed dramatically – as for every child of her generation. Before the war there were plenty of men in her life, not just Micky but many male relatives. The moment war was declared the number of men in her life dwindled to almost nil, and the women took over. Joan, Aunt Pop, Aunt Esther, her maternal grandmother May and Aunt Doll in Birkenhead, provided all the authority and support she needed, and Glenda grew used to a world run by women. Glenda told me, 'I am very grateful for many things, but especially for the way the women in my family just got on with it. Life dealt the women in my family a rather varied deck, but they showed no small grace in dealing with whatever life threw at them. I cannot overstate how important that was to me.' This was not unusual in wartime Britain, of course, but, exceptionally, the women in Glenda's family continued to rule the roost when their men returned. One school friend of Glenda's later said: 'It was an amazingly matriarchal family, and I'm sure that's why Glenda grew up so extremely self-confident as a woman.' Both Glenda and Lynne are clear on one point: Joan was in charge. Glenda states that: 'My mother was definitely the dominant figure in the household, although Dad would be offered up as the ultimate arbiter.' So Glenda grew accustomed, thanks to the war, to a world in which women could not only survive without men, but expected to take the decisions. They might cook, wash and iron for their men, but in the end they were in charge.

The war brought other experiences. Although, along with most of the Wirral, Hoylake remained largely unscathed by the Luftwaffe, Liverpool and Birkenhead suffered sustained assaults, and the effect of war was felt universally. The Wirral was considered to be a possible invasion site, so tank-landing traps were placed along the Dee, and Hilbre Island was declared out of bounds. Rationing meant that every household had to register with a butcher and a grocer, so a yet more regulated society became the accepted norm. Treats acquired a special value – 'We used to eat candle-wax as an alternative to chewing gum,' Glenda remembers. 'The big treat was a pennyworth of peanut butter. If you paid me a million pounds today I would not eat peanut butter.'[6] Self-help and efficiency became even more important ethics than ever, and waste was anathema. Bins were placed on street corners for household waste, which was then taken to local farms as pig food, and the Jacksons even started to breed chickens in their diminutive back yard.

At the same time other major social readjustments were also occurring. During the early months of the phoney war in 1939 some large empty villas in West Kirby were taken over by 'volunteer ladies', who looked after Liverpool evacuees fleeing the expected bomb blasts. For many this brought its own shocks. Liverpool had suffered a prolonged bout of high unemployment, and many of the children who arrived in Meols, Hoylake and West Kirby were dressed in the only set of clothes they had. Some were undernourished, and many carried disease. Nearly all were poorly educated. For the polite world of the Wirral, which had voted Conservative since time immemorial and was to be the safe parliamentary seat of Selwyn Lloyd from 1945 to 1976, this was profoundly shocking, and it was a relief that, when the bombing of Liverpool's docks failed to materialise early on, many dockland mothers took their children back to the city. The clash of classes had a profound effect across the nation, and when Churchill and Attlee united to unseat Chamberlain on the day after Glenda's fourth birthday, a new era of social co-operation was ushered in. Unlike the First World War, in which the wealthy had barely suffered any material privations, the politicians combined to preach that this war would be won only if all shared equally in the 'blood, sweat and tears', and in the essentials of life. Free nurseries for all were started to enable more women to take up war work, and although many schools had to go part-time for lack of teachers, a school meals service began to distribute hot food daily, in vast insulated containers.

For Glenda this new egalitarianism came at just the right time. It meant that from the age of four she was able to attend the nursery section of the infant school in Hoylake, and receive both hot meals for a shilling a day and a free third of a pint of milk (which invariably arrived frozen during the winter and would have to be warmed through by the school's open fire). Glenda now recalls 'the peculiar smell of milk and urine that permeated the place', and, when the Conservatives were in power, never failed to make the political point: 'it is a bitter irony that there were free nursery places then and we can't come up with them now'.[7] After a couple of years at nursery school, Glenda moved on to the Holy Trinity Church of England primary school in Market Street, whose buildings have since been converted, in 1998, into homes. This was a traditional school, which segregated boys and girls until 1948, but Glenda prospered in the long church-like building, under the elderly eye of John Molyneux, headteacher since the twenties. She even enjoyed herself, although she found the uniform uncomfortable, as the navy skirts and jumpers were both made of coarse wool, something she still cannot wear close to her skin without coming out in a rash.

The war had its excitements. On one occasion a German fighter was shot down over Hoylake, and the airman had to be given a police escort, less because of his unpopularity than because of the popularity of his parachute silk. When Glenda was staying with her grandmother in Birkenhead the house opposite was fire bombed, and Glenda saw the Air Raid Patrol wardens racing up and down ladders with buckets of water and stirrup pumps, and removing unexploded incendiary bombs. The Americans arrived with the establishment of an air station at West Kirby, and Glenda's mother forbade her, on pain of death, from asking those staying in Lake

Place for chewing gum. Air-raid shelters appeared in the street and regular air-raid warnings over Hoylake meant many hours spent in the dank darkness and plenty of sleepless nights. Bunks even appeared in the railway stations in Birkenhead, and Glenda remembers standing on Hoylake promenade during the 1941 bombing of Liverpool and watching the vast pall of smoke across the distant city. That April, thanks to a brief home leave for Micky, Glenda was joined by a sister, Gill.

When Germany finally surrendered unconditionally on 8 May 1945, the day before Glenda's ninth birthday, there was an ebullient VE Day celebration in Lake Place, with a lookalike Winston Churchill, but Micky did not come home until several months later. And when in the autumn of 1946 Joan was pregnant again with her third child, Lynne, medical complications (which led to Joan giving up smoking) meant that Glenda spent the Christmas term with her grandmother and Aunt Doll in Birkenhead. Glenda returned to Hoylake just as the fiercely cold winter of 1947 set in, bringing weeks of snow drifts, frozen pipes, a national fuel crisis and the near downfall of the Labour Government. This was the first time in nearly eight years that Glenda had shared a house for any length of time with her father, but because the Lake Place cottage was so small, every night she went to sleep with the Garsides in Evans Road. She had already been having her weekly bath in a tub in Aunt Esther's kitchen since the age of eight.

That summer Glenda sat her eleven-plus exam, which would determine whether she was to attend the local grammar school or the secondary modern. While in Birkenhead Glenda had attended Cathcart Street primary school, and just as at Market Street in Hoylake she had been diligent and successful. Indeed, she came first in the class, and was warmly commended in her school report for her 'all round ability and a pleasant disposition'. But sitting the eleven-plus exam was nerve-racking, especially for a girl of Glenda's background. Another girl who sat the exams that same year, Marjorie Stone, recalls that at the time passing the exam was held to be quite exceptional. 'I always thought it was only for really clever people, and never thought I would be going to the grammar school.' Certainly, going to the grammar school carried hefty expectations, which many poorer families could simply not afford to meet. The school uniform requirements were both extensive and expensive, even just after the war, and girls were expected to have their own gym outfits, hockey sticks and tennis racquets; all the paraphernalia, in short, of the middle classes. Thinly layered social elitism permeated the system.

Glenda, who had worked hard for the exams, recalls the results coming through with meticulous detail. For some reason all the other girls who had passed knew their results before they arrived at school, and friends, family and teachers spent much of the day congratulating them. Because Glenda had not been told that she had passed, everybody assumed she had failed, and she suffered pitying looks all day at school. When Glenda arrived home, however, the letter notifying her that she had passed had finally arrived. Suddenly everyone's attitude to her changed, even among their own family: 'I saw adults whom I had known all my life change their attitude to me twice in the space of a very small time. Contemptible.' It is no surprise that Glenda is scathing about the eleven-plus process and the harsh sentence that it proclaimed over so many children. It was an academic apartheid she detested, because it masqueraded its snobbishness as educational sagacity. Two of her close friends failed the exams that summer, as did two of her sisters later. Nevertheless Glenda not only passed, but, like Margery Stone, won a scholarship, which entitled her to attend the local girls' grammar school for free.

West Kirby Grammar School for Girls sits only a couple of miles from Hoylake in an eminently more refined, more sheltered corner of the Wirral, nestling among the Victorian and Edwardian villas of the lesser gentry. Founded in 1912, it had a Latin motto (*ad metam contendo*, or 'I press towards the mark') and a stirring school hymn ('Onward, Christian Soldiers'). During the war the school had alternated morning and afternoon lessons with Liverpool College for Girls, Grove Street, but by the time Glenda arrived in autumn 1947 the only mark of the inconvenience of these years was the staff tally. For West Kirby Grammar School was almost entirely staffed by spinster women of a certain age. Pre-eminent among these was the humourless Miss Norah Hudson, the headmistress, but there was not a single male teacher and scarcely a married one. There was Miss Griffiths, the art teacher, who 'jumped up and down a lot', the 'very posh' Miss Jennings, the draconian French teacher Miss Powell and the feeble Miss Pope, who taught Latin when the class allowed her. All were unmarried.

For the first two years Glenda behaved impeccably. She was a diligent student and a good member of Gonner house, named after the first chairman of the school governors, Sir Edward Gonner. She even played tennis and was in her house hockey and netball teams. But, as Glenda herself describes:

> When I hit puberty at thirteen the genes kicked in and I became seriously uninterested in scholastic subjects – with a few exceptions – and bored by school in general. I was fat and spotty and suffered terribly from teenage acne. I had no sense of myself as being physically attractive in any way at all – either then or now ... I became part of a group of girls who were less academic. There were cupboards in the classrooms and our great joke was to remove the shelves and sit inside. Then the door would be locked and the key hidden and during the course of the lesson rappings and noises would emanate mysteriously from the cupboard, which we all thought terribly funny.[8]

In fact these childish pranks were not quite so innocent. The teacher who most frequently bore the brunt of Glenda's humour was a Jewish woman called Dr Gasthalter, who had escaped from Austria at the start of the war. Viv James, Glenda's house captain in 1950, remembers that on more than one occasion the girls, including Glenda, would crowd this 'very ugly, tiny little woman' into a corner near the door, and terrify the wits out of her. They were caught and told off for treating the poor woman so appallingly, but, as Viv now recalls with shame, not one of them could have cared less about Miss Guest (as she was known to the girls) and her Holocaust experiences.

When Glenda's rebellious days began everyone tried to sort her and her fellow miscreants out – her mother, Aunt Esther, Miss Hudson, even her house prefects. After a series of misdemeanours Glenda was hauled before a house court because she had inflicted more than five negative house points on Gonner in one half term.

The ritual of a house court was straightforward. The house captain and senior prefects would summon the miscreant and ask in stentorian tones: 'You've lost this house five house points. Don't you care about your house?' Once the reprobate had apologised punishment would be meted out in the form of detention or lines. When Glenda came before the court the house captain was Viv James. Glenda knew that Viv had herself been mischievous prior to becoming house captain. So when the question came – 'Don't you care about your house?' – the shoe was on the other foot, and Viv was terrified that Glenda would recount Viv's misdoings and point out her hypocrisy. There was a seemingly interminable silence while Glenda glared at her house captain, disdain writ clear across her face. But suddenly Glenda realised that Viv was in a tight corner, took pity on her, and abjectly, if sarcastically, confessed her own guilt.

The institutionalised peer-group pressure of the house court and the end-of-term assembly, when all the girls who had faced a court were forced to stand admonished before the whole school, made no difference to Glenda's defiant state of mind. She was in the last year of the School Certificate, and from this time until her exams in 1952, she affected gross apathy about all things scholastic.

Throughout this period Glenda seemed to be seeking attention. The arrival of her sister Gill had meant that Glenda was no longer the sole recipient of her parents' affections. The appearance of Lynne, and then the birth of Liz, during Glenda's last year at school, further reduced Glenda's share of the household attention. Indeed, she was expected to take responsibility for her sisters when her parents were both out at work. It was a role she simultaneously accepted and complained about, arguing that it both made her bossy and left her little time to herself. On one occasion when she was supposed to be looking after Lynne, Glenda walked all the way home before realising that she had left her baby sister in her pram at the library. But it was with Gill that she really fought, 'like cats and dogs', according to Glenda.

Glenda's teenage relationship with her mother was also fraught. Many years later Joan told the *Express* that Glenda had owned up to her in adult life that she had been afraid of Joan because she was always shouting. 'With four of them,' Joan admitted, 'I had to shout. Any mother knows that.'[9] But Joan shouted at Glenda so much that she spent more and more time with Joan Aldridge, who lived in the same road as Aunt Esther, where Glenda had slept since Lynne's birth. Some thirteen years older than Glenda, Joan was already married, and had acquired the independence that Glenda now sought. She was also an extremely good-looking woman, something Glenda feared she was not.

This struck at the heart of Glenda's teenage unhappiness: Glenda hated the way she looked. It is never clear with teenagers which comes first, acne or self-loathing, but Glenda certainly believed that the root of her unhappiness was what she termed her 'ugliness'. She describes herself as:

> a very fat child, and very short – about four feet tall when I was fourteen. And I was terribly, *terribly* spotty. I had *awful* acne. And well, yes, I was just *ugly*. And I was nobody's delight. If you think of yourself as plain – and I certainly did – in fact I tried to think about my looks as little as possible because they were so unpromising – you tend to try and distract from it by sprouting in other directions. Well, I became the form's chief wit. I was the one who could make people laugh, but always, I remember, as a means of compensating for what I lacked in looks.

Glenda was convinced that she was unattractive.

> I was the archetypal fat and spotty teenager, suffering the tortures of the damned because I wasn't like all those model girls in magazines. You *had* to look a certain way then to be acceptable; people didn't do their own thing. I had lank, greasy hair, too. I was the antithesis of what was then regarded as an attractive girl. I minded very much; in a way your confidence stays a bit dented for ever after years like that. But I think now the realisation that my looks would never earn me a penny was a blessing. I knew early on that I'd have to work, work, work if I wanted to amount to much; plums don't drop into plain girls' laps.

It was not, of course, really true. In photos of her as a teenager Glenda scarcely looks fat, for all her asseverations, and there is remarkably little evidence of acne worse than that suffered by almost all children. Nor was Glenda's supposed plainness to prove the end of the story – in later life her ostentatious plainness was to make her a handsome living. Jane Ellison, writing in the *Sunday Telegraph* in 1982, was right when she stated that: 'It is in [Glenda's] face that the key to her star quality is to be found. It is constantly mobile, reflecting with almost painful fidelity every shifting idea, emotion, opinion which she seeks to express.'[10]

Glenda only rarely admits to her own real fantasy 'to look like Audrey Hepburn and be dressed by Givenchy or Jean Muir'. Indeed, she told Michael Parkinson on his chat show in the seventies that she never wanted to be a beauty queen: 'Well, the opportunity would never present itself with my face, really. I mean I was excluded from those particular races when I was born. But all plain ladies occasionally think it would be nice to be beautiful.' But so virulent were – and are – Glenda's assertions that she was and is unattractive that one cannot help wondering exactly who told Glenda that she was ugly. Someone else in the family? Certainly Gill used to scream at her with monotonous regularity, but Glenda knew how to deal with that. Perhaps Micky's long absence during her early years, and his closeness to Gill, made Glenda unhappy and desperate to be more appealing to her father. Gill's presence also exacerbated Glenda's obsession with her looks, as Gill was generally held to be the beauty of the family. And the fact that Elizabeth turned out to be yet another 'pretty little baby' compounded the problem. Whatever the reason, it is clear that Glenda, like many girls her age, suffered from a poor sense of her own self-worth that was so deep-seated that it persuaded her that she was unattractive. It was not that she lacked confidence – she was bold and assertive enough. She became aggressively dismissive of superficial good looks, regularly citing her mother's maxim, 'all cats look grey in the dark', and developing a strong line in classroom wit.

Her self-deprecation also made her transform the Protestant work ethic she had inherited from her parents – 'you got what you earned and you worked for treats; you only read a book when the washing-up was done'[11] – into a deep-seated personal creed of extraordinary rigour. This creed is now so central to Glenda's personality that she will condemn herself for next to nothing. 'I am so craven, I despise myself. I am saying all the time ban the car, ban the car, ban the car, yet I go on stepping into mine and will until someone stops me.' She will accuse herself of profligacy: 'I have no qualms or guilt about buying a lot of books. I'll suddenly decide I want that and I'll buy books. But I will suffer anguish before I'll buy a new Hoover, because at the back of my mind is the feeling that you could actually do it if you got down on your hands and knees with a dustpan and brush.' When one journalist confessed to having recently bought a dishwasher Glenda shrieked at her (at least half in earnest), 'Outrageous. You're a slut and a sloven.'[12]

Between the ages of thirteen and fifteen, then, Glenda experienced a deep internal conflict. Her lack of confidence in her looks led her to seek attention in the only ways she knew, by acting up, refusing to accept the authority of her teachers, joking and jesting – ever the class prankster. For nearly three years she had willing accomplices in a group of close class-mates: Jean Hibbert, Margery Stone, Shirley Smith, Betty Sparks and Jean Rankin. But in Glenda's final year West Kirby Grammar School made an explicit decision to deal with Glenda and her troupe of miscreants. They were to be placed in separate classes in the hope that, thus segregated, the girls' high spirits would be tamed. Only Margery Stone – later Jean Hibbert's sister-in-law – accompanied her. Suddenly Glenda was cut off from her ready audience, and the sense of isolation that this engendered clearly disconcerted her. Myra Kendrick, who taught her English in her final year, recalled that Glenda wrote intelligently about literary subjects, but that 'the change of stream clearly unsettled her. I remember this dark, sullen girl; I could hardly get a spark out of her. Not being with her friends any more, not being with her gang of baddies, she'd landed high and dry in new territory and was disorientated.'[13] The teenage rebel had become a sullen, rather introverted girl, lacking in the social graces, who still showed no interest in academic subjects, despite a voracious appetite for books. Another of Glenda's teachers has always blamed the school for its inability to spot Glenda's talents and channel her energies into something positive, and Margery Stone repeats the charge: 'The school never seemed to notice her potential, so anything Glenda has achieved I would say has been on her own merit.' It was little surprise when, in 1952, she failed to pass the requisite six subjects for her School Certificate, managing to scrape through only in English language, English literature and geography. Glenda confesses now that 'I was never any good at maths and had no affinity for science but I am surprised that I didn't do better at history.'

After failing her exams Glenda had little choice but to seek a job. This was not in itself unusual. The school leaving age was still fifteen, and although West Kirby Grammar School for Girls aspired to intellectual excellence, few of its pupils went on to the sixth form, let alone university. Glenda's childhood ambitions had, in the meantime, bitten the dust one by one: 'I wanted to be a doctor; then I discovered I couldn't stand hypodermic needles. Then I thought I might like to be a Wren, but I got sick crossing the Mersey.' So Glenda started work instead at Boots Cash Chemist in the Crescent in West Kirby. In many ways West Kirby Boots was similar to West Kirby Grammar, with its strict ethic of punctiliousness, deference, cleanliness and propriety. And Boots liked to think of its girls as a cut above the rest. The uniform was simple but rigorously adhered to, and when the manager arrived in the morning he expected the girls to be waiting with clean overalls and clean hands. If a button was missing words were spoken. Each of the girls was given a section of one of the long mahogany counters with glass-fronted drawers at which to serve. Glenda worked at the laxatives and bilious section, but she always aspired to be moved to the far more glamorous cosmetics counter on the other side of the shop, or even to the birth-control section ('but I was considered far too young').

For the sixteen-year-old school-leaver Boots was a stultifying existence, even if it did help pay the family rent. Long days on her feet, poor wages and a dictatorial regime, as well as the simple unremitting tedium of waiting on customers, soon taught Glenda that she must find some other means of making a living and schooled her in the rigours of ambition. Having failed her School Certificate, however, there was little choice but to grin and bear it in the hope that she might at least be promoted from the shop floor to a post in management. This Glenda did for a little over two years, while trying to find other ways of spicing up her life. Key to this was her gradually developing interest in amateur dramatics.

As with nearly every other child in the land, religion had given Glenda her first brief spell in the limelight. Aunt Esther, who thought of Glenda as the child she never had, acted as caretaker of the Hoylake Presbyterian Church, where Glenda had regularly attended Sunday School during her early years. There she gave her first dramatic appearance, playing a crippled shepherd boy with a single line – 'a star in the day' – in the 1941 Holy Trinity Nativity Play. She was, incidentally, an ardent believer, rather taken with the tales of missionaries and gallant saints, and she even toyed with spreading the Gospel for a living herself. A chance mishap made her give up ideas of a religious career, when she won a Sunday School prize, and was presented with a book that she already possessed. The fact that God should clearly have known that she already owned it persuaded the young Glenda that God was worth neither the time nor the energy.

After this Glenda did not tread the boards again in any capacity until she was a teenager, when she started to attend ballet classes run by Laura 'Dinkie' Wicks in nearby Meols. Laura Wicks recalls the first time that Glenda appeared, ostensibly just to watch one of her friends, Jean Hibbert, 'although she seemed incapable of actually sitting still'. After a while Laura asked the young girl if she would like to take part, which she did, although her family was so poor that they could not afford the proper costumes. Aunt Esther soon stepped into the breach, and within a few months Glenda was enjoying weekly classes, fully kitted out in ballet shoes and tutu. Glenda's amateur ballet career never really took off. She had started to learn to dance too late and lacked the ready ease that another eight years of study might have given her, and almost immediately she began to grow at an alarming rate. Nevertheless, she showed no small determination in pursuing this hobby, and infuriated her mother by sending off for a brochure from a fee-paying Russian ballet school, the Légat. And later, at Christmas 1951 Glenda was asked to appear at the YMCA in the annual pantomime, dancing as the wicked witch in *Cinderella*, a performance her friend Joan

Aldridge still remembers: 'She was absolutely fantastic – she stole the show.'

At school, although Glenda had a reputation for reading well in English lessons – Myra Hendrick, her English teacher, recalls that the two of them read *A Midsummer Night's Dream* to the class as a duologue – Glenda showed no interest in the straight theatre. She did not take part in any of the school Shakespeare productions, and was not involved with the Guides and their regular gang shows (although she was briefly a Brownie). Nor, for that matter, was she a great habituée of the theatre. Family visits to the theatre were limited to an occasional pantomime in Liverpool, and Glenda's first experience of classical theatre did not come until July 1950, when West Kirby organised a school trip to see Donald Wolfit as Shylock in *The Merchant of Venice* at the Empire. These Wolfit productions were an annual pilgrimage for the school, which had attended his *King Lear*, *Macbeth*, *Julius Caesar* and *Hamlet* over the previous three years. Many of the girls found the *Merchant* production hilarious – just as they had done when Hamlet's Ghost had fallen off the stage in another Wolfit production – but Glenda found it spell-binding. Despite Wolfit's reputation for melodramatic exaggeration (he is reputed on the last night of Christopher Marlowe's *Tamburlaine the Great* to have stage whispered into the flies, 'Well, Kit, we've done you proud'), Glenda recalls going into the theatre thinking that Shylock was the most loathsome of characters, and coming out with the feeling that he was the most put-upon and oppressed of figures – 'such was the power of the actor'.

Far more important than the theatre in Glenda's early appreci-ation of acting was the cinema, which she adored. She loved every-thing, from Flash Gordon and Ming the Merciless, to classic films with Bette Davis, Katharine Hepburn and Joan Crawford. Even though some of the local picture houses had closed during the war, there were three within easy reach which meant that with mid-week changes of programme Glenda could, if she had the money and the permission, see six films a week. Immediately round the corner, in Market Street, was the Kingsway. 'One could hardly fail to notice the strong, sweet odour of disinfectant', recorded one forties visitor, 'that pervaded the air from the moment you set foot in the cinema. Also very noticeable were the non-stop renditions of popular hit records that preceded the show, contrasting rather unfavourably with the tuneful light orchestral records to be heard at most other "better class" cinemas in those days.'[14] These classier cinemas included the Lighthouse Pavilion, again no more than 200 hundred yards from Glenda's home. Smartest of all, though, was the half-timbered Tudor in West Kirby, which boasted its own gift shop and florist and heavily appliquéd gold satin curtains. When required it could pass muster as a theatre, occasionally hosting minor tours and briefly holding a repertory season in which a young Sheila Hancock appeared. When Glenda served Sheila in Boots one day she was shocked to note that actors must be poorly paid, as her gloves were so threadbare.

Glenda had a keen and uninhibited sense of the dramatic. Jean Hibbert, one of her closest school friends, remembers that even the most high-spirited of the other girls hated the dread moment after games when they would have to disrobe for the showers. They would huddle together, clutching their towels around them, forever putting off the moment of nudity, and trying to avert their eyes from everyone else. Above the West Kirby showers, though, was a series of brass bars that ran the length of the room. Glenda's favourite trick was to swing from bar to bar, stark naked, singing Joseph Locke's latest hit, 'Hear My Song, Violetta', while the more timid girls tried to decide whether to be shocked, intimidated or amused.

It was not only the shower room that saw Glenda's more extravagant side. On one occasion she had herself carried back home from the beach, apparently drowned, much to her mother's fury. On another, she tried to re-enact an Esther Williams scene in Hoylake baths, smiling broadly underwater in the style Williams had made so famous, but which left Glenda spluttering on the side of the pool. If anything her taste ran to the exotic – Maria Montez, the 'Queen of Technicolor', surrounded by cobras – rather than the understated.

When it came to performing in front of a crowd Glenda was an exhibitionist, full of self-confidence, but on an individual level she came across as shy and introverted, and seemed to relish solitude. She was completely uninhibited – happy even to be naked – yet she was firmly convinced that she was unattractive. In time Glenda was to find a partial resolution of these conflicting elements in the theatre, but it was not until the year before she left school, 1951, that she started to show any serious interest in acting, when a change from dancing was suggested to her by her fellow 'Dinkie' dancer, Jean Hibbert. So Glenda applied to one of the several amateur dramatics groups that flourished in the area before the arrival of television, the Hoylake Amateur Operatic and Dramatic Society, which was run by Fred Ferris (who later played a regular part on *Dave Morris' Club Night* on BBC radio). Considered the best of a fairly good bunch, this was also the most snobbish local theatre group, and Glenda, whether because she was too young, or because she was not quite 'one of us', was turned down. Instead Joan Aldridge suggested Glenda should try the less exacting YMCA Players, who put on plays in the then exclusively male YMCA, and were therefore always on the look-out for new actresses.

Fortunately, the YMCA Players had a strong directorial team, with a local commercial artist, Warren Owen, as president and the wife of a local laundry owner and Liberal politician, Joan Banks, as director. Owen was something of a local character, always wearing a velvet jacket and a bright cravat – his directorial style was equally flamboyant. Yet he had a genuine interest in bringing on young actors, and he was particularly helpful to the young Charlie Foster, who was later a senior continuity announcer at Granada television for many years. Just as important was Joan Banks, who had been a professional dancer and actress in her youth, and had only stopped working after a car accident. Her husband, Tom, was both a wealthy local councillor and the regularly unsuccessful Liberal candidate for the Wirral in successive general elections.

Glenda's application to the YMCA Players was successful and in 1952 she appeared in her first play in the old Edwardian Ruabon brick hall of the YMCA. This was not, as others have suggested, Agatha Christie's *Murder at Gleneagles*, but J. B. Priestley's little-known *Mystery of Greenfingers*.[15] Glenda's tiny part gave her little chance to shine, although Joan Aldridge, who was also in the production, recalls her particularly innocent rendition of the line 'Are you a *real* detective?'

There is no evidence of Glenda appearing in any other YMCA

productions in 1952 or 1953, although Joan Aldridge has a distinct memory of Glenda playing an aristocrat in a 1953 production, and being so poor that she could not afford the necessary stockings for the part. Glenda's next chronicled appearance was in 1954, when she played Ethel in *Nothing but the Truth* by James Montgomery, and received her first review from the *Hoylake and West Kirby Advertiser*: 'Glenda Jackson made the most of her opportunities for comedy.' Seven months later she was given her first lead part, playing Margaret Fenwick, a murderous Scottish maid in Roland Pertwee and Harold Dearden's *To Kill a Cat*. Yet again the *Advertiser* remarked upon her: 'Glenda Jackson gave an impressive study of the over-religious maid.' Charlie Foster, who played opposite her, was even more impressed by a flawless Scottish accent. Others in the company also noted Glenda's performances. As Jill Luscombe, whose father did the make-up for the Players, says, 'Warren Owen was constantly imploring us "Try to make your voice carry", but unlike the rest of us, Glenda didn't really have to try. She didn't speak – she shouted.'

With the benefit of hindsight, Glenda's passage into the professional theatre seems inevitable and painless. Ian Woodward, in his 1985 biography of Glenda, maintained that Warren Owen simply challenged Glenda one night as she walked off stage after appearing in *Anastasia*: 'This is what you should be doing, girl – working professionally as an actress. It's what you were born to do. You're just wasting your life at the moment. Why don't you try to get into one of the London drama schools? It's not too late.'[16] So, Woodward suggests, within a week Glenda had applied to RADA, and within a month she was auditioning in London. Glenda added to this impression of effortless success by stating that she applied for RADA only out of boredom, and not from any driving ambition.

In reality, Glenda never appeared in the YMCA Players production of *Anastasia*, and she spent the best part of a year schooling herself as an actress with the help of elocution lessons from Joan Banks – 'trying to eradicate the flat vowels that are part of the Wirral Peninsula sound' – and taking fencing lessons for balance in Liverpool. This was a considerable investment of time, energy and money, which would suggest that Glenda was more determined to get out of 'the bloody chemist's shop' and into the theatre than she now recalls. Charlie Foster, who used to take the bus to visit the Banks household in Caldy for cricket practice (Tom Banks also ran the local gentlemen's cricket team) at the same time as Glenda, when she went for her acting lessons, certainly remembers a 'very determined person, who once she had set her eyes on something was single-minded enough to make sure that she got it'. He was convinced that as long as she got the necessary breaks in the profession she would be a great success. This was not Glenda's schoolmates' view, who felt she was very ordinary – several felt that if anyone was going to be a successful actress it was Gill Jackson, who had started acting with one of the West Kirby theatrical groups and was believed to be more versatile than the rather earnest Glenda. The two eldest Jacksons were getting on so badly by now, that this was incentive enough, if no other had been needed, for Glenda to prove her worth and make her escape from Boots and from Hoylake.

However it happened, Glenda applied to RADA, the only drama school she had heard of (she maintains), in the summer of 1954, and went for audition in the autumn. The trip down to London made her as nervous as the audition itself. 'I had never been away from home before,' she later admitted, 'and I was totally ignorant. But the ignoramus aspect was in a way helpful, because I just went along, did the auditions and left immediately.' Glenda's determination and hard work paid off and she was awarded a place, but there was no guarantee that she would be able to afford to attend drama school. For that she needed at least to win a scholarship to pay for the tuition, and preferably some form of grant from the local authority to cover her living expenses. Ten days after her first audition Glenda presented herself again at RADA for the scholarship auditions. Again she was shocked and delighted to be successful, especially as RADA was prepared to write to Cheshire Education Committee on her behalf to request a fairly sizeable discretionary award – exceptionally, they agreed. Glenda was to start in January 1955.

Neither Joan nor Micky was pleased. The prospect of Glenda moving to the bright lights of London filled them both with horror, and not unnaturally they worried that Glenda would never return. In time they grew accustomed to Glenda's new determination –

for so it had become – to be an actress, and they acquiesced. After all, as Glenda points out, 'they only ever wanted us to be happy'. For all the tensions and jealousies the Jackson family was extremely close-knit, and Glenda's move to London represented the furthest separation, outside war, the family had ever seen. Glenda's parents hated to see her go.

Yet Glenda did not see her future behind a counter selling laxatives, and since her schooling had left her with no readily marketable skills, she was keen to make her way in a field in which she seemed to be able to excel. So Glenda surrendered her Wirral vowels for received pronunciation; she put behind her the days of youthfully exuberant defiance; and she took with her to London a tough working ethic, a belief that she was plain, a confidence in the self-sufficiency of women, and a resolute sense of the task that lay before her.

CHAPTER TWO

※

Work, Work, Work

LONDON, WHEN GLENDA ARRIVED at the start of 1955, was no centre of cosmopolitan fashion, and was characterised by discreet, genteel and moderately affluent charm, rather than the vibrant, questioning style of post-war America or France. The prime minister, Winston Churchill, was approaching his eighty-first birthday and was surrounded by a Cabinet of the *ancien régime*, who busily pursued a general policy of consensual caution.

But London was also the port of entry for all things American, and in the mid-fifties that meant youthful rebellion and raw energy. Marlon Brando, Montgomery Clift and Judy Garland were challenging wan conventionality with a new brand of sexual volatility and every year brought new excitement. In 1955 Brando's *The Wild One* was banned; *Blackboard Jungle* with its title credits song by Bill Hailey and the Comets, 'Rock Around the Clock', led to teenage hysteria in UK cinemas; and James Dean burst on to the scene with *East of Eden* and *Rebel without a Cause* before his fatal car crash in September. For all London's fustiness, signs of a dangerous new era were beginning to appear.

No institution demonstrated this mid-fifties age of transition more acutely than RADA, the Royal Academy of Dramatic Art. Founded in 1904 at the whim (and in the theatre) of the Victorian actor-manager Sir Herbert Beerbohm Tree – who, ironically, believed that acting could not be taught – it had been run since 1909 by one man, the portly seventy-seven-year-old Sir Kenneth Barnes. Sir Kenneth's theatrical provenance was aristocratic. One of his sisters was the actress Dame Irene Vanbrugh, the original Gwendolyn in *The Importance of Being Earnest*, and his other sister,

Violet Vanbrugh, had played opposite Tree and Henry Irving.

With such a principal it was inevitable that RADA should have an air of wistful Edwardian nostalgia about it, but this was exacerbated by the fact that Sir Kenneth had helped the Academy's finances by accepting a large quota of wealthy but untalented girls, whose families saw RADA as a slightly déclassé, but cheap, finishing school. Students still had to check in every day with an ivorene card in the Rainbow Corner of the grandiose main entrance. There was a uniformed doorman and the main staircase and lifts were forbidden for students.

But RADA was already changing. Having finally opened its Vanbrugh Theatre the year before in honour of his two sisters, Sir Kenneth – mirroring Churchill's handover of the premiership to the younger Anthony Eden in April – was to retire at the end of Glenda's first term. His place was to be taken by the eminently more practical director John Fernald, who had two decades of experience as a director in the commercial West End and as director of the Liverpool Playhouse. Moreover, some of the Cheltenham Ladies' College aura had already been dispelled by the arrival of notoriously rough diamonds such as Albert Finney, Peter O'Toole, Roy Kinnear and Alan Bates.

Glenda arrived late for her first term, thanks to a hiccup in the administration of her grant by Cheshire County Council, and by the time she was installed with relatives in Waddington she had missed a full week. Josie Kidd, who shared the two years at RADA with Glenda, remembers her eventual, flurried arrival in the middle of a voice class with her fashionable little box in place of a handbag. Pauline Devaney (later the co-author with her husband Edwin Apps of *All Gas and Gaiters*), who became a close friend, recalls first seeing Glenda arrive in the middle of a fencing lesson. 'I remember it very clearly. She was plump, and not at all like most of the other drama students, because she was direct and straightforward even from the outset – and she was wearing *very* ordinary clothes.' For both Josie and Pauline there was something else that marked Glenda out. As Pauline put it: 'It takes most of us a long time to grow up and know how the world wags. But Glenda was really aware of everything from the very beginning, and it gave her a head start. That really made her stand out.' In Josie's eyes, 'even on that first day she seemed to have the strongest sense of what she was about and a wide-eyed excitement, as if she felt certain that "This is the place I want to be."'

Glenda was indeed certain about her career, and she set about her work with all the determination that had been lacking in her days at West Kirby Grammar. In part she had to – RADA deliberately recruited a large intake, and then weeded people out every term, so you had to work hard to become a RADA finalist. But she was also delighted to be with 'a group of people much the same age as myself, all interested in the same thing', and she started to make friends. Beryl Braithwaite, a Canadian who had already enjoyed some professional success in a North American production of *Alice in Wonderland*, told Glenda of a spare room in the same digs as her in elegant Kew, and she moved in, thoroughly enjoying the much-envied television set, her landlady Mrs Hill's generous food and the new friendship. Beryl, who had resplendent dyed and permed hair, even persuaded Glenda to use hair conditioner for the first time. Pauline Devaney recalls that the three of them (Beryl, Glenda and Pauline) refused to succumb to the artiness of the Academy and spent many hours conspicuously knitting in the canteen.

Thanks to her magnanimous grant from Cheshire County Council Glenda was now relatively well off. She could even afford to eat in the canteen, unlike Pauline, who had to bring sandwiches in every day, but along with most of the students Glenda still spent many of her Friday and Saturday nights working in bars, and when she went home to Hoylake in the holidays she returned to her old place behind the counter in Boots. (A better job than most of the boys at RADA could manage – several were regularly employed on night shifts in the University College Hospital morgue.) There were occasional trips to the theatre, the cinema and the ballet, but since Glenda either lacked the courage, or believed it was wrong, to sneak in during the interval for the second half of a show, she missed out on many of the great performances of the year. For the most part, Glenda's energies were absorbed in her work and she confesses that

> I put my head down and worked very hard. I was sort of
> amazed by people who didn't work hard. I mean, the

social life of RADA was something I only heard about
years afterwards. Friends would say, 'Do you remember
when so-and-so did such-and-such at some party or
other?' and I would have to say, 'No, I wasn't there.' I
wasn't even aware of the intrigues.

Throughout her time at RADA Glenda was a diligent and almost
obsessive worker. Indeed, a summer outing with Pauline to see
Olivier's Stratford season ended in an unexpected row as Glenda
self-righteously announced that 'If I were ever to work at Stratford
I should arrive at least two hours beforehand to prepare.' So
incensed was Pauline by this ludicrous posturing that they spent
the whole journey back to London arguing.

Study at RADA followed the classic *conservatoire* model. There
were obligatory classes in voice production, diction, movement,
fencing and 'technique'. Men and women were taught voice separ-
ately, and each student spent his or her two years in a small group
of fifteen, occasionally combining with actors from another class
for particular productions. Improvisation was still thought of as
dangerously radical. The only regular piece of improvisation was
the basis of the annual Athene Seyler prize, which involved the
elderly comedienne suggesting scenes that the students then had
to enact impromptu. Glenda won the prize in her second year for
a tight-vowelled jolly-hockey-stick impersonation. Method acting
was anathema. (As Noël Coward told one actress who wanted to
know what her motive was for a particular move: 'Your motive, my
dear, is the pay packet at the end of the week.') Prizes were awarded
for 'Grace and Elegance of Movement' (won one year by the *Carry
On* comedienne Joan Sims, who fell down the steps on the way to
receiving her prize).

There were a few wealthy students, such as Diana Potter, who
had a private zoo and regularly brought pythons into classes with
her, and Irish aristocratic scion Tim Seeley. But most had come to
RADA because they wanted to work in the profession, and for all
its failings it was still the best source of contacts in the land. The
staff was a fairly wild miscellany. There was the flirtatious Amy
Boalth, who taught movement and ballet – still one of Glenda's
passions – and a veteran American actor, Edward Burnham, who

took comedy and taught, according to Glenda, 'the old school technique, how to get a laugh lighting a cigarette, how to point a line, and how to polish the soles of our shoes so that audiences would not be offended if we were to cross our legs on stage'. Playwright Hugh Whitemore, who was a couple of years behind Glenda, recalls admiring the voice production teacher Clifford Turner, 'a tall, elegant man who looked more like a diplomat than an actor. He always wore a dark blue suit, a sober tie and shirts with a monogram on the breast, which I thought was the height of sophistication. He had a boomingly resonant voice and seemed to regard his pupils with an amused, benevolent contempt.'[1]

Glenda's dedication took time to pay dividends, as she spent most of her first four terms playing a seemingly endless run of 'maids, charladies and zanies'. She finally surfaced in June 1956, in John Fernald's conventional UK-première production of *The Caucasian Chalk Circle* at the Vanbrugh, but her role meant she never left the balcony (whence she, Josie Kidd and Pauline Devaney declaimed as the chorus).[2] Nevertheless, Glenda later landed some excellent parts which played to her strengths, and were to help her on to the first rung of the career ladder. First was Aristophanes' classical comedy, *The Frogs*, in which Glenda proved to be something of a raw but exhilarating comic genius. Next came a storming success for Glenda as Eliza Doolittle in Shaw's *Pygmalion*.

She was also cast as the ferocious Paulina (she of the great audition speech 'What studied torments, tyrant, hast for me?') in the end-of-term production of *The Winter's Tale*, which was directed by an elderly actress who taught Shakespeare, Nell Carter. Josie, who played Perdita (Pauline Devaney played Hermione), classed this as one of Glenda's great performances: 'It showed that even at a young, puppy-fat age Glenda had the emotional power, the voice and the presence to carry one of the most demanding Shakespearean parts.'

The Winter's Tale, like *Pygmalion*, was given public performances, and the usual round of talent-spotting agents, casting directors and impresarios' assistants attended both. One young agent, Peter Crouch, then working for Peter Glass, took immediate interest in Glenda, and when he had seen both her Eliza and her Paulina, decided to take her on. So began a working relationship that was to last the best part of Glenda's career. Pauline Devaney, who also acquired Crouch as her agent, found him 'a nice chap, genuinely in love with the theatre and with actors', who could be an exceptionally dexterous agent, pushing for auditions, haggling over money, finding ways of introducing his clients to the people that mattered, and picking up on every piece of minor information. Glenda and Peter returned loyalty to each other in equal measure as the years passed, even though the steady round of opening-night receptions, lunches and crush-bar tipples took their professional toll on Peter. It was a working relationship built on trust. As Glenda's ex-husband explains, 'It was just a handshake with them, and the deal was done.' Despite a brief spell when Glenda refused to take Peter's advice, and he in turn gave up on her, he represented her interests in the UK right up until his alcohol-induced death.

It is almost always the case that at any one moment more than 90 per cent of actors are out of work, but at the moment when Glenda started her career the outlook was particularly mixed. On the one hand television was finally coming into its own, offering the prospect of a whole new avenue of employment for actors. Not only had the BBC resumed its television service in 1946 – with its weekly crop of comedies, modern dramas and classic plays – but it had finally won its place in the nation's front rooms with the televising of the Coronation Service in 1953. Moreover, parliament had licensed the new Independent Broadcasting Authority and commercial television had started transmitting on 22 September 1955 – although commercial television did not reach Hoylake and the North West until the following May. Television now had regular drama series – *Armchair Theatre* on ABC, *Sunday Night Theatre*, *Dixon of Dock Green* and *The Grove Family* on BBC – all requiring actors, and with general unemployment also lower than at any other period during peacetime there was a strong likelihood of casual income even in the inevitable 'resting' periods.

But the mainstays of thespian employment, the great local repertory and touring theatres of the provinces, were in decline, partly due to pressure from television. The aptly named impresario Prince Littler was busy closing more than a hundred theatres, the incipient Arts Council only very occasionally acted to resolve the funding breach, and local authorities, newly authorised to subsidise the arts, preferred to build new municipal theatres rather than save old ones. In addition, more than a fifth of London's West End theatres had been either destroyed or damaged in the war. At the same time, again thanks to competition from television, weekly cinema attendances were falling sharply – from 30.5 million at the end of the war to a mere 21.2 million in 1956. Within five years more than a third of the UK's screens would be torn down and attendances would slump to less than 9 million, precipitating a major crisis in the British film industry.

All of which made acting a less than dependable career even if you were Vivien Leigh, Vivien Merchant, Siobhan McKenna (*Saint Joan* opposite Kenneth Williams), Joan Collins or Kim Novak. The one piece of career advice that Glenda most readily recalls came in an exchange with John Fernald. 'You know you're a character actress, don't you?' he asked. 'I suppose so,' replied the hesitant Glenda. 'Well, don't expect to work much before you're forty,' came the dispiritingly robust prognostication.

Glenda herself was more stoical than optimistic about her chances of becoming a leading actress. Josie Kidd recalls sitting on the Gower Street pavement outside RADA on the last day of term and declaring rather grandly, 'I simply can't see myself in rep,' to which Glenda lugubriously replied, 'Well, I can.'

Nevertheless Glenda did have the first prerequisite of a theatrical career, an agent, and thanks to Peter it was not long before she got her first professional job – the tiniest of walk-on parts in *Doctor in the House* at the Worthing repertory theatre on the south coast. Even here John Fernald's prediction proved true as the director, Melville Gillam, told the leading actress in the company, Elizabeth Spriggs, that he was thinking of letting Glenda go after her first week, for the simple reason that he could not think of anything else to cast her in. The exigencies of weekly rep meant that versatile actors, and those who conformed to the strict hierarchy of parts (male and female lead, male and female juvenile lead, male and female character and male and female juvenile character), were most in demand. All juvenile actresses were expected to be five foot four, slim and pretty. Glenda, by contrast, was, in Elizabeth Spriggs' words 'rounded', and although Elizabeth felt there was a tenderness about her that made people feel protective towards her 'she was hardly anyone's idea of a juvenile'. Even Glenda felt that 'I'm not pretty enough to be thought beautiful and not quite plain enough to be considered interesting.'³ Despite Spriggs' pleas to keep her on, Glenda's West Sussex coastal rep career lasted only a week, and she returned to London and to a job at Woolworth's.

Only a few weeks later Glenda was working again, this time in fortnightly rep at the Queen's in Hornchurch, Essex, a dingy theatre that had been opened only four years earlier by Ralph Richardson. She was to work there for nearly seven months. The actress Gwen Watford recalled Glenda at Hornchurch as rather plump and very quiet.

> She was in a bit of awe of everything: watching everybody and learning from watching. In every way she was just a youngster, trying her wings, very much feeling her way. When you're in fortnightly rep like that, the pressure is enormous, the learning, the rehearsing, the playing. She struck me as rather shy. She didn't speak very much.⁴

Only one of the fourteen productions she was in got her any attention – Terence Rattigan's *Separate Tables*, in which Glenda played the student Jean Stratton, during February. By the time it came to the last night of *The White Sheep of the Family*, which played for two weeks from 5 August, Hornchurch felt it had exhausted Glenda's repertoire of maids and waitresses.

According to John Fernald Glenda should now have passed into a further period of unemployment, but within a month of leaving Hornchurch she was appearing at the Arts Theatre Club in Soho, making her professional London debut. The Arts was one of a dozen or so alternative London theatres that had grown up since the war, and thanks to its West End location in Great Newport Street it had become by far the best known. Alec Clunes, the father of the *Men Behaving Badly* actor Martin, had established its reputation with directors like the ubiquitous John Fernald, and since Clunes' death it had hosted a series of striking new plays. Moreover, the attached bar was a favourite hang-out of the young acting fraternity. It was something of a coup for Glenda to be cast in a new play by the American Alex Samuels, *All Kinds of Men*, even though it was, in the words of one cast member, 'a hopeless melodrama', and Glenda's part was insignificant. The cast had a distinguished lead, the bibulous Wilfrid Lawson, an actor in the grand tradition (Clifford Williams described him as 'the most charismatic bundle of nerves I ever saw on stage'). Lawson had had a substantial film career before the war (including the original 1938 screen *Pygmalion*) and had played in a major West End success most years since, most recently *The Rainmaker* at St Martin's, which had run for 228 performances under the direction of Sam Wanamaker. Playing opposite Lawson was a young Miriam Karlin, already well established, although not yet the star of television's *The Rag Trade*. The rest of the cast was, much like Glenda, young and relatively inexperienced. John Nettleton, later an RSC colleague of Glenda's, had to dance with her as the local colour in a brothel, and Susan Hampshire was the ASM.

Of all Glenda's work to date this was her most enjoyable. Wilfrid Lawson, despite his heavy drinking and poor health – he succumbed to pneumonia halfway through the run and had to hand over to John Nettleton – was, Glenda recalls, 'wonderful, wonderful, wonderful'. She delighted in witnessing his nightly transformation:

> at the Arts Theatre you had to go down a long flight of stairs to the stage and between scenes Wilfrid would just stay down there in the wings, scarcely able to catch his breath he was so ill, and then he would go on stage and be suddenly transformed. He made it all seem so effortless.

Miriam Karlin has a rather different memory of Lawson's ability to transcend his physical inadequacies and remembers abandoning a terrifying dress rehearsal – in which a drunken Lawson was giving her 'any old lines' – in a state of desperate anxiety. Lawson stormed into her dressing room to demand an apology from her. Having intended to extract an apology from *him*, she was taken aback, but managed to stutter out that she wouldn't take this kind of behaviour from anyone. Whereupon Lawson stumbled over to her and, drawing from his considerable well of personal charm, said 'well, give us a kiss then'. After that he handed his wallet over to the management, and was only allowed a single drink every night, although

John Nettleton believes that 'it must have been a pretty large measure'.

All Kinds of Men ran for one moderately successful month through to 13 October, and just as unemployment loomed upon the horizon Glenda almost immediately secured yet another job: six months' rep at Crewe, where the Glaswegian director of *All Kinds of Men*, Robert Mitchell, was about to start work.

Crewe is a harsh town, more renowned for its many-platformed railway station than for its Heath Street repertory theatre, but the offer of steady work in a town not many miles from Hoylake was irresistible and Glenda readily accepted the contract – 'half acting, half stage managing and full-time sweeping the floor'. The theatre, recently renamed the New, had had its problems. As audiences dwindled the local newspaper had run a series of pleas for people to attend it, but Armitage Owen, the Welsh playwright, who in 1957 had leased the theatre from the local council for three years, had surrendered in the face of rampant apathy and tried to save money by devoting Saturdays to wrestling. By the middle of February 1958 he had left Crewe and the council was seeking a new lessee. Robert Mitchell had previously made his name in the social- ist Glasgow Unity Theatre, and had formed the Folk Theatre Limited because he believed in 'theatre for the people'. He now decided to take the lease with his wife, the actress Clare Kelly, and started to create a company formed from people he had worked with elsewhere. Anna Welsh, a fellow Glaswegian who had worked with Mitchell in *All Kinds of Men* and several other shows, joined the company, as did her husband, Alan Mishkin, who became the front of house manager. Alan Curtis and Desmond Flanagan, both regulars at Crewe, also joined, and were soon followed by Glenda – 'the baby of the company', as the *Crewe Chronicle* described her. Robert Mitchell ran a fairly adventurous programme of substantial and controversial plays with a left-wing slant – *Look Back in Anger*, *An Inspector Calls*, *The Glass Menagerie* – and it is not surprising that the New continued to have financial difficulties, succumbing during the summer months to a diet of Olde Tyme Music Hall for which Glenda dressed in Edwardian costume and served drinks.

Not long after Glenda's arrival another member of the company was recruited to be stage director and very occasional performer –

Roy Hodges. Roy was a Welshman by birth (Ogmore Vale), though a Lancastrian by upbringing (Warrington). He is eight years older than Glenda ('I was born in 1928, the same year as my patron saint Mickey Mouse'), but his provenance is remarkably similar to hers. His father was in the building trade – a cement contractor for Trollope and Colls – his mother a cleaner. As an actor he had always been cast because of, rather than despite, his working-class credentials. Indeed his first job, playing one of the mining children in *The Corn is Green* at the rep theatre in Lee at the age of fourteen, had come his way thanks to his Welsh accent. Thanks to a wartime shortage of actors he managed to remain at the rep until he was called up for national service in 1946. After two years in the army pay corps he returned to his old profession and spent two years at the Bradford drama school run by Tyrone Guthrie's close friend and colleague, the redoubtable Esmee Church. This led to a more or less steady run of repertory jobs throughout the early and mid-fifties.

But 1957 saw Roy at his least employed and his most impecunious. Even the usual fill-in jobs had dried up, and for virtually the whole of the second half of the year he was out of work. Roy says that

> I had left home at the age of sixteen and this was the only time in my life that I decided to swallow my pride and go back to Warrington. After all, here I was literally starving in London. So my brother, Mervyn, who was a publican in Warrington, managed to get me a job early in 1958 delivering barrels of beer for the brewery. I loathed it and it really took it out of me physically. But it was work.

During national service Roy had been briefly posted to Glasgow and had acted in a couple of productions at Robert Mitchell's Unity Theatre. So, when one day his dray was delivering beer to the theatre in Crewe, and he saw a poster for a production of *The Summer of the Seventeenth Doll*, directed by Robert Mitchell, he decided to write in hope of a job. A few days later Roy was back in Crewe for an interview. A Unity Theatre friend of his, Anna Welsh, caught wind of Roy's meeting with Mitchell and contrived to be hanging around outside the director's office – with her young friend and digs-mate Glenda – just when Roy came out. Apparently she had some idea that her two friends would get on. She introduced them and, as Roy puts it, 'Within a fortnight I was borrowing off her; and I've been borrowing off her ever since.' Glenda admits she threw herself at Roy, but denies that it was love at first sight. Three weeks later Roy and Glenda had taken a room together above a pub and were virtually inseparable.

Although Glenda now complains about Crewe – 'of all the god-forsaken places to meet someone . . .' – Roy's memories of that season are all warm. 'We were a great trio, Anna, Glenda and I, and we carried our happiness around with us.' Money was tight, but a modicum of glamour came their way from time to time. As stage director it was Roy's job to beg, borrow and steal props and furniture for the productions, something at which Roy confesses he was particularly adept.

> I am rather ruthless when I want something, and on one occasion I needed a working four-poster bed. So I asked one of the local landed gentry whether he could oblige, and to our surprise he did. I remember he was out playing polo when the three of us turned up to collect it. But he was so helpful in the end that I think he'd have lent us the whole house if we'd wanted to put it on stage. When the four-poster actually arrived Glenda and I were so impressed we decided we had to sleep in it, which we did. In fact, we even saved money by sleeping on stage every night.

Meanwhile Glenda was doing well in Crewe, and although she started off playing the usual run of walk-ons, she received a good notice for her appearance in *An Inspector Calls* and was given the eponymous lead in *Jane Eyre* in May. This was one of the few occasions on which Glenda and Roy appeared together on stage, and it sent Glenda into regular paroxysms of giggles. 'He had to say, "Come away with me, Jane; I will show you mountains, flowers . . ." and all that rubbish, while the set was changed behind us,' Glenda recalls. 'I used to go on with an open brooch in my hand and force the pin into my palm and stare at a certain spot until I was blind, because if I'd looked at him, I would have had hysterics, *hysterics*. I said afterwards, "Never again."'

For all of these productions Joan and Aunt Esther made the trip from Hoylake with Glenda's YMCA Players colleague Joan Aldridge. On one occasion they overheard a member of the audience extolling the virtues of one of the other actresses in the production before declaring of Glenda: 'Eeh, but she's ugly.' According to Joan Aldridge, all that rescued the moment was the intervention of Robert Mitchell, who announced: 'On the contrary, when Glenda wants to be beautiful she can be absolutely enchanting.' By contrast Roy believes that although Southern audiences might not have taken to Glenda as a natural juvenile lead, Northern ones were far happier 'because she was so plump and wholesome, you see'. Micky, on the occasions when he joined the Hoylake day out, was less convinced, and complained vociferously throughout what he declared to be a completely improbable production of *My Three Angels*. Glenda's own views were down-to-earth: 'The danger of rep, as it was then, was that eventually you fell into a pattern where, indeed, you did give the same performance week after week because that was what you were hired for.'

Within weeks of Roy's arrival in Crewe he and Glenda were contemplating their future. The end of July would see the end of the rep season in Crewe and they would have to decide where to go – back, individually, to Warrington and to Hoylake, or back, perhaps together, to London. Roy recalls broaching the issue with a cautious query: 'Shall we just live together, or would you like to get married?' Glenda decided in favour of marriage. 'Of course, Roy and I could have lived together without getting married, but I personally wouldn't want that,' Glenda explains. 'The people to whom I'm emotionally attached would have been shocked, and it seemed needless to hurt them. I have friends who tell me that marriage is obsolete and that if you try to limit it with a legal document it will fail. But I don't agree.' So one night, after a performance, Glenda transferred a pretty cameo ring with Shakespeare's bust on it on to her engagement finger and Roy and Glenda announced they were engaged to be married. Thanks to a generous gift of £5 from

Roy's brother Mervyn, the wedding itself was to be in London immediately the season ended.

On Saturday 2 August 1958 Roy and Glenda were married at St Marylebone Register Office in London. It was a very low-key affair. 'We looked great,' says Roy, 'but it was far from glamorous.' Glenda had no bridesmaids. Her dress was borrowed from Tarn Bassett, the wealthy second wife of Roy's friend (and Bradford Civic Theatre contemporary), the actor Robert Stephens. The wedding breakfast was a cup of coffee and an iced bun at the Joe Lyons café round the corner, while the honeymoon was a couple of nights at the Bassett/Stephens Chelsea townhouse, where a small party was held that evening. The turnout was low. Apart from the bride and groom and Roy's best man (another Bradford contemporary, Tom Bell) there were twenty present in all. Pauline Devaney was out of town. Anna Welsh was working. And although all of Roy's family made the journey down to London, either through lack of money or lack of support for Glenda's choice of husband – Roy was never quite sure which – Gill was the only Jackson to attend.

The Monday immediately after the wedding they set off for Darlington to rehearse a touring production of 'the new <u>realistic</u> sex play' (as the publicity proclaimed it) by Eugene Hamilton, *A Girl Named Sadie*. Roy had been approached first by the director David Kirk, with whom he had worked before. But when Roy pointed out 'I'm about to be married. Is there a part for my wife?', Glenda was taken on, stage managing, understudying and delivering twice nightly (6.30 and 8.30), a couple of brief lines as an aged grandmother. Glenda and Roy both hated the play, but they made a good new friend, another actor Peter Bromilow, and *Sadie* kept them both employed for nearly three months, touring places as far apart as Portsmouth and the Lake District.

It was not to last, however. One afternoon in Birmingham, Roy and Glenda went to a cinema double bill and had to leave before it was over in order to get to the theatre in time for the first show. Glenda blames the rush-hour traffic in which their bus got caught, while Roy remembers that they took a bus going in the wrong direction, but either way they eventually had to run the last mile to the theatre. Glenda arrived at the stage door just as the other

ASM said Glenda's first line. David Kirk was furious – the most basic rule of the theatre had been flouted. For the first (and last) time Glenda was peremptorily sacked. Roy had fared better than Glenda, as his character did not appear until the end of the first act, and he had managed to get in costume just in time. But when Glenda was sacked he too decided to leave the company, and within days the Hodgeses were on the train to London. As Roy explains:

> We had nothing but our week's wages, which wasn't even enough to pay a deposit on a room. Fortunately we knew someone who ran a terrible boarding house in Victoria and he was prepared to let us have a room, which gave us a week's grace. But we really had absolutely nothing. We even had to pawn Glenda's cameo ring. I remember we got 7/6 for it. Needless to say we were never able to redeem it. If ever I were able to give anything back to Glenda that's the one thing that I would give her.

Fortunately Anna Welsh managed to find Roy and Glenda a room near her in Hampstead, and they put the boarding house behind them after a couple of weeks, but even the Hampstead room was barely adequate. When it came to their first Christmas together they were too poor to get on the train to either Hoylake or Warrington, and Roy can remember Glenda ringing her parents on Christmas Day and crying her heart out. 'She was absolutely distraught and it was the first time that I realised how frighteningly important her family was to her.'

Now began the most dispiriting period of Glenda's life – two and a half years of acting unemployment. There were auditions – even for the Royal Shakespeare Company – but never any parts. She worked. 'Because I had no qualifications and no training that I could sell,' she told me, 'I did a series of soul-destroying jobs which were awful at the time, but I became quite good at lying, pretending I would be there for the rest of my life.' She answered the phones in Peter Crouch's agency; she was a waitress in the 2i's in Soho, where she picked up decent tips; she did clerical work for a big City firm, which was keen to keep her; she worked in the Volkswagen garage in Swiss Cottage, in a television rental shop in Twickenham, in a taxicab office, in British Home Stores, in a phone answering company. In short, she did anything to pay the rent.

Over the next thirty months her life was measured out not just in a shortage of money, but in a run of jobs in which she had no interest. This was a brand of poverty quite different from that of her parents in Hoylake, and it etched itself on Glenda's mind. She had always had a very highly developed work ethic. 'I come from working-class people,' she avers, 'and I suppose it [the work ethic] stems from the fact that they never bought anything unless they actually had the money to pay for it. You never got things, when I was a child, unless you worked for them.' But this period of grinding unemployment gave a new, anxious, element to that ethic: 'If it goes on for long enough, you get a sense that if you're not in work, you'll never work again; and I don't think I'll ever lose that threat hanging over me.'

Yet Glenda retained a strong sense of what she wanted to do. She was, and she readily admits that she still is, intensely ambitious, and although this period depressed her, she was determined that she would work as an actress again. As Marcia Ashton noted when first they met, Glenda 'not only had the talent, but the tenacity as well'. So when, in 1959, Roy was offered work as a Red Coat at the Pwllheli Butlins on the Lleyn Peninsula in North West Wales, performing in the resident company, Glenda resolved at first to stay in London, determined to find theatre work. 'She didn't even last a week on her own, though,' Roy says, 'and within days she was on the train to Pwllheli as I had managed to get her a Blue Coat job.' This meant, in Glenda's words, 'being in charge of reservations and having to tell all the happy holidaymakers who wanted to be in York House that they were in Windsor House. So there. Not an experience I'd care to repeat.'

Roy's memory of the summer season spent at Butlins is warm. 'We had a super place to stay, a delightful cottage in the back yard of a pub, which we shared with another girl because it would have been too expensive otherwise.' But so dispirited was Glenda by the Butlins experience that she made herself seriously ill with acute sinusitis and was forced to spend a fortnight in bed, completely losing her until then voracious appetite. Suddenly she lost pounds in weight – 'so much so that Roy worried I would snap'. Pauline

Devaney recalls that this coincided with a new determination in Glenda:

> She tried very hard to re-create herself. When she was at Butlins she dyed her hair peroxide and started to wear mauve and she made a great effort to be glamorous because she knew she had to do something about her appearance if she was going to work. I think she based herself on Jeanne Moreau who was very popular at the time as a sort of *jolie laide* actress. She also became very strict about dieting – suddenly all the homely cooking went out the window. Potatoes disappeared. It was just meat and veg. Gone was the apple pie and custard she always used to make.

It was as if she had sloughed off her puppy fat, and the new Glenda that returned to London was a thinner, wirier figure with taut cheek bones and a new, shorter, jagged haircut that accentuated the pout of her lips and dispelled the rounded, homely aura that had surrounded her younger self. It is no surprise that when Elizabeth Spriggs met Glenda again, in 1962, she failed to recognise her.

When Roy and Glenda arrived back in London Anna Welsh again came to the rescue, finding them a new, larger room, in King Henry's Road in Swiss Cottage, where they were to stay for the best part of a decade. Still Glenda found no work. Her agent, Peter Crouch, virtually gave up on her, especially when she accepted Blue Coat work. And as 1959 slipped first into 1960, and then 1961, Glenda's spirits ebbed lower and lower. At times she was inconsolable. Roy remembers nights when he would have to call the doctor to King Henry's Road to treat Glenda for all manner of mysterious illnesses that had no name and no cure, but which clearly left Glenda fragile, empty and listless. 'Basically she was just desperate at being out of work and it took an enormous physical toll on her,' he told me. As Pauline Devaney relates:

> I was aware she'd had some kind of breakdown. But they didn't mention it very much. It was very hushed up and anyway I suppose it depends what you mean by a

breakdown. She was certainly very out of work and very miserable. I even remember my mother lending her clothes for auditions. And the worst of it was that Roy was very much in the ascendant and Glenda was reduced to following him around everywhere – which was never very Glenda.

Glenda eventually pulled through. But the brutalising tendency of a profession that is inherently whimsical and has rejection built in to it had changed her. The 'soft, malleable, even vulnerable' character Elizabeth Spriggs worked with in Worthing disappeared, and in its stead there grew a tougher, more resilient woman. The physical change that had come about at Butlins was now matched by an internal emotional restructuring. Counter tedium at Boots had schooled Glenda in ambition, but these endless, power-less months of poverty and under-employment completed that education, transforming her into a determined, square-jawed professional.

Other RADA students believed that the Academy should have prepared actors better for the ordeal of the working theatre. Hugh Whitemore complained:

> We were told how Restoration fops took snuff, but not how to cope with the exhausting routine of weekly rep. Nobody taught us how to talk to an agent, how to make a few pounds as a television extra, how to sign on for the dole. In other words, nobody taught us how to survive. They showed us how to spread the icing, but not how to mix the cake.[5]

It is a point reiterated by Josie Kidd: 'RADA didn't really prepare you for having the hide of a rhinoceros . . . rejection is going to be part of your life . . . you're going to have to sell yourself very hard.'

Glenda toughed it out, writing letters to all the provincial theatres every season, trawling the papers for auditions, preparing new aud-ition pieces, keeping in contact with anyone who might possibly be able to help, and waiting (in the days before answerphones) for phone calls that never came.

Work did eventually materialise, thanks to a *rapprochement* with

Peter Crouch and an old contact, Miriam Brickman, the casting director at the Royal Court who had taken a protective – if rather too occasional to be effective – interest in Glenda's career. When a friend of Miriam's, Antony Page, who was then directing the Dundee repertory theatre, called Miriam at the very last minute for suggestions for a female member to join the company for a brief period before the summer break, she suggested 'my Glenda', and the deal was struck. Glenda was delighted to be back in proper work, especially as Dundee was a well-respected fortnightly rep theatre, performing everything from the obligatory *Salad Days* to *A Streetcar Named Desire*, and Scottish Television had just decided to record a couple of the final productions from the season for transmission later in the year. Moreover, the company then at Dundee was remarkable. The main players of the 1960–61 season were Nicol Williamson, Gawn Grainger and Edward Fox, and they were joined at various points by Brian Cox and Prunella Scales.

Glenda appeared, as Pam, the bride, in *Fools Rush In*, by Kenneth Horne, as Marina in *In Search of Happiness* by Victor Rozov and finally as Katherine in Clifford Hanley's new play, *The Durable Element*. It was an immensely enjoyable time, even if on one occasion Glenda drew the lot as 'the actor least likely to make it' at a backstage party.

Roy, however, was not happy with Glenda spending so many weeks away in Dundee, and when he made a brief weekend visit to see her, he insisted that she come back to London. Glenda was not happy with her husband's autocracy, and her mood was soured by the fact that she had just lost a tooth, but such was her reliance on Roy that she acquiesced. By the middle of June she was on a train back south to London and to another period of unemployment. Peter Crouch was displeased that Glenda was throwing away her few breaks.

The spell at Dundee re-established Glenda's sense of herself as an actress, but it hardly spelt the end of her struggle against unemployment, and the next two years were to see further bouts of bar work. During this time, however, there was at last a steady trickle of engagements. She played a waitress in the Royal Court's second cast production of *The Kitchen*, by Arnold Wesker. Thanks to the director of *The Durable Element*, the actor and television producer John Crockett, early in 1962 she even took over the lead, at twenty-four hours' notice, and with only eight hours' rehearsal, of *The Idiot* with the Ikon Theatre Company at the Lyric, Hammersmith.

In September Roy was taken on as a stage manager at Watford, where Jimmy Perry (who later wrote *Dad's Army*) and his wife Gilda leased the theatre for seasons of weekly rep, which they performed with an ad hoc company that took actors on by the week. Yet again Roy managed to get Glenda a job in the company, although if Glenda had hoped that Watford would turn into a source of regular employment, she was to be disappointed. She received good notices ('Glenda Jackson, pale and edgy, does not overdo the revelation of her anxiety but conveys it and its complex source with authenticity'),[6] and so impressed one of her colleagues, Joyce Marlow, that Joyce rang her own mother to tell her that she had met someone who would be a great West End star as she had both 'the fuck-off confidence and the voice', but after a few weeks the parts ran out. Joyce and her husband Patrick Connor, who also appeared with Glenda, were less impressed by Roy, who accidentally managed to bring the curtain up one night with Joyce practically naked on stage.

So, by the autumn of 1962, although Roy had worked almost non-stop in the theatre, Glenda had spent far more of her career 'resting' than acting, and it was not until 1963 that she enjoyed her first real break.

The ephemeral nature of theatre and the permanence of celluloid and vinyl has determined that Bill Naughton's *Alfie* is best remembered today for Michael Caine and Cilla Black, but the stage production was every bit as emblematic of swinging sixties Britain and was funnier, less sentimental and less misogynist. The language was forthright – one reviewer complained about the incessant use of 'bleedin'' – the issues were treated with raw attention (abortion, casual sex, men's attitude to women), and although Donald McWhinnie was renowned as something of a 'non-director', he cast the play cleverly. John Neville, in a dramatic style as far removed from his long run of Old Vic Shakespearean productions as can be imagined, played the eponymous cockney lad and suddenly the 'best Hamlet of his generation' was a modern actor. As Harold Hobson argued in *The Sunday Times*, 'for a decade Mr Neville has concealed himself in costume and subdued his voice to talking posh. *Alfie* is his moment of revelation. It shows him to be one of our first actors, touching, sincere and very, very comic.'[7] Glenda appeared as one of Alfie's 'birds', Siddie. McWhinnie also cast a set of young unknown actors, Gemma Jones and Patrick Mower, and Glenda's colleague from Watford, Patrick Connor. Other actors were even more of a risk – the Welsh actor who played the abortionist, Norman Wynne, killed himself with Guinness in the middle of the run. When the play opened in June at Bernard Miles' still new Mermaid Theatre in Puddle Dock in the City it so successfully caught the rebellious mood of the age that it proved an instant second hit in a row for Naughton. It transferred to the Duchess Theatre in July and (with a changed cast and new production), to Broadway the following year.

This was Glenda's first part in a truly commercial production in the West End, and although it was not a particularly stretching one, she not only received a couple of complimentary mentions in reviews, but everyone in the company acknowledged that she was exceptional. Marcia Ashton, who played Lily, one of the older roles, recalls that although Glenda had not particularly shone in the early rehearsals, when it came to the first dress rehearsal everybody suddenly sat up the moment she came on stage because 'she was surrounded by this incredible energy'.

This minor breakthrough in Glenda's career, bringing her her longest period of sustained employment to date, was welcome, but it was hardly glamorous and appearing night after night for brief scenes at the beginning and the end of the play was no luxury. In addition, because her dressing room lay next to the wardrobe room and she left stage early on, Glenda invariably made the interval teas. Even at this point in her career she confessed to Marcia to being bored with acting: 'I tell you what, I'm not going to do this for ever. I've got to do something more worthwhile.' Glenda was also shocked by the difference between repertory theatre and the West End:

> The thing that surprised me when I came out of rep into what one always looked up to as the best theatre – which was the West End and then the large, subsidised

companies – was the amount of time and energy that was wasted. The actual quality of the work, and the application to work, was far less than one experienced in the provinces, where, often, the plays were flung on in one or two weeks' time.

The numbing tedium of repetition which is the lot of actors in long West End runs, combined with the appalling backstage state of the Duchess, barely made for an auspicious commercial debut for Glenda – and she and Roy were still poor, living in their single room in King Henry's Road in Swiss Cottage. But Glenda was ambitious, her determination evident in both the almost excessive concentration she applied to her work, and her resolve not to sit on her laurels. She knew better than most that theatrical good fortune would not come her way as a natural right. She would, as life in Hoylake had taught her, have to 'work, work, work', and she was still convinced that 'plums don't fall into plain girls' laps'. So, from the beginning of the production Glenda continued to look for other, better parts, auditioning for other shows and hoping for that elusive major breakthrough.

CHAPTER THREE

———— ✳ ————

Brook, Marowitz and Shakespeare

W HEN THAT BREAKTHROUGH eventually came it was precisely
thanks to her 'alternative' looks and not despite them. For, in the
changing world of sixties British theatre, self-conscious plainness
could, for the first time, be an asset.

Stale, flat but fairly profitable, sums up British theatre of the
time. Two impresarios dominated the realm of red plush velvet
seats. The elder of the two, the sixty-two-year-old Prince Littler,
had made his name with West End pantomimes and imported US
musicals like *Brigadoon* and *Carousel*, whose success had helped him
buy theatres, amalgamate corporations and amass a fortune.

Despite the decline in theatre-going, in 1963 he either owned
or controlled 57 of the regional theatres on the touring circuit and
34 out of 53 'number one' venues (major regional theatres that
could accommodate large touring productions), as well as 18 out
of London's 42 working West End theatres.

As if to complete his control he held a majority share in H. M.
Tennent Productions Ltd, whose managing director was the forty-
five-year-old gay impresario Hugh 'Binkie' Beaumont. Binkie was
austere, self-contained and virtually omnipotent. He shared with
Littler a virtual duopoly in both the commercial and (thanks to a
Treasury exemption on entertainment tax for productions deemed
'worthwhile' by the Arts Council) much of the 'subsidised commercial theatre'. This meant that their artistic values (fine writing that
avoided controversy, opulent staging, star casting, well-made three-
act plays that kept you guessing and ended tidily) were imprinted
upon the whole of the British theatre. For a new generation these
conventions felt like tight, restricting shackles.

There was, if you chose to search it out, an alternative London theatre. The Royal Court Theatre in Sloane Square had reopened in 1952 after a twenty-year spell as a cinema, and in 1956 became the home of George Devine and Tony Richardson's English Stage Company. The company's first season included John Osborne's *Look Back in Anger*, which struck a blow for a new brand of 'kitchen sink' drama that reflected the increasingly confrontational spirit of the age. Later came more adventurous productions of better plays such as John Arden's *Serjeant Musgrave's Dance* in 1959.

In the East End Joan Littlewood and Ewan McColl's Theatre Workshop, treading boldly in the socialist footsteps of the thirties Unity Theatre, had taken up residence in a decaying old music hall, the Theatre Royal, Stratford East. Here they staged the London premières of Brendan Behan's belligerent *The Quare Fellow* (1956) and *The Hostage* (1958); Shelagh Delaney's Salford play *A Taste of Honey* (1958); and, most famously, Littlewood's own musical satire on the First World War, *Oh, What a Lovely War!* in 1963.

Both theatres shared a basic set of convictions: that contemporary commercial theatre was bereft of vision; that theatre should embrace the whole of life; that the hierarchical star system stunted talent; and that theatrical censorship, overseen by the Lord Chamberlain, had to go.

They were not alone – there had been calls for a 'new theatre' since the war. Pre-eminent among those who eschewed the traditions of the past was Peter Hall, the East Anglian son of a railway clerk who had taken over the Arts Theatre Club in 1955, directing the British première of Samuel Beckett's *Waiting for Godot* there in 1956. After triumphantly guest directing *Love's Labour's Lost* that same year and *Cymbeline* in 1957 (both at the Shakespeare Memorial Theatre in Stratford-upon-Avon), Hall took over as Stratford's artistic director. Almost instantly he set about creating a major semi-permanent repertory company which would stage challenging new British and foreign plays. Committed to greater ensemble playing, he persuaded luminaries like Peggy Ashcroft to make two- or three-year commitments to the company. In order to give the company a London showcase he raided Stratford's reserves to take a protracted lease on the Aldwych Theatre in the West End – something he achieved only by outsmarting the lessor, Prince

Littler. And with a keen eye for marketing he campaigned for a new name. In 1961 the Shakespeare Memorial Theatre became the Royal Shakespeare Company.

With the support of the RSC's chairman, Fordham Flower, Hall drafted in directors with a similar commitment to reshaping the theatre. First John Barton was summoned from Cambridge where he was a fellow at King's College, and where he had directed vividly natural Shakespeare productions for the Marlowe Society. Next to join the team in 1960 was Michel Saint-Denis, the sixty-three-year-old French director whose attempts to transform the theatre had included the thirties London Theatre Studio, the Comédie de l'Est in Paris and the formation, with George Devine, of the Old Vic School, immediately after the Second World War.[1] The last of the directors to arrive was the most influential. Peter Brook, who was still only thirty-seven in 1962, was already a theatre legend. At twenty-one he had directed *Love's Labour's Lost* at Stratford, at twenty-five *Measure for Measure* with John Gielgud, and at twenty-nine *Titus Andronicus* with Laurence Olivier. He had also taken the commercial theatre by storm, with Broadway and West End hits to his name, several of them under the Beaumont umbrella, and he had directed more contentious productions such as Truman Capote's black musical *House of Flowers* in New York.

More important, however, was Brook's growing frustration with the unquestioned assumptions upon which so much of contemporary theatre was based. From 1956 on – the year not only of *Look Back in Anger* but also of the first London visit of Bertolt Brecht's *Berliner Ensemble* – he penned regular broadsides against the mannered declamatory theatre of the day. Even the most basic elements of theatre had to be questioned if it was to have any value because 'what once passed for language is now seen to be lifeless and in no way expressive of what really goes on in human beings, what once passed for plot is now seen not to be plot at all, what once passed for character is now seen to be only a stereotyped set of masks'.[2]

It was through the influential bi-monthly radical theatre journal, *Encore*, in which these Brook manifestos appeared, that he came to learn of the work of a surly young New Yorker who had come to train at the London Academy of Music and Dramatic Art, LAMDA. Charles Marowitz too was angry at the complacency of

English theatre, but he focused more on the working actor, a 'prisoner in a profession which meticulously develops his spite, ambition, deceit and envy'.[3] The answer had to be the creation of a permanent company 'which is unconventional enough to have ideals and stable enough to work towards realising them. When this happens, a new ethic will evolve, and a better theatre.'[4]

Marowitz's attempts at shaping this 'better theatre' had been far less conformist than Brook's. He had set up a fringe group, In-Stage, in a minuscule garret in Fitzroy Square, where he had tried out the wilder ideas of Beckett and Artaud. Brook's *Encore* manifestos appealed to his innate sense of anarchy, so early in 1962 he invited Brook to see his In-Stage production of Ray Abell's quirky short play *A Little Something for the Maid*. By the middle of the year they were hatching plans for an experimental theatre group under the aegis of the RSC, and Marowitz was working as Brook's assistant on his acclaimed and enormously successful *King Lear*, with Paul Scofield magnificently catching Brook's sense of enveloping nothingness.

In the meantime work was progressing on the experimental group. Peter Hall had used most of the RSC's first year of Arts Council subsidy in 1962 (£90,000) to pay for an experimental season at the Arts Theatre Club, with productions of Middleton's *Women Beware Women*, David Rudkin's *succès de scandale Afore Night Come* and Maxim Gorky's horrendously depressing *Lower Depths*.

To Brook's eye this was still very safe experimentation. Brook was keen to stage Jean Genet's *Les Paravents*, known in English as *The Screens*. This was controversial in itself as it dealt with the mindless autocracy of French rule in Algeria, and had already been turned down by the Lord Chamberlain on the basis that it was deeply offensive to one of Britain's closest allies. It was, however, perfectly legal to mount productions of plays that would otherwise be banned, as long as the audience was deemed to be a private club – the Arts Theatre Club was one of many venues where such plays could be put on beyond the censor's reach.

More troublesome was the conviction shared by both Brook and Marowitz that there simply were not enough actors either within the RSC or on the wider market who had the skills and the training to perform with the rawness and disciplined recklessness that the

Genet piece demanded. After all Brook had been expostulating since 1959: 'Why are our actors lazy and passionless? Why do so few of them do more than two hours a day?'[5] He was convinced that 'England destroys artists', and saw a theatre 'subsidised to the hilt' as the only hope of training a new breed of actors. So he and Marowitz designed their new RSC experimental group as a theatrical finishing school, preparing a group of actors in techniques that would make possible the 'better theatre' they both espoused. Brook stated that: 'Its appeal must be that it can *dare completely*: that it can *dare* offer any author with a completely uncommercial idea, a stage *immediately*. It would be an actor's studio of writers, it would be our avant-garde.'[6]

By the time Glenda was opening in *Alfie* in the summer of 1963 Brook and Marowitz had the subsidy they needed – from the Gulbenkian Foundation – and the political backing – from Peter Hall – for a twelve-week experiment with up to twelve actors (in the end there were ten) on £12 a week, and with no requirement to produce anything for public consumption at the end. Finding actors who were willing and able to indulge in such wild new techniques was not easy. 'We were looking for marginal people,' Brook told me, 'those on the outside. But most people who wanted to be actors in those days were busy grooming themselves to be respectable.'

Marowitz devised a new style of auditions. Instead of declaiming a set speech, the actors' individualistic and declamatory instincts would be frustrated by group workshops with plenty of improvisational games. They would be asked to repeat their prepared speech, but in a completely different and inappropriate character – and then to do it again, before taking part in an hour-long group exercise with five or six other actors. This was completely unheard of at the time. Despite the fact that a place in the RSC was something most young actors would kill for, and despite Brook's soaring reputation, many actors turned tail and fled. Others had their agents ring to cancel the auditions. It became part of the RSC's many legends that one actor went home after his taxing audition and took his own life. But, slowly, others – in Brook's words 'a good group of cookies' – came on board. Jonathan Burn was cast after an audition with six others that involved playing with a ball that became first Yorick's skull and then the globe on Atlas's back, and Richard Dare, an older actor who had appeared with Glenda at Watford, also signed up, along with Leon Lissek, Freda Dowie, Rob Inglis, Robert Lloyd, Susan Williamson and a Canadian, Alexis Kanner.

Glenda was more than eager to impress the celebrated Peter Brook, whom she already admired 'as a sort of god', so she laboured hard at a less conventional audition piece. By the day she came to audition there were two places left for women, one of which was taken early in the morning by Mary Allen, a young actress. How Glenda then won the final place is still a matter of dispute between Marowitz and Brook.[7]

Either way, both Brook and Marowitz acknowledge the extra-ordinary power of those first impressions. 'In came a very curious figure, a hidden, shy and yet aggressive, badly dressed girl who seemed resentful of everything,' says Brook. She let it slip that she hated audition speeches, so she had prepared a short story by Dorothy Parker, which she delivered. Brook asked her to do it again, first as a street salesman, then as if addressing a political meeting, and finally as a woman incarcerated in a psychiatric hospital by her husband and trying to convince others of her sanity. Whatever they threw at her in the four-hour audition workout, she threw back in double measure. Marowitz recalls watching her

> stark nutty eyes shifting slowly in her head like arc-lights; feeling that behind her studied stillness was a cobra ready to spring or an hysteric ready to break down; choosing my words carefully and getting back short, orderly answers that betrayed the very minimum of feeling and information; being perpetually conscious of a smoulder-ing intelligence rating both my questions and her own answers as she shifted her focus from within or without, mimicking the mechanism of a hyper-sensitive tape-recorder that could fast-forward to rewind with the flick of an invisible switch.[8]

Brook was no less mesmerised 'by the sudden plunges she took and by her intensity'.[9] But he also noticed something curious in one so evidently unrestrained: 'I had seldom encountered anyone so determined to be concealed. She hid behind an ugly thick overcoat, a scarf, a woollen hat, a scowl, half-closed eyes and a sarcastic, defensive voice.'[10]

Also auditioning that day was another exceptional young actress called Eileen Atkins, who did a powerful, if more conventional audition soon after Glenda. This left Brook and Marowitz with a straight choice for the last place. Marowitz believes not only that there was pressure from elsewhere in the RSC to take Eileen, but also that he was so fervent in trying to persuade Brook to take Glenda that Brook thought Marowitz had sexual designs on her. Brook's memory, however, is different. As he wrote to Marowitz,

> We both weighed one against the other from all points of view and were both sharing a real question and a genuine indecision. There was no moment when you fought against me for Glenda. What my very exact memory has recorded is how the question was ultimately clinched. You said: 'I've got an idea that Glenda's marriage has just broken up – she's all screwed up and I think that's a better starting point for the sort of work we're going to do rather than Eileen, who seems comfortably settled down.'[11]

There was no truth to his suspicions. Glenda and Roy certainly knew how to row. Indeed, their first big bust-up came only weeks after their wedding when Roy had decided to go home after the Saturday-evening performance of *Sadie* to watch Bette Davis in *Now Voyager* on television. Glenda, who had to stay behind until early in the morning to strike the show, was furious that Roy had refused to pick her up from the theatre and had 'left me to walk the dark deserted streets of Darlington'. But these full-throttle, sometimes public rows were no more than grist to their theatrical and still passionate love life. As Glenda admits:

> Control is part of my nature. I suppose the closest I've come to uncontrollable passion is when I've really lost my temper, and that is an extremely unpleasant experience which makes me shake for two days afterwards. I throw anything that comes to hand; crockery, ornaments and I've even swept everything off a shelf with great

abandon. It all goes in what seems to be the most salient direction. And afterwards it's always very salutary because I have to do all the sweeping up.[12]

It comes as no surprise that Timothy West thought of Roy as 'the least likely person in the world to be married to Glenda, because he was not quite up to all the strife', but Pauline Devaney believes that these dramatic arguments were cathartic and harmless for both Roy and Glenda. They were still very much a couple and the years of Glenda's unemployment had cemented their dependence on each other.

Glenda's air of being 'screwed-up' was derived instead from the fact that she was totally different, on many levels, from other actresses of the time: her looks were unconventional and her attempts at glamour were conspicuously unsuccessful; she was an evidently curious mixture, an uninhibited introvert in an extrovert's profession; she was hungry for success, yet she reeked of disdainful defiance. Moreover, Glenda intentionally fostered a disturbed air while acting for Peter Brook. As Pauline Devaney put it to me: 'Glenda is a very hard worker and just as with any other part of her professional life she worked extremely hard at her image.'

What also helped Glenda win the day, though, was the fact that, according to Roy: 'We had seen Brook's *Irma La Douce* and we knew that to work with Brook was to work with God. He was *the* guru and she wanted it more than I have ever seen anyone want anything in my life.' And so began the most taxing period of her career. Brook and Marowitz were both passionate about their work and there were no half measures. The rehearsals, or daily experimental workshops, which lasted a full eight weeks, were every bit as arduous and unusual as the auditions, deliberately pushing the actors to extremes, confounding their easy notions of how to convey emotions, frustrating their inveterate desire to deliver a text.

Jonathan Burn recalls that on the first morning, in the Church Hall off Sloane Square, before any kind of introduction to the other actors, each of them was given something to bang with and something to bang on. They had 'to explore the range of their instrument' by bashing ladles on tin cans and tin cans on the floor. They rapped the floor with their forehead, a knuckle, an elbow, a knee. And once they had done all this 'exploration' they rapped out a series of rhythms: in unison with others, in harmony, syncopated, accelerated, decelerated, in pairs, in threes, alone. Then they graduated to other 'instruments' – broom handles, tennis racquets and empty crates – playing out pitched battles and scenes from *Romeo and Juliet* in a wild symphony of metallic tinkles and brass percussions.

More was to follow, with a whole series of games and exercises dreamed up by Marowitz to realise Brook's aspiration to a form of theatre 'that would not depend on anecdote or character or even verbal messages, but which would communicate *directly* to an audience through a combination of all its elements – sound, gesture, the visual relationship between actors and objects'.[13] One such exercise involved reducing an improvised scene of a sensitive man trying to get rid of his over-fond girlfriend to a series of communicative sounds – or grunts. This was meant to teach the actors how to find their own 'new theatrical language'. Some of the results of this work were impressive, but no sooner had the actors learnt how to please or impress Brook than he would put them through another round of exercises that completely confounded what had just been done – all in the name of forcing them to delve deeper into themselves. It is scarcely surprising that at times the actors felt used and abused. So convoluted were the ensuing emotional power games that Brook could come across as a manipulative dictator and Jonathan Burn would ask himself, 'Was Brook doing that because he disliked you or because he *wanted* you to think he disliked you?'

Although at first terrified that she would not be up to it, Glenda revelled in all this. The sense of disciplined energy, of channelled wildness, appealed both to the puritan and the rebel within her. Glenda would often go further than anyone else, pushing the boundaries of taste and testing her own vast reserves of moral courage. She appeared scornful of those who would take the easy route. She delighted in Brook's mind games, the power play of rehearsals and the opportunity to search within herself to find a more profound truth. She also, of course, liked the stable income – with *Alfie* in performance and the RSC in rehearsal she and Roy finally escaped poverty.

After three or four weeks, though, there was a great surge of anger in the company, and several of the actors demanded that Brook and Marowitz also take part in the exercises. Glenda, the last to join the company, was the first to speak out. This time the directors held their ground. The next battle hinged on Brook's decision to invite Michel Saint-Denis to work with the company for a day on the use of masks; something neither Brook nor Marowitz had ever used before. There had been grumbles the previous evening, when Saint-Denis' visit had been announced, but on the morning it was Glenda who first mounted a rebellion, arguing that the whole point of the group was to find out what could truthfully be expressed *without* the use of extraneous conventions and props – the masks were completely at odds with this, and Brook should know better. Brook was chastened, angered and impressed by the arrogance of this unknown actress, so Saint-Denis was politely asked to leave, and work resumed.

For all Brook's theoretical austerity, he is a showman at heart and he soon felt the need to put the company on show. By week eight it was deemed that the company had gelled enough to put on a performance of their 'work in progress' for an invited audience. Variously described as 'a nutty little programme of surrealist vaudeville'[14] (Marowitz) or 'an avant-garde revue' (Brook), this show ran at the LAMDA theatre from 12 January 1964 for five weeks and put an end to Glenda's appearance in *Alfie*. Brook explained in the programme notes that he had decided to call the evening's entertainment *The Theatre of Cruelty* in homage to the radical French theatrical guru Antonin Artaud. Brook had long been an admirer of Artaud, and later, in his own seminal book *The Open Space*, described him as an 'illuminated genius', as a 'prophet in the desert ... railing against the sterility of the theatre', and as the inventor of 'a Holy Theatre in which the blazing centre speaks through those forms closest to it. A theatre working like the plague, by intoxication, by infection, by analogy, by magic; a theatre in which the play, the event itself, stands in place of a text.'[15] Despite his admiration, however, Brook recognised that Artaud needed some explanation to a London audience, as did the Theatre of Cruelty. 'Artaud', he explained, 'used the word "cruelty" not to invoke sadism, but to call us towards a theatre more rigorous, or even, if we could follow him that far, pitiless to us all.'[16] In fact,

Artaud was even more specific: 'from a mental viewpoint, cruelty means strictness, diligence, unrelenting decisiveness, irreversible and absolute determination'.[17] This was a rather recondite understanding of cruelty and for years Brook had to field questions about his supposedly dubious sadistic taste, but the austerity of the vision espoused in Brook's – or Artaud's – Holy Theatre was fierce. Brook was keen to assert that 'This group is not a showcase for people looking for future stars, but one which hopes to be accepted per se. It isn't trying to make news; it hopes to provoke wide discussion.'[18]

It certainly did.

The programme consisted of two nonsense text pieces by Paul Abelman, two versions of Artaud's *Spurt of Blood*, a wordless dramatisation of a short story by Robbe-Grillet, two collages by Brook, three scenes from *The Screens* (which were soon dropped), short pieces by Ray Bradbury and Cyril Connolly, a collage *Hamlet* devised by Marowitz and two improvised 'free' scenes. Elements changed frequently. One night the national anthem was played at the end of the show and the audience stood (as convention then dictated), only to be disconcerted that no sooner had the tape finished than it started again. It took three or four replays before the audience reluctantly abandoned the theatre. Glenda and the Canadian actor Alexis Kanner, whom Marowitz describes as 'the most obnoxious members of the company' and who shared nothing so much as their dislike for each other, performed a surrealist piece by Paul Abelman for five weeks with a completely new sub-text every night – much to Marowitz's admiration. But most of the LAMDA show still bore the marks of conventional theatre. Several of the sketches could easily have come from situation comedies and, unlike the purist work of Artaud, many of the aspects of the performance were based on accessible images of modern life, while the *Hamlet* collage ('O what a rogue and peasant slave am I' was given by Alexis Kanner hanging above the audience) depended for its wit on an audience that was well versed in the play.

One part of the evening's entertainment took on a life of its own, however, and in the process established Glenda in a sixties emblematic role; 1963 had been a year of national and international iconic events. In January the Wykehamist Leader of the Opposition, Hugh Gaitskell, suddenly died, and a month later the grammar-school boy Harold Wilson took over the reins of a reinvigorated Labour Party. In October, just as rehearsals for the Theatre of Cruelty got under weigh, the sixty-seven-year-old patrician Harold Macmillan handed over the Tory leadership and the premiership to the sixty-year-old aristocrat Sir Alec Douglas-Home. In the meantime the Government had faced a major scandal concerning the Tory War Minister John Profumo and a call-girl, Christine Keeler. Profumo denied having an affair with Keeler, who was also linked to a Soviet naval attaché. When the evidence of his affair emerged he was forced to confess that he had lied to the House of Commons – and to resign. With both the Cold War and the sexual revolution of the sixties at full pelt, the names of Profumo and Keeler became emblematic of the changing social order. The defining political moment of the year came in the middle of rehearsals, when, on 22 November, John Fitzgerald Kennedy was shot on his way to lunch in Dallas. The amateur camera work that captured the event was to be transmitted around the world and images of his wife Jackie – both in the car as her husband died and at the funeral – were etched in the collective memories of the Western world.

Brook realised that there could be 'a strange correspondence between this world heroine and this rejected whore' and he put together the outline for a sketch which he thought might suit Glenda's anarchic left-wing sympathies. Central to the sketch, which Brook called 'The Public Bath', was a searing image he recalled of Christine Keeler's ritual humiliation, when on her arrival in prison she was stripped and washed in public because it was assumed that she would be filthy, despite the fact that she was a very expensive – and therefore doubtless thoroughly cleaned and perfumed – prostitute.

For the purposes of the season, the LAMDA theatre had been turned around so that the tiered seating area was now the acting arena, and the audience sat on the stage. This gave the actors a steeply raked platform with an elevated entrance at the back. At the start of Brook's sequence Glenda appeared at the top of the high stairway that led down between the seats, wearing the conventional costume of a high-class whore: a tight black dress, black stockings and high heels. She was Christine Keeler. She began to strip, simply removing her clothes without seductiveness. Presently she was entirely naked, but still with no sense of sexual allure. Here was a naked body, no more, no less. A judge recited over her. While men begged her for sex she was led, still naked and still impersonally asexual, down to the floor of the theatre, where she was placed in a metal bath. When she stepped out of the bath she was reclothed in shapeless prison garments with thick stockings and clumsy shoes. She knelt by the bath, which became a coffin. She was Jackie Kennedy. Men offered her condolences. The coffin was carried away.

Although Peggy Ashcroft had appeared naked once in a club performance in 1932 of *Fraulein Elsa*, in 1964 nudity was still the prerogative of the porn show and unheard-of in the straight theatre. There had been considerable doubt in Brook and Marowitz's minds as to whether Glenda would actually go through with it, not least because it seemed to go against both the puritanical element of her nature and her upbringing. In rehearsals she mimed the strip until the last dress rehearsal, when there was an amazing tension in the air. Would she go ahead or would she turn around and rebel again? When the moment came she tossed her head, as if to defy the world to think it shameful, and with 'dry, undramatic resignation' (Marowitz) proceeded to strip. When she stood naked Brook believed that 'of all her integrities it was clear her integrity to her work would be the strongest'. The day when Brook first suggested the scene Glenda raised it with Roy. 'He wants me to strip,' she told him. 'What do you think?' Roy admits now that his ambition for her, as well as Glenda's, pushed him into telling her, 'Of course you must do it.' When it came to the first night, though, he was furious.

He was not the only member of the audience to be outraged by the evening's entertainment, although the fact that the LAMDA Theatre was a private, 'members only' club (so avoiding censorship) meant that it was witnessed by a self-selecting audience of liberal theatrical cognoscenti. Glenda's nudity led to complaints, although Brook, not Glenda, took the blame. A couple of the members of the cast noted that Glenda had ugly, painful-looking varicose veins. But in the main there were only plaudits for Glenda's performance, and the 'public bath' acquired a reputation as the apotheosis of sixties theatre – not a mere representation of events, but an event in itself. Glenda Jackson, this unknown, almost coarse, out-of-town actress with unconventional looks, stormed her way defiantly into the forefront of the sexual revolution.

This was not entirely what Glenda had intended. She had entered the profession with no ambition to change the shape of British theatre, nor had she particularly fixed views about the politics of sexual liberalisation. If anything, Glenda was the least likely person to demand sexual freedom. She had married Roy soon after meeting him because she believed it was morally better to be married than to live in sin. Roy was her only lover, and their relationship was remarkably conservative. Roy partly attributes this to his upbringing.

> My mother worked as a cleaner for twenty-eight years, but my father was so determined that a woman's place was in the home that she hid it from him all those years and he went to his grave not knowing she'd ever worked. And I inherited that. I even remember telling Glenda when we first got married, 'If ever you become more successful than me, that's it.' And Glenda replied, 'Well, there's no chance of that, is there?'

Glenda's family was equally conservative, and although she and Roy were great friends with the actor Peter Bromilow right up until his death, his sexual adventures and love of handcuffs, whips and bondage remained an incomprehensible mystery to them both. Glenda was an unlikely campaigner for sexual liberation, yet her work, first at the RSC and later in film, was to play a vital part, in Roy's words, 'in the birth of girl power, stirring the cauldron of women's lib and bringing a real neurotic edge to the theatre'.

Despite any incongruities, Brook's rigour of thought was vitally important to Glenda. She admits: 'I wasn't prepared for Peter Brook's extraordinary way of working, but I adored it. Admittedly by the end of the Theatre of Cruelty I never wanted to hear the word Artaud again.'[19] And she came to respect Brook with a careful eye, nicknaming him 'the Buddha'. 'Ah, the time and effort, suffering the boredom,' she recalled. 'But you will never work with a director as remarkable as him. He doesn't settle for boundaries. With Brook everything is possible.'[20]

By Christmas time the company knew that once the season was over in February they were going to be working on Genet's *The Screens*, which was to be performed in front of the Lord Chamberlain in the hope of gaining a licence for a full production. Brook was not particularly interested in performing the whole of the play, which he thought unnecessarily repetitive, but work began on twelve or thirteen scenes.

This involved another two months of rehearsal, still working in the arduous, abstract, improvisational way to which the actors were now growing accustomed. One of Brook's friends, the Russian film director Grigori Kozintsev, attended a rehearsal and drew a vivid picture of the day's Artaudian proceedings: 'frenzy, hoarse shouts, furious gabbling, bursts of complete incomprehensibility, howls and now and then a sort of hoarse barking; hysteria and the grotesque; the actors themselves painted spots (fire? blood?) on the white screens; fantastic stuffed birds, ritual rhythms, masks'.[21]

The Lord Chamberlain, Lord Cobbold, and a selection of theatre worthies had a private viewing of the production in the Donmar warehouse in then unfashionably sordid Soho. At that time it was quite literally a warehouse, with no stage or auditorium. The set consisted of white screens on castors, on which the actors would daub or throw paint to suggest scenery or an emotional effect. Martin Esslin, then resident dramaturg at the RSC, recalls that 'in one of the last scenes the peasants set fire to the colonialists' houses by painting the fire with red paint on white screens; after the performance the audiences rushed to grab these – they were some of the best action paintings you have ever seen'.[22] For all the excitement of the production the Lord Chamberlain was not impressed, and yet again he refused the play a licence on the grounds of possible offence to the French, so the show had only a few performances.

Just as the company was coming to terms with the fact that *The Screens* was never going to come to mainstage fruition, and several were contemplating unemployment, out of the blue Martin Esslin received the text of an anarchic and apocalyptic play, *Marat/Sade*, by the German playwright Peter Weiss. The play was still in performance in Berlin, but was looking for a British production. Would the RSC be interested? After a quick skim through, an excited Esslin rang Brook to tell him this was the play he had been looking for, and had it translated overnight by a colleague in the BBC. Brook was transfixed and persuaded the RSC to snap up the rights the very next day, thereby outwitting Ken Tynan, who was now Esslin's opposite number at the National Theatre (then based at the Old Vic), and who had already gone to Berlin to see the play for the National. Brook flew out to see the show, and although he found the production tame, he saw immediately that here was a play that would be an exact match for Artaudian principles. The Theatre of Cruelty company would have to be enlarged, but their newly acquired skills would finally be put to use.

Brook set about creating this new company while taking *King Lear* on tour in Russia and Scandinavia. Only five actors remained from the original group: Jonathan Burn, Robert Lloyd, Susan Williamson, Leon Lissek and Glenda, all of whom were finally put on long-term RSC contracts. Glenda was confident enough to make Brook beg her to accept a 'play as cast' contract, which guaranteed her employment for a whole season, although it meant that she had to accept whatever part she was offered. She rejoiced in the irony that she had failed two RSC auditions before appearing in front of Marowitz and Brook. The company also needed strong text-based actors and singers, and Clive Revill and the gravel-voiced Irish actor Patrick Magee were drafted in to play Marat and de Sade respectively. Elizabeth Spriggs, who had worked with Glenda twice before, turned down a part in a four-and-a-half-month tour of Clifford Williams' production of *The Comedy of Errors* to play one of the clowns. Others also joined the cast: Freddie Jones; Timothy West; Michael Williams; Henry Woolf, who later married Susan Williamson; a young Ian Richardson in the part of the herald; and Clifford Rose, Albany in *King Lear*, whom Brook offered the part of the warder of the asylum, Coulmier, a part he repeated in the 1997 Royal National Theatre production.

Diana Rigg was less fortunate. Despite an outstanding recent performance as Cordelia, and despite a promise of the part of Charlotte Corday, in the middle of the *Lear* tour a barely contrite Brook informed her that he had cast Glenda instead of her. Spriggs recalls seeing her flee the room in tears. Days later Rigg announced she was leaving the RSC to play Emma Peel in *The Avengers*, and everyone was led to believe that Glenda had inherited her part.

In equal parts gruelling, disturbing, frightening, sickening and fascinating, *The Persecution and Assassination of Marat as performed by the Inmates of the Asylum of Charenton under the Direction of the Marquis de Sade* (to give it its full title) is one of the most ferociously innovative plays of the twentieth century. Essentially it consists of a debate, ostensibly scripted by de Sade, between himself and the French revolutionary Marat, who lies cooling his appallingly itchy skin in a hip-bath in a pose reminiscent of the painting by David. Marat preaches revolutionary violence, de Sade the unlocking of the cells of the inner self by cruel, unfettered imagination. Around this philosophical debate is set the story of the French Revolution, which climaxes, after two abortive trips to Marat's house, in his murder at the hands of Charlotte Corday. All the parts in this play within a play are taken by disturbed inmates, and the action is regularly interrupted by bursts of singing ('Fifteen glorious years'), by wildly enacted scenes from the Revolution, and by musical history lessons given by four of the inmates dressed up as clowns. The only character who consistently remembers his lines is de Sade, and the others frequently succumb to their personal problems. Corday is played by a narcoleptic who regularly falls asleep and has to lie down on the ground. Her lover Duperret, supposedly a polite Girondist deputy, is played by an erotomaniac, who continually loses his self-control and thrusts his erection at the somnolent Corday. Occasionally the inmates run riot and the asylum warders have to douse them down with water, put them in straitjackets, or force them into one of the baths that the designer Sally Jacobs, who had worked in both the Theatre of Cruelty and *The Screens*, had sunken into the floor of the Aldwych revolve.

Brook, now working without Marowitz, wanted a very different production from the Berlin version he had seen. The actors were not just to present madness, but to 'be' mad, to 'face their own violence', and to draw on personal reserves of irrationality. His first approach in rehearsal was to get the actors to do anything they could think of, 'in a wild way'.[23] Next was to get everyone, through improvisation and open discussion, to recall instances of madness among their family or their friends, and to act them out. The company were given books by de Sade, Artaud and Ezra Pound to read; they were shown classic depictions of madness by Brueghel and Hogarth, and the 'black' paintings of Goya, which were painted out of the depths of Goya's deaf madness. Clifford Rose, by dint of playing one of the few 'sane' characters, did not attend the first two weeks of rehearsal but, once all the other actors were well advanced in their various clinical forms of insanity, was brought in dressed as a doctor to try and calm everyone down.

Six weeks into rehearsals the company were shown a couple of films, one of a dramatic performance in a French asylum, the other of a ritual in Nigeria. Brook later pointed out:

> The play is about madness as it was in 1808 – before
> drugs, before treatment, when a different social attitude
> to the insane made them behave differently, and so on.
> For this the actor had no outside model – he looked at
> faces in Goya not as models to imitate but as prods to
> encourage his confidence in following the stronger and
> more worrying of his inner impulses. He had to allow
> himself to serve these voices completely; and in parting
> from outside models, he was taking greater risks. He had
> to cultivate an act of possession.[24]

Of course this possession could never be complete. Lines still had to be delivered on cue, and the machinery of theatre still had to work. Robert Lloyd recalled:

> Every night I had to do a run from the back, in a strait-
> jacket, up to a bath-top that was lying on its side. It was
> quite a narrow ridge to run up and then jump off at the
> end, and it was dangerous to do if the bath-top wasn't
> being supported. And I'd look down a few lines before I
> had to do the run and I'd see this slobbering lunatic,
> John Harwood, with foam coming out of his mouth,
> rocking and moving, and yet on the same cue every night,
> for all those months his right foot would come out and
> he would support the bath-top, spot on and the person
> in front of him would move a hand round and support
> it from the other side, and that was it . . . There was a safe
> framework, but it looked so dangerous in the theatre.[25]

Brook was aiming at a theatrical experience that forced the audience to confront the very darkest side not only of humanity, but also of themselves. The parade of erotomaniacs, syphilitics, catatonics, schizophrenics, paranoiacs and manic depressives, with their howlings, wild songs, lust and suppurating sores, had to have structure, pace and rhythm, but the sense of ever edging closer to dangerous chaos had to hang in the air.

Glenda's performance was shockingly courageous. Jonathan Burns found playing madness 'a doddle', and Timothy West and Henry Woolf found a convenient way out: 'We decided that our kind of madness required a great deal of medication, so we spent a great deal of the play asleep in the corner and when it was our turn to do something one of the cast came over and woke us up with a kick. Peter Brook thought this was very inventive.' Glenda's part demanded a tougher discipline. The inmate who plays Charlotte Corday has few lines, but her presence on the stage is central. This meant that Glenda had nothing to draw on but her own darker resources. All the unhappiness, resentfulness, self-destructiveness and aggression she was capable of were channelled into a disconcertingly frightening portrayal. Some moments were truly disturbing. At one point she threw herself off a fourteen-foot ladder into the arms of the lunatic cast beneath. At another, at her own suggestion, according to Albert Hunt, who worked with Brook as an assistant, 'she used her hair [to whip de Sade], sometimes holding it in her hand, sometimes letting it hang freely; she would lovingly caress his bare shoulders with it and lash him as she flicked her head; inmates' whistling accompanied the strokes building to a climax as Sade collapsed on the phrase "the severed genitals of men"'.[26]

The play opened at the Aldwych on 20 August 1964. Brook saved his *coup de grâce* for the finale, when the warders lost control and the inmates set about raping the nuns and killing the weakest. With chaos everywhere a stage manager walked on stage and blew a whistle, at which point all the actors stopped acting and turned to look at the audience. They moved down stage and as the audience began to applaud, the actors started a slow, hostile, rhythmic handclap back at them.

The production excited immediate controversy. Despite having been granted the Lord Chamberlain's licence, it reeked of disrespect for the established certainties and, with *Afore Night Come*, it soon became one of the polite critics' *bêtes noires*. The chattering classes took sides with remarkable alacrity. Prince Littler's young brother Emile, who was on the RSC's Executive Council and who had been piqued when Hall took a lease on his brother's theatre, the Aldwych, instead of his own, the Cambridge, was furious. In an interview with the *Evening News* on 24 August 1964 he declared that these plays were out of keeping with the Queen's royal patronage: 'They are dirty plays. They do not belong, or should not, to the Royal Shakespeare Company.' Another RSC governor, Maurice Colbourne, objected to what he saw as the RSC poking fun at the Lord Chamberlain. The critic Ivor Brown wrote to Fordham Flower in November: 'If, as I surmise, Peter Brook is a big influence on Stratford and Aldwych policy, I think this is a pity since he appears to have so strong a proclivity for horrors. His craftsmanship is not in dispute, his taste is (incidentally, his favourites Artaud and Sade were both insane).'[27]

For others the *Marat/Sade* was the most potent proof that English theatre was not yet dead. Bernard Levin wrote in the *Daily Mail* that it was 'without doubt one of the half-dozen most amazing achievements that the English theatre has seen in my lifetime', while Harold Pinter was so impressed that he considered it to prove that 'the RSC bestrides the world – I must say it – like a colossus'.[28] The actor Jack Shepherd was deeply impressed by Glenda's performance. 'I was completely in awe of her energy,' he told me. 'You truly felt that she would stab Marat. That actress might be so out of control that she might actually kill him. It was like the Medusa just before she turns you to stone. I was completely intimidated.' Joan and Micky, who travelled down to London for the show, only volunteered that it was a shame that Glenda could not sing very well.

So began the 'dirty plays' row that was to rage for the next four years until the abolition, in 1968, of the Lord Chamberlain – thanks to the Secretary of State for the Arts, Jennie Lee, but against the wishes of Harold Wilson, who missed the relevant Cabinet meeting.

As a full member of the company on £30 a week since February, Glenda had not just been busy on the *Marat/Sade*. While rehearsing the *Marat/Sade* Glenda spent evenings and spare days understudying other RSC productions. Most understudies are never needed, and throughout three months backstage with Timothy West and Freddie Jones on Pinter's own production of *The Birthday Party*, Glenda was the only one to go on stage when Janet Suzman had laryngitis. Suzman recalls that everyone thought Glenda was so good it was 'rather a shame' when Janet recuperated and rejoined the cast.

The days of understudying, however, had ended with the summer opening of the *Marat/Sade*. Rave reviews and the special attention of all the RSC directors suddenly propelled Glenda into the front row of the younger generation of actors. She almost immediately started new RSC rehearsals in the Donmar warehouse, having been cast as Bellamira in Clifford Williams' production of Christopher Marlowe's *The Jew of Malta*, and the moment that opened she returned to rehearsal for a radio play by John Arden and Margaretta D'Arcy. When a brief respite came at the end of the year, with only performances of the Weiss and Marlowe plays in repertory to contend with, Glenda must have been only too happy to relax.

As for *The Jew of Malta*, Williams' production to celebrate the 400th anniversary of Marlowe's birth was only its second outing this century, and proved to be another triumph to follow Williams' wildly successful first RSC show, *The Comedy of Errors*. Despite having been thrown together at the last minute at Peter Hall's behest to fill a three-week gap while Brook put the finishing touches to *King Lear* in 1962, *The Comedy of Errors* had been lambasted by Hall at the very last minute. Hall repeated this trick with *The Jew of Malta*, taking little interest in the production until the penultimate dress rehearsal, at the end of which he asked Williams if he could take 'a couple of minutes' to give some notes to the company. Instead he spent two hours rubbishing the production. As a result Clive Revill, who was playing the Jew, entirely lost his confidence, and rehearsals had to be abandoned for three full days while the company recuperated. Several of the cast had had profound misgivings about the production since the first day of rehearsals, when John Nettleton recalls Williams coming in after a fortnight of 'research' in Malta, announcing that 'we're all going on a voyage of discovery'. Contrary to expectations the show received rave reviews and became yet another jewel in the RSC's crown – thanks, in Timothy West's view, to the fact that 'basically we played it for laughs'. Several felt that Williams had won some fortuitous and unearned praise.

By Christmas 1964 Glenda was well and truly ensconced in the Aldwych wing of the RSC, but it was not until the New Year, when she briefly shared an RSC tied cottage in Stratford-upon-Avon with the actress Patsy Byrne, that she broke into the Shakespearean preserve. It was a different world. In London there was plenty of companionship backstage and in rehearsal, but when the working day was over the diaspora began. At Stratford, in contrast, there was no getting away from the company. There were not just rehearsals and performances, but classes in verse-speaking, voice, movement and masks to attend, and when the day's work was done everybody met again in the pub. To all intents and purposes the seventy or so actors lived a communal life, and although Glenda now has a reputation as a 'quick trapper', in that she speeds off home the moment the work is done, during 1965 she (and Roy when he briefly joined her) played a full part in the social activities of the company, even becoming a regular green-room bridge player. Glenda was at her most clubbable and open, enjoying the new freedom that success afforded her, pleased for once to have Roy in tow rather than the other way round, and delighted to have at least temporary respite from poverty. Janet Suzman, with whom she slipped off to the Birmingham rep one afternoon to see Olivier as Othello, found her 'admirably modern, moody and aggressive', and delighted in their jovial rudeness to each other.

Michael Pennington, who was fresh out of Cambridge, found her a stimulating colleague: 'I was very impressed and awed to be working with this extraordinary woman whose unsentimental, bleak style, absolutely without flourish, was something quite new. She gained a reputation for taking enormous risks with cues.' It has been said that Glenda made many actors feel insecure or unsettled during this period, but even those who, like Clifford Rose, found Glenda 'very tough and quite spiky', admired her 'phenomenal commitment', and Donald Burton, who played Horatio, recalls her 'as a very warm person: completely without rancour'.

Yet Glenda did not really enjoy Stratford, and her stay was not entirely successful, thanks to some poor casting. The opening production of the season was John Barton's production of *Love's Labour's Lost*. This was as different a theatrical experience as can be imagined from the days of rolling on the floor for Peter Brook. Barton, a lanky, bearded eccentric (he had a reputation for chewing Gillette razor blades because he liked the sense of control it gave him) was always something of a theoretician, but in 1965 he was at his most scholastic. His vision of *Love's Labour's Lost* was strictly Elizabethan, which entailed baldpates, shaved eyelashes, tight stomachers and enormous farthingales for the women, while the men appeared dashing and elegant. It was not a particularly enjoyable production, and when the cast tried on the costumes for the first time Janet Suzman, Katie Barker and Glenda tottered on stage left, barely able to move or breathe, while four of the men bounded on stage right. Glenda and Janet immediately screeched to a halt and declared, almost in unison, '*we* are not appearing with *them*'. At which stage the diminutive Katie Barker fainted in a heap of velvet and corsetry, as if to prove the point that such precise period detail would strangle the play. So intense was Glenda and Janet's determination not to go on stage looking ludicrously ugly that they simply left her lying on the stage while they argued with Barton – who eventually caved in. Glenda might be prepared to appear naked for her art, but not with a baldpate and an exorbitant wig – or at least not yet.

In the summer of 1965 Glenda worked with Peter Hall for the first and last time. She played Ophelia in Hall's most risky *Hamlet*, which drew very deliberately on the anarchic ethos of the sixties. Hamlet was played by the twenty-four-year-old David Warner (Henry VI in *The War of the Roses* in 1962 and the butler in *Titanic* in 1997) as a febrile undergraduate in a long red scarf. Here was no romantic hero – Donald Sinden described Warner 'as a tall spotty youth who had not woken up'[29] – but an emblem of the angry younger generation. This was radically different from any other *Hamlet* to date. Hall was so worried that the production was too aggressively modern for the critics that he warned the cast on the eve of the Press night that, although they would get appalling reviews, this was still one of the most important productions of the decade and that it would remain in the repertoire for two years.

As it turned out, he was right. All the reviews were hostile except for Ronald Bryden in the *New Statesman*, yet *Hamlet* was an enormous box-office success, and it came to achieve a cult status, especially among the young. Every night there were interminable queues of teenagers clamouring for David Warner at the stage door, and the production passed into legend as the 'student' *Hamlet* that caught the spirit of the age long before the Paris student uprisings in 1968.

The critics made no exceptions for Glenda. For B. A. Young (in the *Financial Times*) she was too much in command of everything. For W. A. Darlington (in the *Daily Telegraph*) she was 'entirely sophisticated and with her wits so much about her that it is absurd to think that she could credibly lose them'. Only Penelope Gilliatt in the *Observer* rated her performance, noting that 'she makes Ophelia exceptional and electric, with an intelligence that harasses the court and a scornful authority full of Hamlet's own distaste', and recommending that Glenda should play Hamlet. Others agreed with the criticisms. Hall says he wanted 'a very emotional, very passionate actress, who suppresses all that till the last moment', but felt that Glenda lacked the sensitivity to restrain her strength until the mad scene. Janet Suzman, who followed Glenda in the role, says that 'the mad scene was rather Glendoid', Elizabeth Spriggs thought the performance was just a pale imitation of Glenda's Charlotte Corday, and blamed Hall for miscasting her, while Joyce Marlow felt that Glenda knew she was miscast which was why she overdid the aggression. Timothy West, one of the few London RSC actors to make the transition with Glenda to Stratford, was unconvinced by either of her Avonside appearances: 'She just played the Princess of France as the daughter of Charlotte Corday. It was quite wrong – a Peter Brook residue really. If only she'd had the courage or been amenable enough to advice, she should have said "Right, I've done that. Now for something new."' Although Glenda was shaken by the notices,[30] she was unrepentant, refusing to portray Ophelia as weak. 'Weak people don't break,' she points out, 'they bend. It's only the seemingly strong people who snap. The madness has to come as a surprise to everyone.'

If Glenda found it difficult to restrain herself in character she also found it tough holding back on her views in rehearsal. Nearly every actor she then worked with says how amazed they were that this still inexperienced actress was prepared to take on any director, including Hall. Hall believes there was a belligerence about her, as if she was saying 'You'd better jolly well prove why this is a good play and a good way of working – otherwise there'll be trouble', and that she had it in her to bully a director if he allowed her. This was partly her refusal to accept bullshit, but it also seemed bred of a desire to taunt authority and see how far she could go. With Brook this could be fascinating. As far as Hall was concerned it came too close to insubordination, especially when, from the ranks of the RSC, Glenda offered her own thoughts on him to a trendy sixties magazine, *Nova*: 'I do wish', she declared, '[Peter Hall] would stop pretending to be so bloody nice and simple and democratic when really he's very complicated and ambitious and a dictator. You have to have a boss. All right.'[31] (Interestingly, Hall still blames Glenda for an additional comment carried in the article – 'he's power mad' – but these were actually the words of another actor in the company, Roy Dotrice.) Speaking fifteen years later Glenda condescended: 'I have to say I don't really regard Peter Hall highly as a director and, therefore, I wasn't really looking for inspiration or guidance from him.'[32] Her view of Hall today is no more complimentary: 'I don't think I would ever use the word "joy" in connection with *that* man. There *is* someone who is manipulative,' she told me.

Glenda did not stay in *Hamlet* for long. From the moment it had opened in August, she had begun to rehearse with Peter Brook in London while commuting up to Stratford for the two Shakespeare productions. Brook's latest venture was another gruelling evening's entertainment by Peter Weiss, *The Investigation*, in which Glenda and Penelope Keith played all the women witnesses at Auschwitz and which opened in October (and which brought Glenda and John Nettleton together again).

By now it had also been decided to take the *Marat/Sade*, after fresh rehearsals with a slightly altered cast, and a week of performances in London, to New York, where it opened at the Martin Beck Theater on 27 December 1965. If anything the new production was more exciting than ever. Ian Richardson, now playing Marat, gave the philosophical debate with de Sade a more biting edge, and the play arrived in the United States with perfect timing. Not only, thanks to the Beatles, the Rolling Stones and the 'white heat' of Harold Wilson, were all things British in vogue, but the very theme of the play – political assassination – was extremely topical. If a British audience was intrigued by the play the Americans responded with heart and soul. The advance booking broke all records. Night after night the audiences stood and cheered and demanded that the cast come back on stage. So hot were the tickets that during one matinée Clifford Rose noticed two young faces craning up at him from beneath the grills in the stage, where they had managed to crawl in. And the reviewers were ecstatic, often catching the play's intent more accurately than their British counterparts. 'The audience becomes implicated in the confusion,' wrote Wilfred Sheed in the *Commonweal*.

> The night I was there people began to applaud their favorite ideas, only to waver when they realized that the avowed lunatics on the stage were clapping even louder ... The uncertainty reached a screaming crescendo at the end when the lunatics ... solemnly applauded the audience: de Sade and Weiss have obliterated all distinctions – the monkeys are outside the bars, the visitors inside.[33]

The actor George Segal found the play worked so ferociously on his dark side that he fled the theatre suffering from acute claustrophobia.

The cast found themselves the focus of attention for New York society, and there was a steady stream of invitations to glamorous parties. At one such event at the White House Brook met Senator Bobby Kennedy, brother of the assassinated president, who confessed that he had tried unsuccessfully to chat Glenda up. Brook tried to change the subject by suggesting that the senator should come to see the play, but he declined on the grounds that its theme was too close to home. Two years later, while running for the Democrat presidential nomination in 1968, Bobby was himself assassinated.

Glenda also met Bette Davis, although Roy was far more impressed by this than Glenda. When Glenda was invited to appear on the television programme *Good Morning America* she was sent advance notice of the questions, and she asked Roy how she should reply to 'Which American would you most like to meet?' Roy, not Glenda, first thought of Miss Davis. When Bette turned up backstage at the *Marat/Sade*, Roy was outraged to hear her, supposing him to be Glenda's dresser, declare in stentorian tones, 'Out – just Glenda.' 'After all,' Roy complained, 'it was me who wanted to meet Bette Davis all along, not Glenda.' Throughout this whirlwind of celebrity Glenda remained remarkably down to earth, sporting a £2.5/- Marks and Spencer cotton dress to meet Jackie Kennedy, and sending back home $140 worth of towels that she had bought in the sales. Some of the offers received by company members were more salacious than glamorous. Patrick Magee was asked by one woman whether he would mind tattooing the word Mississippi on the lips of her vagina and was requested by 'a hoodlum' to offer Glenda a fur coat in exchange for a chance to meet her. Jonathan Burn even managed to talk his way into a menswear consultancy deal at one of the New York department stores – and the freedom of Las Vegas – on the strength of appearing in the play.

The production had its own traumas as well. One night a member of the audience died; another night Patrick Magee suffered a heart attack and had to walk off stage clutching his chest while the rest of the cast carried on; one of the musicians, Richard Kallinan, would unexpectedly thrash away at the drums or shout out 'Three Cheers for Dixie' in the middle of a scene; an actor developed severe rheumatism from sporting a straitjacket every night; and Glenda described the backstage atmosphere: 'It's like an asylum. People twitching, slobber running down their chins, everyone preparing to isolate themselves from reality.'[34]

The play ran in New York for 144 performances, and could have run far longer if several of the cast – including Glenda – had not made it clear that they feared for their sanity if they continued. Peter Brook picked up a Tony award for best director en route, but of all the acting company Glenda stole the limelight, winning the *Variety* magazine award for most promising actress, and narrowly missing a Tony award for best actress, which was carried off by Zoe Caldwell.

Despite eight excruciating bouts of madness a week, Glenda

enjoyed her stay in New York, especially once Roy had joined her out there. And she made a lifelong friend of an actress who was then appearing in a theatre in the same street. In fact it was Roy who met the broad-accented New Yorker Brenda Vaccaro first, as he had taken advantage of his position as Glenda's husband to get tickets for all the hottest shows in town, one of which was *Cactus Flower*, starring Lauren Bacall and Brenda Vaccaro. 'When I was out getting fresh bagels the next morning,' Roy told me, 'I saw this crazy thing walking her dog just outside where we were staying. It was Brenda and I told her she had been wonderful in the show and invited her to Glenda's party that night.' From that night on the vivacious, rough-edged actress – later the star of John Schlesinger's *Midnight Cowboy* and lover of Michael Douglas – became one of Glenda's closest and longest-serving friends.

It is difficult to imagine a less likely pairing than Brenda and Glenda: one with a gloriously sophisticated vulgarity bred of Italian American East Coast money; the other steely ambition distilled out of generations of Wirral poverty. Yet Glenda's taste in friends has always been catholic and it is frequently the totally unconstrained side of her that real friends latch on to, not the die-hard professional, and she always responds in kind. At school it was the naughty troupe of Jean Hibbert, Marjorie Stone, Shirley Smith, Betty Sparks and Jean Rankin. At RADA it was the appearance-conscious Beryl Braithwaite and the glamorous but down-to-earth Pauline Devaney. In her thirties it was the self-assured Anna Welsh, Brenda Vaccaro and the sexually extravagant Peter Bromilow. Later in life there would be others, all of whom shared a deep sense of loyalty to close friends.

During these early years of success a series of factors conspired to restrict Glenda's circle of friends. At the top of the list, of course, was Glenda's own predilection for quality rather than quantity. The closeness of her family made her value the long-established, unquestioning bonds of blood far more than the superficial, transient acquaintances of the theatre. Moreover, she loved candour – at times this made her seem a spiky, uncongenial colleague, and an uncomfortable friend for any but the strong-hearted. Her success also bred new insecurities and made easy friendship impossible for her. Her timetable left her little time for casual pleasantries, and her intense domesticity left her only too delighted to return home and put her feet up the moment the day's work was done. She also hated the sycophancy of those who sought to flatter her, and success made her more sceptical than ever. As Pauline Devaney, who had a substantial spell in the limelight herself, with the success of her television series *All Gas and Gaiters*, explains:

> People aren't very kind to famous people. You end up paying for everything and people expect you to sing for your supper with hilarious anecdotes. It's a great strain. You end up being so distrustful of people. So it's no surprise that Glenda just doesn't want any of that. And she can't stand weakness in other people – that's her strength and her weakness. As a result Glenda can be a rather lonely figure, because there are very few people who are sort of equal to her so that she can relax.

Glenda was by now a significant, much talked-about, 'arriving', theatrical celebrity, and she had to learn to deal with the rather unreal atmosphere that can attend such celebrity. Roy now garnered new friends and shaped Glenda's social life, and friendship became an ever more costly process for her.

CHAPTER FOUR

---><---

Making a Name

ON 15 OCTOBER 1964 Harold Wilson had won Labour's first general election victory for thirteen years. Within a couple of hours of entering Downing Street he was dealing with intractable problems abroad. As he recorded:

> The Chinese had, the previous day, exploded their first nuclear weapon ... There was a telegram appraising the situation in the Soviet Union following the overthrow, less than twenty-four hours earlier, of Mr Khrushchev ... There was a telephone call from President [Lyndon] Johnson ... And grimmest of all, there was the economic news.[1]

The president's phone call was no mere courtesy. Johnson needed British foreign policy support almost as much as Britain was to need US dollars. For in the first week of August the North Vietnamese had attacked two US destroyers in the Gulf of Tonkin. The US Senate had immediately authorised retaliatory attacks on the Communist forces of North Vietnam, backing up the large number of US troops already stationed in South Vietnam to train the Saigon government troops in their war against the insurgent guerrilla group, the Vietcong. By the time Glenda had arrived in New York for the *Marat/Sade* the Americans were already hopelessly mired in a war that over the next eight years was to see two million Vietnamese killed, another three million wounded and about twelve million people made refugees.

From the outset Brook had wondered how theatre could make the horror of this conflict, and the ethical dilemmas it posed, real to a London audience. Although many of the moral scandals of the war were yet to break – My Lai was not until 1968 and many US atrocities were not known until the early seventies – there was already plenty of raw material for a devastating assault on the consciences of Middle England. In June 1963 a Buddhist monk had set fire to himself in protest at the US-backed Diem government's religious discrimination. Napalm was being used extensively, as was the defoliant Agent Orange, which deprived the guerrillas of cover by clearing vast reaches of the jungle. Thousands of civilians had been slaughtered by both sides in the conflict, many of them mistaken for guerrillas. And the great imperialist nation, the USA, despite tentative moral support from Britain, was being humbled in a war it seemed it might not win.

Early in 1966 Brook set about developing a theatrical event that would explore what people sitting in Britain could and should do about the Vietnam War. It was not that Brook had an answer to offer the politicians. Geoffrey Reeves, who worked on the production, thinks Brook 'did not expect the show to convert anybody', and Glenda believes that 'unlike many of the company he was not particularly anti-American'. Instead he wanted to force an audience to think hard, and to 'plant a seed of change, so that when people were later confronted by situations, they might begin to react in a different way'.[2]

Brook read assiduously about Vietnam and gathered a directorial team. As with the Theatre of Cruelty season there was no formal text. The actors, working with the directorial and writing team, were to find within themselves an unflinching severity of expression that could communicate Vietnam directly to the audience. The cast of twenty-four drew on Brook's by now well-established group of actors: Mary Allen, Leon Lissek and Robert Lloyd from the Theatre of Cruelty; and Clifford Rose, Barry Stanton and Michael Williams from the *Marat/Sade* were all drafted in. There would be sixteen weeks of rehearsal (although two weeks of that were spent filming the *Marat/Sade*), and to ensure the total commitment of the company, every Friday Brook told the cast that anyone who did not wish to continue could simply not turn up after lunch. The raw material came from a phenomenal array of experts: the American director, Joe Chaikin, who worked on Americanisms; a Vietnamese

Buddhist monk who looked as if he was on the verge of tears; Chaing Lui, a Chinese theatre expert, who taught the company how to perform the Vietnamese Story of the Mosquito in strict mime; war correspondents and subversive militants.

The most exciting and challenging of all the visitors was the great Polish director (or in Henry Woolf's words 'a fashionable theatre fascist') Jerzy Grotowski, who spent ten days in August working with the inner core of the company, including Glenda, Barry Stanton, Henry Woolf and Clifford Rose. If Brook's gospel had a touch of austerity about it, Grotowski's was pure mordant asceticism – Clifford Rose described a rehearsal as 'a sort of Buddhist retreat for masochists'. He demanded not just a tidy rehearsal room but a floor so clean you could kiss it. He believed that only by pushing an actor to the very limits of his physical and emotional endurance – and beyond – could the director really see what he was capable of, and that only through pain could an actor break through the obstacles to theatrical truthfulness. Each day for the first fortnight of August he sat – dark-glassed and chain smoking – with one of his own actors, Ryszard Cieslak, barking out commands that Brook then translated: 'You will now follow the instructor.' Each actor was given, according to Brook, 'a series of shocks: the shock of confronting himself in the face of simple irrefutable challenges; the shock of catching sight of his own evasions, tricks and clichés; the shock of sensing something of his own vast and untapped resources; the shock of being forced to question why he is an actor at all'.[3]

Although Glenda has always been one of the least evasive of actors, she was not spared Grotowski's attention. Indeed, one whole day was devoted to her. Albert Hunt, who as an assistant to Brook witnessed the battle of wills between the Polish director and Glenda, believes that Brook told Grotowski on his first day that she had immense talent, but that she kept it all inside her and was never out of control. Could Grotowski break down her control in order to build her up again? Brook, who acknowledges the power games that he and Glenda played with each other, cannot recall deliberately setting this up, but it is clear that Grotowski tried to break her will. In Brook's words 'he gave her hell, pushing her all the time, trying one obstacle; that's not right; another; again'.

The first bout of Grotowski's assault on Glenda's self-will was simple. The rest of the company chased her round and round the rehearsal room for three hours, while he squeaked (according to Henry Woolf) 'in authoritarian French, "Now you are a deer and you others are bloodthirsty hounds, now you've escaped from a concentration camp and they are guards relentlessly pursuing you" until he ran out of commands'. Woolf thinks that Glenda was meant to have 'collapsed sobbing and confessed her errors', but since she was still intact there was a second round in the afternoon.

This time she and another actor were playing without words a scene from *Romeo and Juliet*. Juliet invites Romeo in secret to her bed. As they are making love there is a knock at the door. Romeo tries to jump up to escape, but Juliet instinctively pulls him back into an embrace. Finally Romeo breaks away and escapes over the balcony. The first time the scene was played, the episode on the bed was very brief, and one of the actors made the sound of the knock on the door. Then Grotowski got them to do it again, but this time he would provide the knock on the door. The scene started and soon the two actors were locked in their supposedly passionate embrace. Grotowski let the scene run – and run. After a few minutes he moved the actor so that he was lying fully on top of Glenda. Another twenty minutes of silent writhing passed with Glenda (in Albert Hunt's words) 'obviously trying to avoid being involved in passionate kisses while pretending to respond to them'. Finally Grotowski gave the knock and Glenda sprang away with considerable relief – only to have to pull Romeo back for another embrace.

The tension was immense. Glenda could easily have broken down in anger, in tears. It felt to Albert Hunt rather like 'bear-baiting' but he was delighted that there were 'no signs that Grotowski had broken through'.[4] Perhaps all was not quite so sadistic as it sounds; Brook, who was not entirely convinced that the exercise was useful, recalls that when it was over Grotowski walked over to Glenda and ruffled her hair – the first sign of tenderness that week.

It is easy to understand why any actor should chose to forget such an explicitly deliberate display of autocracy. In Glenda's case the affront to her privacy was close to a violation, and she now has no memory of the Romeo and Juliet episode, despite the fact that

Albert Hunt, Barry Stanton and Henry Woolf all recall it. She does recall an intense feeling that the Grotowski exercise was 'a dehumanising waste of time'. That evening she rang Brook to tell him that if rehearsals were going to continue in this vein they would have to do so without her. Brook, and Grotowski, relented.

Once the Grotowski fortnight was over the task of putting together a workable text started in earnest, with Denis Cannan joining the team to write the second half of the show. Rehearsals still featured a perplexing and arduous number of experiments. One day five of the cast – Glenda, Clifford Rose, Mark Jones, Michael Williams and Robert Lloyd – had to spend the morning imagining they did not exist and slowly discovering human senses and feelings. In the afternoon they were each placed with their eyes closed at one end of a wooden bench and told to think about Vietnam. As soon as they were willing to give up any one part of what constituted their life in order to stop the war, they could take one step forward. If they were willing to follow the Quaker Norman Morrison's example and commit suicide, they could step off the bench. Only Robert Lloyd got to step five, most to four.

The rehearsals were not all so earnest, and on two occasions Glenda led a light-hearted revolt. When Brook came in one morning and told the cast to surprise him, Glenda urged him to close his eyes. When he opened them again the cast had absconded to the pub. On another occasion Brook had persuaded the company to leave the stage at the end of act one wearing paper bags on their heads 'to suggest the fog of war'. The cast found the exercise confusing and dangerous, and Glenda hated stepping into the audience because it felt as if the safe fourth wall between the stage and the audience had been destroyed. Glenda suggested to Brook and the rest of the directorial team that it would give them some helpful insights if they wore the bags for a while, perhaps sitting in a circle. Brook agreed and the team sat in solemn silence with the bags on their heads while Glenda silently ushered the rest of the company down the stairs and off to the pub. 'In fact,' Glenda told me, 'the cast chickened out when we got to the bottom of the stairs, but we were delighted when we returned to see through the glass in the doors that the directors were still dutifully awaiting some great theatrical apotheosis.' Brook tried to puncture the actors' delight in their prank by announcing as they came back into the room, 'We thought you had all gone off to the pub.'

By September the show – to be called, opaquely, *US* (and known as U.S., us) – was taking shape. The first half was performed in front of Peter Hall and the second half was given a first reading, while a copy of the script was sent to the Lord Chamberlain. Cobbold was furious and demanded that George Farmer, the new chairman of the RSC, then on a fishing holiday in Scotland, prevent the show from going ahead because it was 'bestial, anti-American and Communist'. Farmer flew down to London to see a runthrough at the Donmar warehouse before taking Brook and Hall to see the Lord Chamberlain over sherry at St James's Palace. It was eventually agreed that the production could go ahead, but not without cuts.

The show opened on 13 October after a host of last-minute changes. When the cast first donned their costumes Brook decided to scrap them in favour of 'whatever you wore to the theatre this morning'. (This disconcerted Mary Allen, who had sported an expensive new Chanel suit as she was going on to a polite reception.) The set kept on altering. Lines were cut between the final preview and the first night. And there were problems with the planned live video sequences because the paging system in the next-door hotel interfered with the monitors.

Yet again the dramatic focus of the play centred on the several parts played by Glenda, whose coruscating attack on middle-class assumptions provided fodder for the critics. At the climax of the play she demanded:

> So you end the war in Vietnam. Where's the next one? Thailand, Chile, Alabama? I WANT IT TO GET WORSE!! I want it to come HERE! ... I would like to smell the explosion of frightened bowels over the English Sunday-morning smell of gin and the roasting joint and hyacinths. I would like to see an English dog play on an English lawn with part of a burned hand. I would like to see a gas grenade go off at an English flower show, and nice English ladies crawling and swallowing each other's sick ... I want it to go on ... Like lust it goes on because

we want it. And as we lust, we suspect most of all those
who shout loudest, 'No'.[5]

The evening ended with typical Brookian panache. Robert Lloyd
would open a box full of butterflies on the centre of the stage and
let them escape. As they fluttered into the wings he would take
hold of one, light a match and set fire to it – or so it seemed. In
fact the 'butterfly' was no more than a piece of paper, but the sense
of anger in the audience was palpable every night. For the curtain
call the company then came on stage and stood in silence – yet
another surly ending. So disturbing was this finale that even the
one-time *enfant terrible* Ken Tynan was unsettled enough on the
press night to break the silence with a petulant 'Are you waiting
for us, or are we waiting for you?'

(The story of the butterflies, incidentally, is worth telling in
more detail. When Peggy Ashcroft went to see *US* she adored the
burning of the butterflies, which symbolised the destruction of all
that is delicate and beautiful. A few nights later, however, one of
the butterflies distracted the audience by fluttering down from the
wings during her main soliloquy in *Days in the Trees* by Marguerite
Duras, and she had no compunction about slamming her hand
down on the table and killing it. Roy Kinnear, who was playing
the lead in *The Thwarting of Baron Bollingrew*, similarly suffered at
the hands of the butterflies. During the play he had to fire a shotgun
at a distant animal. One night a butterfly landed on the very edge
of his gun, just as it was meant to go off. The shot was fired, but
Kinnear could not resist the temptation to shout 'missed', at which
the audience collapsed in laughter, along with most of the cast.
Even Paul Scofield had a line ready for any spare butterflies that
might appear in his cellar barbershop in *Staircase*.)

Yet again controversy raged around Brook and the RSC. In the
House of Commons Sir Knox Cunningham called for the Arts
Minister Jennie Lee to cut the RSC's Arts Council grant. Martin
Esslin, writing in *The New York Times*, wanted it retitled 'The
Persecution and Assassination of Uncle Sam and the English liberal
as performed by the inmates of the RSC under the direction of
Peter Brook'. Hilary Spurling attacked the 'cheap, facile ambiva-
lence' of the play's attitude to Vietnam in the *Spectator*, and Ken

Tynan accused it of 'shallow and factitious pessimism' in the *Theatre Quarterly*.[6] Several members of the cast felt that it was 'very well-intentioned but ultimately flawed'. And members of the audience regularly tried to intervene in the conflagration of the butterflies. Other critics, though, were enthralled. John Robinson, the controversially liberal Bishop of Woolwich, described it in the *Guardian* as an epic piece of modern liturgy. Irving Wardle wrote in *The Times* that 'detachment is finally broken down. I have never before experienced this so fully in a theatre', and *US* was successful enough to fill fifty performances at the Aldwych over the next six months.

Brook was proud of the play:

> *US* used a multitude of contradictory techniques to change direction and to change levels. It aimed to put the incompatible side by side. But this wasn't drama. This was in a way seduction – it used a contemporary, highly perishable fun-language to woo and annoy the spectator into joining in the turning over of basically repellent themes. All this was preparation, like all the many phases of a bullfight that precede the kill. We aimed not at a kill but at what bullfighters call 'the moment of truth'. The moment of truth was also our one moment of drama, the one moment perhaps of tragedy, the one and only confrontation. This was when at the very end all pretence of play-acting ceased and actor and audience together paused, at a moment when they and Vietnam were looking one another in the face.[7]

Glenda herself thought it was a valiant attempt. She recalled with candour one young girl's visit to her dressing room after the play:

> She was crying and couldn't speak and stood there, shaking. She was looking to me for some kind of restitution of her equilibrium that we had destroyed or had distorted and there was absolutely nothing I could do except get her a taxi and hope she'd get home. The truth of it was that all I was really concerned with was (a) getting a drink because I was so parched by the end of the second act and (b) getting myself home.[8]

Once *US* had opened Glenda was at something of a loose end, having worked solidly for the RSC since late 1963. The lengthy period of *US* rehearsals had been interrupted only for the filming of the *Marat/Sade* and Glenda was not contracted to appear in any further RSC shows. Instead, at the start of 1967, while still appearing in repertory in *US*, she was offered both a part in Bill Gaskill's production of *The Three Sisters* at the Royal Court and associate membership of the RSC (a largely honorific title). *The Three Sisters*, which opened in April and ran for fifty-three performances, was something of a theatrical curiosity thanks to the casting of the pop singer Marianne Faithfull, whose lover Mick Jagger made Glenda seethe with fury when he offended every rule in the thespian book by appearing backstage only moments before the curtain went up for the opening night. Faithfull seemed so natural to Peter Hall that he found Glenda rather stale and mannered in comparison. Jack Shepherd, who also acted in the production, was not convinced by her performance either. 'There's no need for Masha to be quite as scathing as Glenda was – the tender qualities didn't come through anywhere near as strongly as they should.' For all the production's troubles, the pairing of Glenda and Marianne sold well at the box office, and the Royal Court made a respectable £8,000 profit.

Although Glenda was now a minor theatrical celebrity the work was not flooding in. She spent part of the summer making a film version of *US*, called *Tell Me Lies* in the UK and *Benefit of the Doubt* in America, and she was cast opposite Peter McEnery and Diane Cilento in Peter Medak's low-budget film *Negatives*. Neither of these provided anything like the rigour and excitement – or the public profile – of Glenda's earlier work with Brook, so when, later in the year, Charles Marowitz approached her with a play, *Fanghorn* by David Pinner, in which she would play a leather-clad bullwhip-toting lesbian seductress, she was only too pleased to oblige. Glenda adored the role, which involved shaving off the First Secretary to the Minister of Defence's RAF-style moustache in a ritual castration. Unfortunately, despite a first night at the Fortune Theatre, attended by London's glitterati, the critics and the public were not so keen on Tamara Fanghorn, and the play closed after only seven performances.

Meanwhile Glenda's mentor Brook was in Paris devoting much

of his time and energy to 'the luminous presence of Madame de Salzmann', a disciple of the spiritualist Gurdjieff. His next production did not open until March 1968 – Seneca's *Oedipus* with John Gielgud and Irene Worth at the Old Vic, in a visceral translation by Ted Hughes. It was a revolutionarily ritualistic production of a play that is often considered unplayable. By this time Brook had also accepted an invitation from the great French actor/manager Jean-Louis Barrault (best known in Britain for his appearance as Baptiste in *Les Enfants du Paradis* but then running a festival called the Théâtre des Nations) to assemble a multinational company in Paris (nine British, five Americans from the Open Theater, seven French and one Noh-trained Japanese) for an experimental workshop on *The Tempest*. Inevitably Glenda was high on Brook's list for the company, as were several others from the *US* cast, including Barry Stanton. Glenda and Roy were planning to go on holiday to the Bahamas, but Brook agreed that she could join the company in Paris once work had started, and further agreed to her flying back to London to do some post-synching for *Negatives*. Days after the opening of *Oedipus* Brook started work in a vast (150- by 40-foot, 25-foot-high) stone gallery intended for tapestry exhibitions at the Mobilier National, a furniture storehouse in Les Gobelins, which had been provided by the French government.

Those who live by the sword die by the sword, and it must be one of the stronger ironies of modern theatre that the director who gave London its most aggressive critique of the Vietnam War was soon to have his own work curtailed by political demonstrations. Just as Brook started work the student committee of March 22 was evicted from the Sorbonne and the 1968 *événements* began. The first he knew of the movement that was soon to sweep Continental Europe was when he went to pick up one of the cast from the airport, and found himself caught in complete gridlock for several hours. He was soon blessing the makers of Volvo for constructing a vehicle so heavy that, when all the other cars in his street had been dragged to the barricades, his was left behind, unharmed.

At first the multinational company was largely unaffected by the call to strike, although some of the French actors immediately left to fling themselves into the theatre of the streets, and work continued for a month. But the fact that the workshop was funded by the government soon told against it, and when Barrault was both identified as bourgeois by the students and as insufficiently robust in his defence of the government when his theatre, l'Odéon, was invaded, he was fired. The project immediately fell apart. The French actors stayed behind while Glenda and the rest of the company fled to catch the last flights out of France before petrol and engine fuel ran out.

Back in England Brook tried to put together the money to continue, while the actors waited, unemployed. This was a difficult time for Glenda, who could have been earning good money elsewhere, and who had only agreed to the project because of the opportunity of working with Brook again. With new offers arriving every week and no real certainty of the *Tempest* project restarting she was keen to be released. Barry Stanton recalls a long company discussion in Trevor Nunn's office at the Aldwych, and overhearing Glenda desperately trying to back out of the company in an hour-long phone call to Brook, who was by now in Paris again. Brook's insistence that without her he would have to abandon the project finally persuaded her to continue, and despite funding problems workshop rehearsals soon started in a converted train shed in Camden Town, the Roundhouse.

Glenda's heart was no longer in the work, though, and it was only a matter of time before she found an excuse to leave. This came one day when Brook sent the cast up into the rafters while he showed the project off to some wealthy women who were considering giving him financial backing. In the process of clambering around in order to make suitably tempestuous noises, Glenda managed to dislodge some duckboards, and would have come crashing through the roof to the floor thirty foot beneath if she had not fallen astride a metal strut. Shaken, Glenda decided that her days of physical risk-taking were over and left the *Tempest* rehearsals, citing ill-health. The project continued, and a performance was given in July 1968, but by then Glenda had departed from the RSC.

Through the years at the RSC Glenda's relationship with Peter Brook defined both her career and her personal development. Glenda described to Charles Marowitz the experience of working with Brook in glowing terms:

When I was in rep there was no such thing really as a director, in the contemporary sense. You were given your moves, pretty much as they were in the French's acting edition, and the set was pretty much as it had been in the West End, where the play had usually started. The director gave you notes like 'slower' or 'faster' or 'react on that'. That was really my sum of knowledge of directors until I worked with you and Brook, and then suddenly a whole new kind of theatre was opened up to me and I realised that was the sort of theatre that interested me most. What I can never understand, talking about Brook, is when people cite him as an example of an autocratic dictator of productions when in fact, the reverse is the case, for he just sits and says nothing for weeks and months and you have to find it yourself. Then he will suddenly come in and orchestrate it. What is interesting working with Brook is that he is looking as much as you, to see if there is anything to be *found*, whereas with other directors you know they start out from the premise that there is a production to be discovered. Brook starts out thinking: is there a production to be discovered?

For all their differences, the Oxford graduate and the assistant at Boots shared much in common. They had rapidly fixed on each other as sparring partners, soul-mates and creative accomplices. Brook said that:

> There was between us an instant complicity, a telepathic communication needing a minimum of explanations. Like Jeanne [Moreau] Glenda seized any suggestion and at once made it her own. But her special quality was an organic originality that made whatever she did unexpected, different, though never quirky – she bypassed clichés to reveal a truer and more sharply observed facet of human behaviour.[9]

There were frequent rows. They delighted in staring each other out and throughout their protracted unspoken battle for supremacy it seemed to other members of the cast, in Barry Stanton's words, that although Glenda was Brook's favourite, 'he never quite cracked her'. Timothy West saw it slightly differently:

> Glenda adopted a kind of persona, which I thought was designed for Peter Brook – and he rather got off on it. After all, you can pretty well have *carte blanche* playing a part like Charlotte Corday, but she chose to go to the very edge. I thought that the persona she developed had not much to do with her really. She was pushed into it by the success of the Theatre of Cruelty – and she played up to it.

Brook had certainly changed her. Glenda had become a bright, intelligent, even austerely erudite actress who relished a theatre of passionately held ideas, a theatre of ritual, of self-discipline; an ambitious woman who knew her own mind and who had grown swiftly in intellectual confidence. Clever but unschooled, sexually assertive yet still convinced of her plainness, she now met perfectly the spirit of the age.

CHAPTER FIVE

———— ✳ ————

Motherhood and Movies

BY THE SUMMER OF 1968 Glenda was thirty-two, she had been a professional actress for eleven years and her tenth wedding anniversary was due on 2 August, yet two of her strongest ambitions – to be a mother and a film star – remained unfulfilled. As is often the way with the ambitious, Glenda managed to time the realisation of both her dreams immaculately – but only just.

Ever since she had acted as surrogate mother for her younger sisters Glenda had wanted to be a mother. She and Roy had tried for children from their marriage onwards, even when they could scarcely have afforded to support a growing family. Glenda looked on her friends who had children with envy and took up the cause of several children's charities, but it was not until the night of her return from Paris, when she and Roy (who was touring) managed to meet up in Salisbury, that her first child was conceived. And she did not know that she was pregnant until June 1968.

This was not entirely convenient. For a start she was in Brook's experimental group at the Roundhouse, and while she was to play the symbol of fertility, the goddess Ceres, the strenuous activity of a Brook production was not designed for a woman with child. More importantly, Glenda had just been cast in a film – and, as she had confessed to the *Evening Standard* in March, 'at the moment, what I want more than anything in the world is to go into films. It seems that there is much greater freedom of approach somehow.'[1] Most professional women can, if they want, work virtually through to full term, but pregnancy almost invariably precludes work for an actress for at least five months even before she has any time to spend with the new baby. In Glenda's case this was even more problematic as the film, *Women in Love*, was to be based on the novel by D. H. Lawrence, which focuses on sex and sexuality, and Glenda was to play a couple of scenes naked. An evidently rounded naked Glenda was unlikely to be able to disguise her condition.

Glenda found out that she was pregnant a few days after starting shooting in Derbyshire, when she came down to London to have her hair done. As with most things, she asked Roy for his advice. Should she tell the director and risk losing the part? Roy thought that on balance she probably should. She was determined to play the part, however.

Women in Love had all the marks of a potential box-office success. The cast was impressive. Alan Bates was an established film actor who had appeared in *The Entertainer* with Olivier, Richardson and Finney and starred in the elegiac movie *Whistle Down the Wind*, at the start of the sixties – and he had just played Gabriel Oak in John Schlesinger's successful *Far from the Madding Crowd*; Oliver Reed's route to stardom had been rather more brutish, but with a clutch of Hammer Horror and Michael Winner films to his credit he was certainly 'box office'. There was also an impressive screenplay from the American Larry Kramer, and the original novel's controversial nature made it probable that the film would attract publicity and audiences.

Moreover, the director was a wilder and less disciplined – but equally visionary – version of Peter Brook. Ken Russell had started his professional life as a dancer and began directing at the age of thirty-two in 1959 when he was recruited in a pub by the producer Huw Weldon to work on the television documentary series *Monitor*. Here he fumbled his way through a run of documentaries before landing on the idea of semi-dramatised pieces on composers, which earned him a reputation as an exciting, controversial and innovative director. His first feature film, *French Dressing*, came out modestly in 1963 and was followed in 1967 by *Billion Dollar Brain*, starring Michael Caine.

Despite the fact that Russell had very little money with which to make *Women in Love* (so little that Bates and Reed were persuaded to work for just a share of the profits – an almost unheard-of practice in those days), Glenda and Peter Crouch had mounted an assiduous campaign for a part in the film. Russell granted her a reading and then a screen test, but at that stage was only impressed by her varicose veins, which he told her would have to go. Russell was not the first to notice the unsightly veins. When she appeared in *The Kitchen*, the play's author Arnold Wesker thought that her legs were so marred by these ugly protruding veins that she would never succeed as an actress, but he was impressed when he was told, falsely, that they were painted on for the part. When Russell complained about them Glenda scarcely hesitated before stripping them out. At the same time Peter Crouch made sure Russell was shown the film of the *Marat/Sade*. Impressed by the subtlety of Glenda's film performance – all minute movements of the eye and internalised hysteria made convincing by its physical simplicity – Russell succumbed and Glenda was offered the part of the domineering Midland sculptress Gudrun Brangwen.

Casting the other parts for *Women in Love* had been an arduous job. To get Oliver Reed, whom he had directed in a *Monitor* biopic on Debussy, Russell had to clamber up a mountain in the Alps, where Reed was filming *Hannibal Brooks* for Michael Winner; and when Reed discovered he was to play a naked wrestling scene with another man he stormed into Russell's sitting room and started to enact it, throwing the corpulent director across the room. In order to keep Reed on board Russell was forced to accept changes to the screenplay. All this occurred in 1967, months before Russell cast either of the women's parts. For Ursula he wanted Jennie Linden, whom he had to chase into Wales, where she had gone into hiding after the birth of her son Rupert – expressly because she had resolved not to work for at least four months. Finally she was persuaded by a late-night visit on a Sunday from Russell, Kramer and the producer Marty Rosen to her parents' house. At the last minute Russell also decided to swap the two male roles.

The four main characters were only able to gather together for the first time for a reading as filming was about to start. Oliver Reed described the scene in Russell's house:

> Suddenly this woman sat on a chair on the other side of the room, and this rather plain truck started to make the air move. So I just mumbled my lines, because I had no identity towards Glenda. I didn't know her from Eve;

never heard of her. I'd heard of Shakespeare, but not this truck sitting across the room from me. Unlike her I wasn't associated with *art*: I made commercial films. I love motor cars, and you can judge a car by its pitch; and suddenly I'd met a truck, no less, and when its engine started to rev I began to realise it had a different pitch to what I'd expected. Glenda was like a Ford truck with a highly tuned V8 engine in it. If an engine is properly tuned it doesn't care about the road. So, more than making the air move, she began to eat up the road very quickly, because she didn't care about the hypocrisy of the old structure of cinema, the star system and the casting couch. Glenda didn't take that route. She came straight from the dust of the theatre and she began to growl.[2]

Despite Roy's advice that Glenda should tell Russell that she was pregnant, she failed to do so. Roy explains, 'Glenda is a great procrastinator. She always has been.' She delayed in case Russell decided to change his mind – one of the cast had been sacked after a single day of rehearsal, and she did not feel secure enough to start talking about ways of hiding her growing belly. She did tell Jennie Linden, however, admitting to a sense of relief that pregnancy was likely to make her breasts grow, just as Jennie's own had thanks to her recent pregnancy. 'It's just as well,' declared Glenda. 'Neither of us is going to worry about taking our jumpers off in this film.' After a few weeks of filming, though, Glenda's condition became so abundantly clear that she had no choice. She owned up to Kramer and Rosen – who were furious – and Russell. Fortunately the rushes had just come out, and Russell was so delighted with Glenda's performance that he was only too happy to delay shooting some of Glenda's naked scenes until her breasts had filled out yet further.

Apart from trying to hide Glenda's pregnancy, filming was remarkably straightforward, and although the relationship between Glenda and Reed was sometimes heated, if anything this added piquancy to the on-screen battle of wills. On one notable occasion Glenda refused to accept Russell and Reed's reading of one of the sex scenes. Reed's version of events is shot through with his usual insecurities, but is nevertheless revealing:

> Russell and I were trying to convince her that I should rape her and be the dominant factor in that particular love scene. She was so aggressive about it, saying no, *she* should dominate *me*. In the end we had to call in the producers, because this unknown girl was being so headstrong ... She thought she had to rape me, had to completely dominate me, had to climb on top and be the aggressor. But she wasn't experienced enough to know that to be on top is not the be-all and end-all of the conquest. I don't think she would ever have compromised had she not believed that there was still enough superstition left in male vanity to warrant the leading man, and the director, to think that she should be underneath getting fucked for the things that she said.[3]

In fact, Glenda hated the sexual politics of Lawrence's novel and was keen to make Gudrun far less quiescent than Russell had originally intended. She was acutely perceptive about portrayals of women that she thought were simply inaccurate or improbable, and this battle with Reed was only one of many minor instances of rebellion whereby Glenda tried to make the woman Lawrence and Russell wrote more realistic. She was also determined not to be eclipsed by the better-known male leads.

One of Glenda's friends, the Polish actor Vladek Sheybal, played the homosexual Loerke with whom Gudrun shares a bed in Switzerland. Despite their friendship Glenda made sure that she dominated even his scenes. When they had finished a fantasy scene which Sheybal himself had suggested to Russell and Sheybal saw the rushes he realised that the whole scene was interspersed with close-up shots of Glenda reacting to Sheybal, shots to which he had not been party. On asking Russell when they had been done he discovered that Glenda had rung up Russell in the middle of the night to persuade him to shoot her 'counterpoint' to Sheybal's 'brilliant' performance. Clearly Glenda was determined that this would be her film if it was to be anyone's.

Ken Russell was about as different from Peter Brook as a director could be. Ostentatious, flamboyant and obsessed with the look of the film, he had none of Brook's cerebral qualities or austerity, yet Glenda found him a joy to work with:

> He doesn't know anything about acting, and he leaves you alone. He spends hours on the background detail, on the sets and costumes, on how it's all going to look, and you just get on with it. I think the ideal thing about working with him is that you can surprise him as a director, and I think that is essential for actors. He gives you the sense that what you're doing is important, that what everybody is doing is important, that everyone is joined together to get the very best possible results they can. And that's a very important work atmosphere to create.

Certainly Glenda worked extremely hard in *Women in Love*. Despite being well advanced in her pregnancy, she was rigorously determined to give her all and not to let on to the rest of the cast that she was slowly having her costumes let out – even when filming the difficult rape scenes up in Gateshead. This professionalism, ambition, determination – however you choose to read it – was also at the heart of Glenda's willingness to strip for the film. Glenda has always been dismissive of anyone who has even questioned why a 'serious' actor like her should agree to appear naked. It was a theme she returned to time and time again. 'How on earth', she demanded, 'could any woman involved in the D. H. Lawrence story with all its erotic relationships not take her clothes off in the love scenes? It is easy to say, but in fact it is true – where nudity is essential to the role it would be fraudulent to shrink from it.'[4]

At this time, despite five years of almost continuous work, Glenda and Roy were still far from wealthy. Roy's own theatrical career had dried up, and although there had been occasional bouts of work as an ASM he had taken increasingly to following in Glenda's footsteps. In Stratford, in New York and on the set of *Women in Love* Roy was ever-present, making coffee, providing advice and support, but not officially employed. Glenda's earnings did, however, mean that they were better off and – at the suggestion of

Pauline Devaney and her husband Edwin Apps, who had moved south of the Thames with their new son Barnaby – the couple abandoned the noisy and minuscule flat in King Henry's Road, Swiss Cottage, for a flat that was still small, but in the far more pleasant, almost rural, Blackheath, which nestles like a village in a quiet triangle between Lewisham and Greenwich in south-east London.

It was from the rented flat in Blackheath that Glenda hurried to St Thomas' Hospital in Lewisham on 6 February 1969 for what was to be a painful labour, culminating, after several hours, in the birth of a son, Daniel. Glenda was delighted and has since often described the birth of Daniel as 'the highest point' of her life:

> They had to knock me out because he got stuck and I came to on a trolley with drips in my arms and asked, 'What did I have?' and they said, 'Oh, a boy' – totally unconcerned you know. Then I came around again, at two in the afternoon, and this little white bundle was brought in for me to see. I felt as though I was just the delivery van that Dan had arrived in.[5]

Glenda had resolved that she would not work for at least four months after Dan's birth, and when she did go back, for a short television play, she felt so guilty that she retreated to her home. But as Roy was not working someone had to bring in a salary, and when Ken Russell approached her about a version of the life of the Russian composer Tchaikovsky, which was to start filming in September 1969, she was delighted. Dan believes that the Hodges family was still so poor that for lack of a pram or a cot he spent most of the first six months of his life in a drawer – which his parents kindly kept open in case he cried.[6] *The Music Lovers*, however, gave Glenda and Roy financial freedom and they finally bought both a car and a place of their own. So with their six-month-old baby, the Hodgeses moved with their new Triumph Herald to an Edwardian house in Hervey Road, off Shooters Hill, that cost them all of £8,500. With the rest of Glenda's advances she bought Joan and Micky 10 Alderley Road, 200 yards from Lake Place in Hoylake. Joan Aldridge thought it was a typically thoughtful and sensitive act from Glenda, not removing her parents from the world they knew and loved, but giving them financial ease after so many years of privation. Glenda's mother was delighted to be able to offer people sherry in the front room and, in time, show off her daughter's many awards. Needless to say this did little to endear Glenda to her sister Gill who was now married to Stan, a local chemist she had met in the West Kirby amateur dramatic group. When they were children they rowed, but as adults and while the rest of the family, in Pauline Devaney's words, 'delighted in sharing in Glenda's success', Gill kept herself apart. One of Glenda's new-found pleasures came from taking the family on holiday, so there were trips to Cyprus, Sicily and the Caribbean, but Gill refused to go along. Gill's response to Joan's collection of Glenda's awards was typical. 'It's like a bloody shrine in here,' she complained.

The coincidence of Glenda's soaring success and Daniel's birth meant that Roy now formally agreed to adopt the role of house-husband. Today the concept of house-husband is still not common, and the reversal of the traditional male and female roles can be problematic – especially when it is not as a result of a conscious choice but of the relative fortunes of the two partners. In the sixties and seventies, however versatile a relationship one had, such a career disparity could appear a snub to the manliness of the husband. And for all her ardent feminism both Roy and Glenda were always remarkably conventional, schooled, as they both asserted, in the same working-class traditions. Liberal in their attitudes towards others, their own lifestyle was very conservative. In Hollywood in 1971 she declared, 'I'm not doing any of the things actresses are supposed to do here. I'm not on drugs. I'm not throwing fits of temperament. I'm not fighting for any causes. Damnit, I'm not even living in sin.'[7] Indeed, Ken Colley recalls Glenda turning on her heels at a New York party 'the moment the white powder appeared'. Although Glenda was a passionate feminist she was extremely traditional in the way she ran her home. When at home she would vacuum the house and make sure that there was a meal on her husband's table simply because 'that was the way I was brought up. I can remember my father sitting in front of the fire telling my mother, "The fire's gone out. Come and light it." '

She felt guilty about going to work and leaving Daniel at home with Roy, and even when she was staying in a hotel she would rearrange the furniture and clean out the ashtrays. She was also less than convinced by the 'professional feminists'. A later colleague, Bridget Armstrong, recalls that when they were shooting scenes for *The Incredible Sarah* the glamorous *Playboy*-posing feminist Gloria Steinem turned up at the Compleat Angler in Marlow to see Glenda. Glenda instantly begged Bridget to go down and 'keep her happy' so that she would only have to spend a few minutes with her. In the event Glenda was lucky, as Steinem told Bridget 'I can't be long. I've a bit of rough trade waiting in the limo.'

So Roy became an unlikely house-husband and Glenda resumed her career, back on a film set with Ken Russell. *The Music Lovers*, with a screenplay by Melvyn Bragg, was based on *Beloved Friend*, a contentious Tchaikovsky biography by Catherine Drinker Bowen and Barbara von Meck, which maintained that the composer was a closet homosexual who had attempted to cover his tracks by marrying the nymphomaniac Nina Milukova and had taken his own life by drinking typhoid water.

While biopic was the genre in which Russell had made his name, this was to be a Russell *pièce de résistance*. He saw his task in grand terms, describing the theme of the film as 'love itself' and wanting to portray all the various forms it played in Tchaikovsky's life and music – 'the romantic, the incestuous, the homosexual and the maternal'.[8] To achieve this he was happy to shock, and the imagery he conjured up certainly startled and repelled. Having been deserted by her husband, Nina, played by Glenda, ends the film in a hellhole of a mental asylum, sitting astride an open grill through which men rudely thrust their fingers in search of her vagina. It is not surprising that Barry Norman wrote in the *Daily Mail*: 'when there's a bit of fraught acting to be done people nearly always send for Jackson'.[9]

Earlier in the film one of the most graphic and disturbing images is of Glenda writhing around naked on the floor of a train carriage, working herself into a frenzy of orgiastic pleasure once Tchaikovsky has failed to make love to her – a scene which Glenda's election agent later feared the BBC would show on election night in 1992. As Glenda described it 'you see this horrible skeletal figure writhing around and it's enough to put you off sex for the rest of your life. You're meant to experience the repugnance which Tchaikovsky, a homosexual, feels for his wife. It came off. It worked.'[10] To get the mood right for filming this episode Russell rigged up speakers next to the train to blast out a chunk of Shostakovich's *The Execution of Stepan Razin* (which is not the soundtrack for the scene in the film). In Glenda's own words:

> They started rocking the coach to simulate the movement of the train. First a champagne bucket, glasses, a chicken, knives and forks fell on me and I'm covered with broken glass and superficial cuts and Ken is there shouting 'Wipe the blood off her, clean her up; it will never show.' Then heavy luggage fell on me and Russell said, 'Never mind, get on with it, the bruising doesn't show.' Then the cameraman [the eminent Dougie Slocombe, who was kneeling in the luggage rack] falls right into my lap and he says, 'OK, it's all right, I'm a married man.'[11]

Russell's worries were rather different:

> I thought, here's this lady from the RSC lying naked like a piece of meat on the floor, being bombarded with this music. I wonder it it's distracting her from what she thinks she should be doing in this scene. So I said, 'Glenda, I know you don't usually work like this. In the RSC I know it's all hours of intellectual chat with Peter Brook. Would you prefer to do the scene without the music?' Like lightning, she said, 'Christ, if you stopped the music I couldn't do it.' Which was fine, because I'd made up my mind I was going to use it anyway, whatever her answer. So I played it louder than ever. After the film I sent her a record of it, which I'm sure she burned immediately.

Perhaps one of the most striking elements of *The Music Lovers*, however, is the fact that for much of the film Glenda looks outstandingly beautiful. Glenda has always been more than candid about her own beauty or lack of it – as she announced during the filming of *The Music Lovers*: 'me as me wouldn't stop a tortoise. I don't think my face is my fortune'.[12] Or when suggesting the shaving of the top of her head during the filming of *Elizabeth R*: 'Let's face it, it isn't exactly a face that can be enhanced by powder and puff. One brushing of mascara and my eyes disappear like little raisins in a bun of unbaked dough. It's very sad.'

Film and theatre critics have delighted in trawling out witty ways of agreeing. Jack de Manio coined 'the face that launched a thousand dredgers', but Peter Evans in the *People* was typical of his colleagues: 'at first sight it is a factory face, more gargoyle than coquette. The sort of face you once saw travelling third-class in northern towns. A face worn like a battle scar from the old days of class warfare.'[13] Yet in *The Music Lovers* Glenda looks stunning, radiating sexual confidence, and sweeping from coy allure to sultry pout to impassioned, dangerous anger with apparent ease. Charles Marowitz is convinced that Glenda knows how to make herself beautiful. 'When the actress decides to generate the kind of beauty required by a particular character, be it a trendy career girl or the dashing young Queen Elizabeth, that bony raw, disproportioned face can become utterly transformed.' Pauline Devaney agrees, recalling one party at L'Escargot in London at which Glenda turned up. 'I remember being shocked at how beautiful she looked, but it was because she was acting beautiful. She knows how to create that beauty.' Dougie Slocombe had always attributed this to her almost severe cheekbones.

At times Glenda seems to revel in being badly dressed: 'I'm quite sure I'll never be recognised ... because I never look outside like I look in anything I act in. I go out looking absolutely dreadful. People come to the house and think I'm the char – well, I am really. I'd hate to think I couldn't go out looking dreadful.'[14] Herein lies a contradiction. For in 1972 she admitted to *Vogue* that

> For someone who inevitably looks like a badly-packaged parcel of cast-offs, I worry enormously over clothes. Part of the problem is an inability to see myself as I really am – very 'ish'. Shortish, thinnish, plainish, palish. My mind's-eye has me gliding through the fashion salons of the world, an elegant mysterious, fantastical giraffe. On the aforementioned creature the clothes I buy would undoubtedly look good. In fact, I tend always to look like a lampshade and find myself hoping no one will notice me hiding inside my clothes.[15]

Yet in costume and on screen Glenda managed to convey a sexual confidence that was in equal measure alluring and disturbing. Victor Davis in the *Express* wrote that 'whatever medium she appears in, Jackson is compulsive viewing'. In no film was this more true than *The Music Lovers*.[16]

Midway through the filming of *The Music Lovers* (and after a tussle with the censor) *Women in Love* had opened. Latterday critics have tended to be snide about Russell's cinematic exuberance, his interpolation of other Lawrence material and the ostentation of scenes like the two sisters swimming naked or dancing in front of the bulls, the orgiastic chaos of the Loerke sequence and the infamous nude wrestling. But the film was undoubtedly a landmark in British film history, rendering a complex novel in an equally dense cinematic language, and those who disliked Ken Russell's style were mollified by the strength of the original novel. The film broke UK box-office records. In the US the *New York Daily News* described it as 'a visual stunner and very likely the most sensuous film ever made'. Glenda, with a performance that was both concentrated and exuberant, took many of the plaudits for a daring performance in a daring film. She was greeted as 'the most exciting actress of the year' by Victor Davis in the *Daily Express*, and *Time* announced, obliquely, that 'Jackson overcame both Russell and the difficult role of Gudrun with her range and depth of talent, conveying dark sensuality without the usual physical equipment'.[17] *Variety* similarly declared of Glenda (ironically, in the light of *The Music Lovers*), 'the girl's no stunner in the looks department, but she has punch and intelligence which gives a sharp edge to all her scenes'.

Such reviews and the assiduous publicity machine behind the film meant that Glenda first received an Oscar nomination for best actress – up against Ali MacGraw in *Love Story*, Carrie Snodgress in *Diary of a Mad Housewife*, Sarah Miles in *Ryan's Daughter* and Jane Alexander in *The Great White Hope* – and then, on 15 April 1971, an actual Oscar. Apparently unconcerned by the outcome of her nomination, Glenda neither went to the ceremony in Los Angeles, nor stayed up to await the result, so John Mills' daughter accepted it on her behalf from Walter Matthau, and the movie mogul Hal B. Wallis came to Britain for a formal presentation.

Glenda heard the news very early in the morning from none other than her supposed idol, Bette Davis. Roy, who was the first to answer the phone and was still smarting from Miss Davis' peremptory dismissal of him from Glenda's dressing room in New York, was tempted to reply to her 'Who's that?' with 'Glenda's dresser', but he restrained himself enough to pass the phone over to Glenda. 'You've won. You've won,' screamed Bette down the phone. 'It was nice of her to call,' rasped Glenda, 'but I could have done with the extra hour in bed.'

The Oscar added further glitter (Glenda has always delighted in the fact that after a couple of years' polishing by her mother the gold of her Oscars wore off and exposed the base metal underneath) to a career that was already in the ascendant. Even before the American opening of *Women in Love* Glenda had been able, for the first time, to choose from a selection of job offers. Russell wanted her to play a sexually obsessed, hunchbacked seventeenth-century nun in his next venture, *The Devils*; John Schlesinger, the director of *Midnight Cowboy* and *Billy Liar*, approached her about his next film *Sunday, Bloody Sunday*; Roman Polanski wanted her to bare all as Lady Macbeth and there was talk of a series for the BBC. With Peter Crouch's advice Glenda made her decisions fairly swiftly, declining Polanski on the grounds that she did not fancy six weeks on location 'walking through that damned gorse for no money'. 'No,' she also wrote to Russell, 'I don't want to do another sexually neurotic woman.' Russell was furious, presuming that he had a claim on the actress whose career he believed he had built, and he put Glenda's rejection down to the fact that he had changed the original script, removing a final scene in which people would come and pay homage to Glenda's severed head in a glass casket. Russell let it be known that Glenda had 'loved the idea of her head in a casket and everyone worshipping her on their knees. And with all that gone, she'd just have been back in the madhouse again.' In a fit of pique Russell fired off an abrasively rude letter to Glenda and an offer of the part to Vanessa Redgrave (who was also being considered by Schlesinger), effectively leaving the path open for Glenda to start work on *Sunday, Bloody Sunday* before finalising the deal with the BBC.

John Schlesinger had just had a great success with *Midnight*

Cowboy, featuring Jon Voigt and Glenda's great friend Brenda Vaccaro, and United Artists had effectively given him carte blanche for his next film. *Sunday, Bloody Sunday* developed as 'the most personal' of all Schlesinger's films as it dealt with an older Jewish man who had an affair with a younger man, an experience Schlesinger had lived through himself, although he was not able to say this so openly at the time when the film was made. Schlesinger had mentioned the original idea to his long-term colleague Joe Janni, but the screenplay had grown out of a series of long personal discussions Schlesinger had had with the film critic of the *Observer* and wife of John Osborne, Penny Gilliatt, while editing *Far from the Madding Crowd*. Gilliatt's screenplay made the young man bisexual and gave him a female lover – the character played by Glenda. Schlesinger's relationship with Gilliatt was seriously strained by the experience of working together, not least because Gilliatt was keen on keeping any physical contact between the two men in long shots and in silhouette, the exact opposite of what Schlesinger intended. A new writer, David Sherwin, had to be brought in to finish off several of the scenes. Schlesinger declared that 'it's impossible to have a friendship with a critic', and never forgave her for having the printer put on the back of the published script, 'Miss Gilliatt first thought of this screenplay on a train in Switzerland, on her way to see Vladimir Nabokov.' As he put it, 'How's that for intellectual pretension (and a lie)?'[18]

There were other difficulties with the production. Although Schlesinger had plenty of money for the film he had difficulty casting the leads. Paul Scofield turned the part down, Peter Finch was originally unavailable and Ian Bannen had to pull out of the film due to ill health after only a few days. Coincidentally, Peter Finch had an MGM project, *Man's Fate*, axed after four years of preparation, leaving him free. Finch's agent Olive Harding rang him from London with Schlesinger's renewed offer of the part of Daniel Hirsch. 'I'm not a queer,' came Finch's automatic response, topped by Olive's 'No, dear, but I'd like to see you play one to prove you are an actor.'[19]

Schlesinger was at first decidedly nervous about casting Glenda. Several years earlier he had observed her from a distance when they were both working in different wings of the RSC. Then he saw her as 'rather scary and strident' and it was not until seeing *Women in Love* that he had even conceived of her for the part. In the end they developed a strong rapport:

> I loved her because I was so surprised by the sort of camp, bawdy sense of humour she has. She was great fun to work with, which was simply not a quality I had associated with her. While they were setting the lights we used to sit there in our canvas chairs and howl with laughter, and because I had been awarded a CBE (Commander of the British Empire), in the midst of shooting she would send me up all the time, asking, 'Commander, am I standing in the right position?'

Filming, which ran from March to August 1970, was not straightforward. Glenda had to wear a wig throughout as Russell had shaved her head for *The Music Lovers*, and in addition Schlesinger wanted two weeks of rehearsals in which Finch and Glenda could explore this relationship triangle, which Glenda enjoyed and Finch hated. When it came to filming, Murray Head, who Schlesinger thinks was badly miscast as the young bisexual lover, was so self-involved he would turn up without any idea of what scene they were doing. The problems with the script became so insurmountable that filming was stopped while Joe Janni schooled Sherwin in crisis writing. 'The stars', Sherwin recorded, 'eye me warily as I approach each morning across the jumble of wires and brute lights with their latest lines. Usually apprehension turns to relief but the weeks become months and our nerves are at snapping point.'[20]

Schlesinger believed that Finch was a 'deeply complex man' and that this was inescapable in his performance (he recalls him suddenly stopping the action one day and screaming, 'I've lost it! I've lost it! Please don't let's do any more!').[21] Glenda found Schlesinger equally complicated:

> When you meet John he is seemingly so confident and so multi-faceted, so widely and deeply cultured and cultivated; the surprising thing about him is that on the set, he is the most nervous person there. There is a ritual that has to be gone through every morning whereby he

says: 'The rushes are awful. We're making a piece of shit here, why are we doing this?' He talks himself up to the point where he is saying 'Well, no, it's really rather good, isn't it?' That's the pattern of it and that vulnerability of directors in a working situation was something that I hadn't experienced before.[22]

Despite these complications the film was another success for Glenda, winning her more rave reviews and a second Oscar nomination for best actress while Vanessa Redgrave suffered ignominy in *The Devils*. Ken Russell was dismissive of the film, accusing it of being decorated 'with a good deal of window-dressing in order to drape the middle-class leading characters with a cloak of reality',[23] but it did well at the Venice Film Festival and in both Britain and the US. Schlesinger now worries that the film has not enough humour and is not assertive enough as a gay film, but Glenda defends its, at the time controversial, theme:

> He treated the homosexual relationship in a way that was neither prurient nor supercilious. It is actually said in the film that it is entirely possible for men to love men in the way that other men love women. There was balance to it, in that it was about unrequited love as much as about sexual acts. It was quite unsensational.[24]

By the time of the Oscar ceremony in April 1972 (she lost to Jane Fonda in *Klute*) Glenda had already completed a major new series for the BBC, it had been screened and she had completed another film with one of the other 1971 nominees, Vanessa Redgrave. In an acting career that lasted thirty-five years Glenda did remarkably little work for television: a few plays; an appearance in a Le Carré adaptation; and a few appearances on other people's shows. Yet, of all the parts she ever played, she is most associated with a BBC series that had originally been devised as a sequel to the 1970 BBC2 series *The Six Wives of Henry VIII*. This had featured Keith Michell, Annette Crosbie and Dorothy Tutin and had been so successful that its audience of 4 million for the Catherine Howard episode beat the viewing figures for BBC1.

Elizabeth R, in which Glenda famously played the English queen from childhood to crabbed old age, took the same shape – six ninety-minute separate but interlinked dramas, each produced by a different writing and production team. There was a lengthy rehearsal period for each episode, which was then filmed at the BBC's Studio 1 in Acton, and there was a similarly classical cast to that of the previous year. Some of Glenda's former colleagues joined her: John Nettleton from *All Kinds of Men*, who was delighted that her recent success had not made her 'starry', Clifford Rose and Michael Williams from *Marat/Sade*, Rachel Kempson, Robert Hardy, Leonard Sachs, Ronald Hines, Bernard Hepton and Daphne Slater. Glenda was as rigorous as ever in her approach to the part. She learnt how to ride side-saddle for the opening sequence, archery, calligraphy and how to play the virginal. She endured hours of make-up every morning, allowing Dawn Allcock, her make-up artist, to build a suitably Tudor nose for her, and offered to have the pate of her head shaved – yet again – for authenticity's sake. Roy confessed that it was a shock to see her half-bald head on the pillow every morning for the seven months of filming, and she shocked others too. Bridget Armstrong, who was then filming *Platonov or Wild Honey*, with Peter Eyre, Siân Phillips and Rex Harrison in the next-door studio, recalls that during their excessive ten weeks of rehearsal Harrison refused to eat in the canteen, so his Rolls Royce arrived every lunchtime and he would sit out in the parking lot quaffing champagne. One day he reeled into the rehearsal room after his Bollinger lunch declaiming, 'I've just seen the most ghastly sight. Glenda Jackson in the lift. A green face with pock marks all over.' Harrison is said subsequently to have observed that he was not sure whether this was Glenda in make-up or not.

When filming was complete, early in 1971, everyone on the production was certain that it was to be a success – the producer, Roderick Graham, credited it to Glenda's 'fantastic sense of danger. You never know what she'll do next. She can go from total woman to total politician in mid-sentence.'[25] To celebrate there was a big party at the *Rocky Horror Show* in the King's Road before the first screening on BBC2, which ran from 17 February to 24 March. So popular was the series that it was instantly repeated on BBC1 and it began to sell round the world, even before it scooped Glenda a couple of Emmies the following year, as best actress in a series and best actress in a single television performance. As ever, someone else picked up the awards on Glenda's behalf – Julie Andrews.

Only six weeks after the filming of the last episode of *Elizabeth R* Glenda was yet again playing the virgin queen, this time on location at Shepperton for a Hollywood version of a recent best-selling biography of Mary Stuart by Lady Antonia Fraser. Hal B. Wallis persuaded Glenda to take the part in *Mary, Queen of Scots*, doubtless influenced by a shrewd perception that US audiences would delight in the on-screen confrontations between Britain's two most lacerating performers, Glenda and Vanessa Redgrave, who was to play the Scottish queen. History maintains that the two queens never met, but Wallis managed two rebarbative encounters, which Glenda defended on the grounds that 'just because no one recorded it doesn't mean they never saw each other'. This was more a commercial star vehicle for Redgrave, Jackson and Trevor Howard than a serious historical film: the screenplay veered from the banal to the ludicrous; and the direction, by Charles Jarrott, was too lumbering to capture anything of value from the distinguished cast. Trevor Howard turned to Glenda one day to moan, 'There has got to be a better script than this we can do together one day.'[26] He had to wait seven years for *Stevie*.

Thanks to advice from Peter Crouch Glenda was reluctant to reprise her role in *Elizabeth R*. This meant Wallis did not get Glenda cheap, as she insisted that her scenes all had to be filmed in three and a half weeks, before boredom could affect her performance. Wallis recalled that 'it meant a major reworking of the script. We wanted her, we had to put up with it.' Such assertiveness revealed not only her usual candour and a refusal to kowtow to anyone, even if they were one of the most powerful figures in Hollywood, but also a growing confidence in her own bankability. Glenda now knew that there was plenty of work out there for her, and she could start to demand her price. Invariably, this consisted of a script, a director and a cast that she respected, and she later berated herself for this, the first film that she felt ashamed of appearing in. 'One really shouldn't do films like that,' she declared, 'especially if like me you're a silly cow and talk about your artistic principles and then go blithely into productions which you know bloody well are going to make you compromise and betray them.'[27]

CHAPTER SIX

A Touch of Class

GLENDA WAS NOW a major international star. She had won theatrical awards in Britain and the US, she had an Oscar and two Emmies, and, above all, her name would help guarantee sales for a film both in Britain and, more importantly, across the Atlantic, where all things British were very much in vogue in the early seventies. There were more offers from Hollywood for parts in productions to be made in Britain. Richard Fleischer wanted her to play in *The Brontës*, and the Romanian producer Samuel Bronston (of *El Cid*) wanted her for another historical epic to be entitled *Isabella of Spain*.

More important than her new-found status was the fact that as a result of *Elizabeth R* Glenda was asked to appear on the BBC's *Morecambe and Wise Show* in the summer of 1971. (When Glenda had received her Oscar her head had been shaved for *Elizabeth R*, so when she was photographed for the world's media the next day she had to cover it with a bizarre arrangement of bandannas. When Eric Morecambe saw her that night on the news he had rung Ernie Wise to tell him, 'She's dressed up as Tonto. Look, Ern, Tonto's won the Oscar.') Glenda has stated that her appearance on the show was the apotheosis of her acting career so often that she almost apologises for it nowadays, as if it is just a line for the media, but the truth is that Glenda had always enjoyed comedy – the prize she won at RADA was for her comic improvisation. Her appearances with Eric Morecambe and Ernie Wise were also genuinely ground-breaking. When the show's producer, John Ammonds, first suggested that they should invite Glenda on to the show, Eric bet him that she would not agree to appear because she was a serious actress and would not take kindly to the light-hearted abuse that they would throw at her, let alone agree to one of the innovations the comic duo was proposing – namely putting a famous personality in a completely incongruous situation. In later shows this would mean Shirley Bassey singing in enormous heavy boots; and newsreader Angela Rippon showing her legs.

Glenda's first appearance featured Ernie Wise trying to persuade 'the Academy-award-winning' serious classical actress to appear in his latest play, a spoof *Antony and Cleopatra*. Eric treated her to the usual ritual abuse when she first walked on stage, telling her 'Excuse me, Miss or Madam, as the case may be. I'm afraid you can't step up here. Only professional performers are allowed up here in front of the cameras. Go back to your seat. This isn't *The Generation Game.*' Glenda had to suffer the ignominy of Ernie's doggerel: 'All men are fools and what makes them fools is beauty like what I have got'; and appalling jokes, 'Desdemona! More like Des O'Connor'. But she adored her first *Morecambe and Wise Show*, enjoying the extraordinary rigour with which they approached even the slightest of material, rehearsing and refining for days before performing in front of a studio audience. She valued the advice they gave her ('Louder, faster') and appreciated the vast wealth of experience they represented, from every aspect of theatre, circus and variety. The palpable sense of excitement she betrayed revealed, as George Segal noted, that 'there is a vaudevillian in there, striving to get out'.

And Glenda was good. Not only did she enter into the spirit of the programme – letting down her hair but never revealing that she thought what she was doing was funny – but she was genuinely witty herself. So witty that she was asked back for the Christmas special in 1971, with André Previn ('You're playing *all* the wrong notes.' 'No, they're just not in the right order.') and Shirley Bassey. This time she performed a Fred Astaire and Ginger Rogers pastiche with Eric and Ernie, even contributing a few warbled notes of 'I won't dance, don't ask me', a couple of tap sequences and a selection of high kicks before falling off the back of the top of a sequinned staircase. The following year she was back for another Christmas show, and with five appearances in total she was the only guest to appear more than three times, becoming as much a part of the nation's Christmas as Eric and Ernie themselves, at a time when they could command audiences of upwards of 28 million. These were classic moments of British comedy: Glenda, Eric and Ernie performing a ludicrous faux Egyptian sand dance; Glenda entreating Eric to apply a non-existent asp to her breast; Glenda kissing Eric as if he was on his way to work with eight or nine increasingly passionate 'goodbyes', before Ernie, the 'real' husband arrives with a surprised 'hello'. Glenda was an excellent foil, rising beautifully to the bait every time.

ERIC: Dame Glenda.
GLENDA: Dame Glenda? I'm sorry, Eric, it's just plain 'Glenda'.
ERIC: Oh dear.
ERNIE: Oh dear.
GLENDA: Is something wrong?
ERIC: Well, it's just that, you see, nowadays we only work with *titled* people.

Appearing as a guest star on *The Morecambe and Wise Show* won Glenda her next major part. The veteran American producer and director Melvin Frank was looking for an actress to star opposite George Segal in a sparky, semi-autobiographical romantic comedy (*A Touch of Class*) that he had written. Frank was an established Hollywood 'pro'. Born in 1913, he and Norman Panama had worked as joint writers and directors for the Hollywood comic masters Bob Hope, Lucille Ball, Phil Silvers and Danny Kaye. Together they had written the famous scene in *The Court Jester* when Danny Kaye and Robert Middleton try to remember whether the pellet with the poison is in the chalice from the palace, the vessel with the pestle or the flagon with the dragon and which one holds the brew which is true – a model of Frank's delight in terse word-play and his ability to tailor a script to an individual star.

When he saw Glenda's Ginger Rogers routine in 1971 he was so impressed that he got on the phone to her the next morning and set about altering the screenplay to accommodate a British, rather than an American, lead. Glenda immediately agreed to do the film:

One never knows at the beginning of a project what will happen at the end. How boring it would be if one did. There is never any one overriding reason why you decide to do a job. In the case of *A Touch of Class* I suppose there was a desire somewhere in the back of my mind, to work in an American situation and actually, I found that really invigorating. I really love the Americans' energy, the sense of attack they bring to a film. It is utterly and refreshingly professional.

Filming was to start in May.

In the meantime *Isabella of Spain*, which Glenda had also agreed to do, fell through, and she was suddenly left with six weeks to fill from the start of April 1972, neatly allowing her just enough time to do her second film opposite Oliver Reed, *The Triple Echo*, based on a novella by H. E. Bates. Graham Cottle, who had bought the rights and adapted it, had secured Glenda and Oliver Reed before finding a director. Michael Apted, who eventually directed it, had had a long apprenticeship in television but had never made a film before. 'The producers had wanted someone rather more substantial [than me] to make the film,' he told me, '[but] it was a question of making do with whoever was available.' Perhaps because she was given right of refusal over Apted Glenda was very protective of him, and when it came to filming she behaved, to Apted's mind, impeccably.

Ian Woodward, a previous biographer of Glenda, maintained that Glenda was a recalcitrant member of *The Triple Echo* cast and stated that 'visitors to the set noticed that Glenda, with a scarf over her 1940s wig and gum boots on her feet, invariably sat alone on a rickety canvas chair between takes, almost cold-shouldered by the other actors and totally ignored by Reed'.[1] In fact Glenda was deliberately making life easier for her inexperienced director. Apted was used to homely stars like Violet Carson (Ena Sharples) and Pat Phoenix from *Coronation Street*. They could play the prima donna in their own way, but Reed was a full-scale movie star with a very dominating personality. He had already proved himself something of a nightmare by demanding changes to the script, and he insisted on a very different style of working. Apted was immensely grateful to Glenda when she decided that since Reed was to be present only for a little over a week there was little point in going 'head to head' with him, and that she would not insist on her way of working. Even so, Apted was so on edge that when they filmed the first shot – Glenda milking a cow – the cameras started rolling, the clapperboard snapped and there was a long, expectant silence because he had forgotten to say 'action'. In the end Simon Ralph, the first assistant director, had to whisper the magic word in Apted's ear before the scene could begin.

Glenda was also very good-humoured about various filming problems with her co-star Brian Deacon's wigs and with the small derelict cottage near Salisbury in which they were shooting (and which was subsequently bought by the British screenwriter Michael Thomas). This was also Brian Deacon's first movie, and Apted was so protective of him that when he was filming a close-up on Glenda with Deacon delivering lines off-camera, Apted actually praised Deacon instead of Glenda. All this Glenda took contentedly in her stride. There were rumours that Glenda was behaving badly on the set, and a BBC documentary on the filming seems to show a difficult Glenda at work, but Apted (who says 'I am pretty thin-skinned about actors shouting at me, so I would have remembered it') does not remember anything of the kind. Ken Colley, who plays one of the other soldiers, and who had also worked with Glenda on *The Music Lovers*, found her affable and approachable.

The film is a subtle and deeply charged piece and remains both one of Glenda's strongest performances and the piece of which she is most proud. The plot, dismissed by some as fanciful, deals with a woman living alone (because her husband is a prisoner-of-war) in 1942 on a remote English farm. When a young soldier, played by Brian Deacon, appears, crossing her land, she takes to him and they start a passionate affair. On an impulse he decides to desert, and in order to hide him she disguises him as her sister. Claustro-phobia soon rots the relationship and when a lascivious and bullish sergeant appears (Reed) and starts trying to seduce both 'sisters', Deacon agrees to go to an army Christmas ball to spite Glenda. Still supposing Deacon to be a woman Reed attempts to seduce him, and when he is met with resistance attempts to rape him, whereupon Reed realises his mistake. Deacon flees, and Reed catches up with him at Glenda's farm. In the final scene Glenda is seen at an upper window looking down on Reed and the captured Deacon. She raises a shotgun and shoots not Reed but Deacon.

Reed agreed with Glenda that 'as antagonists, we worked together better in *The Triple Echo* for Michael Apted than we did as lovers for Russell', and delighting in his own misogyny he declared that 'in the end when she pointed her rifle at me and her lover, there was a gasp of dismay from the bra burners when Brian Deacon dropped'.[2]

The film, which cost £200,000 to make, did well enough in Britain, and very well in Continental Europe, especially France, but thanks to a legal bankruptcy wrangle which went on for several years it did not have a proper US release. When it finally appeared in the States it sank without trace, having been packaged as a sex-ploitation movie and retitled *Soldier in Skirts*.

With *The Triple Echo* complete, after a brief pit-stop at Hervey Road, Glenda moved on to *A Touch of Class*, which – apart from a few weeks in Marbella – was to be filmed in studios at Kensal Rise in North London. If *Women in Love* was to be the great critical success of her film career, this was to be her greatest box-office one, grossing more than $20 million in its first year. As with most two-hander movies the key was to lie in the chemistry between the leads. Segal, like Glenda, was no typical Hollywood actor, having spent much of his career in the theatre, but he had played the younger man in the Burton/Taylor movie of *Who's Afraid of Virginia Woolf?*, and having spotted him in *The Owl and the Pussycat* with Barbra Streisand, Frank had decided to cast him – the part had originally been intended for Dustin Hoffman.

When Anthea Disney visited the set of another Jackson/Segal movie five years later she reported in the *Daily Mail* that the two actors could scarcely abide each other, but in fact the relationship between them was close and their public antagonism was no more than a type of sibling rivalry. Segal confesses as much: 'It's fun to be around Glenda, because she has so many opinions. There's a kind of austere purity about someone like that and it's so tempting to take an opposite view when she comes on strong – and that's when she fires up.' It is a point he also made to Anthea Disney:

The first time I made any real contact with her was over Paul Scofield. He's God to her. So I became acrimonious about him, found fault, criticised. We insulted each other – at least we insulted each other's opinions. She loves it. That's the relationship she has with her sisters and with certain other people. She can be very acid with people, really cut them, but if you cut back you're suddenly in a duel and it starts to get fun. And that's brothers and sisters; they're the only ones who have the right to criticise each other.[3]

This delight in verbal combat was invaluable in *A Touch of Class*, as the film featured a tempestuous and frequently caustic extramarital affair between a married American living in London and a fashion designer divorcee uncharacteristically throwing caution to the wind. The element of rivalry was at the very heart of their performance. Glenda comments revealingly on Segal: 'He doesn't hang about . . . you throw something and he catches it and tosses it back. I liked that directness very much.'[4] Segal, staying in Tony Bennett's apartment in Grosvenor Square, also enjoyed himself, so much so that on one occasion he failed to turn up for filming, only to be discovered fast asleep in a boat on the Serpentine – a professional lapse for which Glenda gave him hell – but he admits: 'It was fun being bossed around by her because I'm a youngest child and she's the oldest.'

Frank, described by cast member Michael Elwyn as 'a cuddlier but less talented Billy Wilder', also noted, 'Take after take in one very complicated scene, calling for Segal to go into a complete rage, brought a perfectly matching response from Glenda no matter how much he varied the intensity of his performance. It was extraordinary.'[5] Yet Frank did not get off scot-free. As with *Women in Love* Glenda was determined that the character she was playing would bear at least some resemblance to reality, and she took Frank to task for what were, to her, evident mistakes. The film seemed to suggest that it would be far more difficult for the man to find ways of creating time for the various assignations. Glenda felt that it would be at least as difficult for the woman and so some extra scenes were written in. It was a subject on which Glenda was ardent:

What is hard is that one is increasingly aware of the absurd characters purporting to be female that one is asked to play . . . There are films that do have marvellous parts for women in them, but they're still carrying through a rather prehistoric view of how women react . . . It's very difficult as a woman to break out of that. It's very difficult to actually realise that so many of one's responses are invisibly indelibly programmed. It's amazing listening to the conversations of relatives like my mother and aunt. They are women who have worked every single day of their lives. They know just how hard it is for women. They know that in most working-class homes it is the woman who keeps family and household together. And yet they would no more think of expecting my father to go out and bring in a bucket of coal after work than they would fly to the moon, although they've worked all day and will probably work all night. They accept that that is a woman's lot. What is terrific is that women are not accepting it.[6]

Glenda's feminist assertiveness with Frank was not the only thing to astound other members of the cast. Equally shocking was the fact that this ostentatiously unfashionable actress was playing a fashion designer. When she first turned up in a scruffy T-shirt and a short crop Segal could scarcely believe that she would be able to carry off the part of the sophisticated Vicky Allessio. Yet when the Jean Muir costumes and the wig arrived it suddenly made sense, and Glenda gave one of her sexiest performances. As on so many occasions, Glenda knew how to turn on the glamour, despite the fact that she prefers to dress very plainly, delighting in the fact that she can 'schlep round Sainsbury's without anyone recognising me'.

I don't like the starry sort of life. I think of myself as an actress. I'm not a personality as such. I have nothing of myself that I can sell in that sense and I think that if you lose touch with actuality, with the way life is lived by most people, you lose the roots into acting really. The more remote you become from people the more difficult it is to act I think. Most lives are not comprised of enormous tragedies or enormous joys, but they are comprised of tiny little pin-pricks, of having to queue at the butchers, or it's raining when you're waiting for a bus. And these things, I think, it's very important to keep within your frame of reference.

This is part of an understandable conscious attempt to keep her private and her public lives separate, and prevent unwelcome intrusion into her life. Paradoxically, given that she does not want to become remote from ordinary people, it also lends Glenda an air of ambiguity, which can border on the aloof.

Segal maintains that a similar sexual ambivalence made *A Touch of Class*:

> She feels the stirrings of sexuality, but it confuses her and makes her angry. She projects more sexuality than any other actress I know, certainly more than any American movie stars, who do a kind of imitation of it. I found our love scenes were so illuminating, because they revealed areas of which I'd been completely unaware . . . The first time I kissed her, well, there was all that sexual energy, I guess, that had been held down and kept in check, because we'd been together for a long time by then, it was explosive and each time I kissed her the passion grew more intense. That's why the movie shimmers.

Glenda's many strengths and the new acting style she adopted for the film – she was 'a bundle of live wire fun' according to Michael Elwyn – could not save the movie from some of its problems, notably a very imperfect ending. Glenda was not convinced by the film either. In later years she has been dismissive of this period of her career. In 1990 she told the *Evening Standard* magazine: 'It's not that the work was light-weight, it was just pointless. I don't find acting easy at the best of times, and if you are ashamed of what you're doing, it's too painful a process. You might as well commit yourself to something you have respect for.'

Despite Glenda's doubts the film won her a new round of plaudits and a second Oscar. Once more she was dismissive of the award, refusing to attend the ceremony and boldly telling the Press that 'Now my mum has a proper set of bookends.' Yet a second Oscar was a significant achievement by any standard; an honour then only accorded to seven actresses (Luise Rainer, Elizabeth Taylor, Olivia de Havilland, Vivien Leigh, Katharine Hepburn, Bette Davis and Ingrid Bergman – Jane Fonda, Jodie Foster and Sally Field came later). It virtually guaranteed Glenda plenty of offers of work, even if the quality of the material on offer was not consistent, and she had to be careful not to appear blasé about her success. She told her friend Charles Marowitz that:

> It's really a three-day wonder, you know, and it doesn't make all the difference that people think. It's nice the day you hear the news, and it's nice on the day they actually give you the statuette and maybe twenty-four hours after that. It doesn't really stretch much further than that. And it doesn't mean that every film script gets sent to you. You don't get the pick of the cream. The cream is a very small proportion of the work that is circulating at any given time. I get dreadful scripts sent to me most of the time and the good ones – now as before – are very rare indeed.

Yet she was delighted to receive a congratulatory telegram urging her to 'stick with us' if she wanted another Oscar – from Morecambe and Wise.

Glenda's next film, which was already lined up before *A Touch of Class* was completed, was not to be anywhere near as happy an experience, for Glenda, her co-star Peter Finch, the director and the financiers. *Bequest to the Nation* had started life as a television play by Terence Rattigan about the romance between Admiral Nelson and the hefty, vulgar Emma Hamilton. Hal B. Wallis, by now on his third historical movie in a row, had decided it was ripe for transfer to the big screen. In a curious move Wallis had drafted in the successful director of television classic serials, the Welshman James Cellan Jones, who had never made a feature film before. Partly out of personal habit and partly due to uncertainty about Cellan Jones' inexperience, Wallis kept a very tight grip on the

Glenda (right), ready for the open-air baths in Hoylake, with her school-friend Marjorie Stone.

Glenda, kneeling, and Jean Hibbert pose at Laura 'Dinkie' Wicks' ballet school in Meols.

Glenda's first appearance (far right) in a play, as a maid in the Hoylake YMCA Players production of *Mystery at Greenfingers*. Her friend Joan Hadwin is far left.

Glenda's publicity still when she was appearing in rep in Crewe, where she met her future husband Roy Hodges. Note the fashionable haircut.

Roy Hodges and Glenda Jackson pose for photos after their wedding ceremony at St Marylebone Register Office.

Glenda's first award-winning role, in the *Marat/Sade*. Charlotte Corday murders the French revolutionary leader Marat (Ian Richardson) in his bath, watched over by the Marquis de Sade (Patrick Magee) and other inmates of the Asylum at Charenton.

The toast of Broadway, during the New York run of the *Marat/Sade*.

Glenda with Jennie Linden in *Women in Love*.

The young baby Daniel with his parents in Blackheath. Glenda described the birth of her only son as the greatest moment of her life.

One of several harrowing scenes from Ken Russell's *The Music Lovers*. Glenda, as Tchaikovsky's once beautiful bride Nina Milukova, spreads her legs above the madhouse grating.

John Schlesinger's daring and highly personal *Sunday, Bloody Sunday*, in which Glenda played Alex Greville in a love triangle with a bi-sexual designer (Murray Head, centre) and a doctor (Peter Finch).

Above The Hodges family – Glenda, Daniel and Roy, in John Schlesinger's house.

Glenda's second appearance as the Virgin Queen, Elizabeth I, this time in *Mary, Queen of Scots*.

Glenda appears in the *Morecambe and Wise Show*: 'All men are fools and what makes them fools is having beauty like what I have got.'

film, specifying that Cellan Jones could not have Liz Taylor as she was unreliable, and that he had to have Glenda for the part of Lady Hamilton, because she was 'far hotter'. Cellan Jones told me that 'this effectively signed the film's death warrant as Glenda was hopelessly miscast'. Lady Hamilton was a large woman – more than fourteen stone – and the film even included a scene in which she had to be forcibly strapped into her dress. With a bulging actress this might have been funny, but with an angular Glenda it was simply surreal. False breasts were made for her, but had to be discarded because of the cut of Hamilton's Empire dresses.

There were other problems. There was no money to go to sea. To re-create the Battle of Trafalgar, Cellan Jones had to make do with one day at Dartmouth, another day filming cannon fire, an afternoon playing with model ships and old footage from *Hornblower*. A wholly inappropriate ship filmed in three-quarter profile had to masquerade as a three-master. All of which made Glenda intensely unhappy. She mocked the script, which Rattigan, who was ill with cancer, had little time to redraft. She was rude to Anthony Quayle who also appeared in the film and, according to Cellan Jones, she gave Peter Finch, with whom she had worked happily in *Sunday, Bloody Sunday*, an appalling time, despite the fact that he was already not in the best of health and contracted cold sores whenever he was stressed.

Cellan Jones says that:

> It's very difficult to put one's finger on the numerous reasons why she made him so uncomfortable and insecure . . . she wouldn't talk to him at all, except when working; she ran to the dressing room the moment a shot was over; she discussed something of mutual interest only through me; she wouldn't look him in the eye; she screamed when I had to restage in order not to show Finchy's nervous cold sore.

Glenda's relationship with Cellan Jones was frosty in the extreme, and she took umbrage when he asked her tartly for 'more Wirral and less Blackheath', in reference to the fact that Emma Hamilton was from Glenda's own part of the country. But it was not until midway through the three weeks of Glenda's time filming that real antagonism set in. Cellan Jones was preparing a scene with Margaret Leighton, the fine but arthritic actress who was playing Lady Nelson, when Glenda imperiously bellowed from the other end of the set that she wanted to see the director – if that was what he called himself – in her dressing room at lunchtime. Cellan Jones arrived and the two embarked upon a lengthy and acrimonious row. Director and actress only just managed to get through the rest of the film. In the end, the breakdown between star and director was so complete that Hal Wallis surreptitiously directed Glenda in most of the post-synch dialogue. Cellan Jones was furious that this had happened behind his back and threw a tantrum in front of Wallis, insisting that the dialogue be redone by him. Yet he credits Glenda 'with at least enough professionalism to improve her performance in the dubbing theatre under my direction by a hundred per cent even if she hated my guts'.

Glenda's extraordinary behaviour did not, however, end with the last roll of film. When the film was on the verge of release and she was doing the usual round of publicity interviews, she launched a vicious assault on her own performance, declaring in the *Guardian*'s women's page that this was 'the worst piece of over-acting I've ever committed', and telling *The Sunday Times* that her whole performance was just 'bash-bash-bash'[7] and then redoubling her attack on television before bowing out of the film's royal première.

In retrospect Cellan Jones is very forgiving of Glenda's outrageous behaviour, maintaining that it arose because she knew she was miscast and felt guilty that she was getting £70,000 – the same as Rattigan – for only three weeks' work, compared, for instance, to Cellan Jones himself, who earned £10,000 for the whole project. But at the time he, Finch and Rattigan were all furious. Alexander Walker and Derek Malcolm both condemned her behaviour as 'unethical'. According to Cellan Jones, Rattigan, while pointing out that Glenda had not yet offered to return the £70,000, tartly argued that Glenda had played Emma 'as a mean-spirited bitch, instead of a great-hearted whore, but I suppose that is her range'.

Glenda, without a shred of remorse, maintained:

> I should never have done it. I don't like Rattigan's stuff
> and I don't know how to play it. Also I loathed the

director. Instead of doing what I should have done which was to scream and rage and behave like a spoilt Hollywood star, I behaved very well. When I was asked about the film I had to tell the truth and the truth was that I was fucking terrible in it. It's not a good film anyway.[8]

Needless to say this approach did not earn Glenda any new friends. Glenda *had* screamed and raged and behaved like a Hollywood star. A better stance would have been to say that she was saddened that the film had not turned out quite as everyone had hoped. Glenda still argues that 'I didn't criticise the film, only my own performance in it – which was rubbishy – and that criticism was accurate.'

Tact never came as high on Glenda's list of virtues as professionalism and candour. As Marowitz put it, recalling early rows in the RSC:

Some of her problems have been that she has worked with people who did not share her degree of commitment, English amateurs who were happy to make a pass at a performance for a bit of a lark. So many English actors see a performance in terms of where it will lead, rather than in its own right. But Glenda was always completely focused on the task in hand and it made her seem dismissive of others when all she was really doing was setting herself high standards.

Moreover, by the time of *Bequest to the Nation* Glenda had formed a very clear understanding of what film acting required, and she had little time for those who wanted to do things another way. In the theatre she was renowned for leaving the rehearsal room the moment the day was over. Actors would complain to Peter Crouch about it, and she would readily admit that she was 'anti-sociable'. In films this solitary attitude was a professional style. When asked whether she found it stimulating to work with people such as Tony Britton, she revealed her opinion that the cinematic process has little to do with traditional thespian camaraderie:

I have to be honest with you and say that acting for a film is not like that. The most interesting thing to work for is the camera. The camera is absolutely fascinated by what you are doing; you never have to work for its interest or its attention because it is totally absorbed in what you are doing. That concentration of energy you get on a film set is something that I find enormously helpful, but acting with other actors on a film is very much a jigsaw process . . . you obviously work with people and there is that interchange and interplay, but the really interesting thing to work for is the camera.[9]

It is not surprising that often the best relationships Glenda established on set were with the cinematographers.

Single-mindedly Glenda focused entirely on her work, and because she concentrated so exclusively on her performance she always tried to find as much time as possible to herself, conserving energy in her dressing room during the long periods of waiting that filming requires. When things stood in her way frustration could turn into acerbic anger and she would take on anyone, from fellow actors to the most powerful of Hollywood directors and producers. This often won her the grateful admiration of less adventurous performers. As Jennie Linden, who worked with Glenda on *Women in Love*, says: 'Glenda's the sort of person who would say what I always wished I had the courage to say on set. In so many ways Glenda's a perfectionist and she had a courage about her person that was very enviable if you didn't possess it.' Even if it led to often appallingly self-centred behaviour it took genuine courage for Glenda to stick to her resolutely exacting standards. Glenda's early life – Boots, poverty, unemployment – had not prepared her for the high-life of a movie star, nor for the opportunity to wield power and influence. All too easily she came across as aggressive instead of assertive, stubborn instead of determined, aloof instead of introverted and insecure.

Moreover, by the end of 1972 Glenda was more than a little disenchanted with the world of big-budget movies, and was questioning the whole idea of acting as a profession. She declared to a journalist on the set of *Bequest to the Nation* that she was now thinking of retiring because 'all I want is a breather to be with Roy and Danny and catch up on my other loves – gardening and reading'. And she told the *Sunday Telegraph* in April 1973: 'I suppose it is true, this is a trivial profession. I think of all the energy I pour into what may turn out to be a very unimportant film and I feel it should be channelled into something more worthwhile, helping the homeless or the handicapped.'

1973 and 1974 were to be quiet years for Glenda, almost the quietest in her career. Since 1968 she had been working exclusively in films, largely because she had been vociferous in her condemnation of the working conditions in many London theatres and the suburbanite mentality of many playgoers, but also partly because she felt that cinema afforded her so many more possibilities. Now, a combination of factors made her turn back to the theatre. Not only had she two bad experiences of film work within a year, but she was also being offered more interesting theatre work: Rosalind for the RSC at Stratford, and Beckett's *Not I* at the Royal Court. In addition, she was looking for work that would allow her more time with Dan, who was just starting school. Finally, when she spoke to Peter Brook on the phone on the first night of his spell-binding *Midsummer Night's Dream* 1972 season at the Aldwych, where it had arrived after Stratford-upon-Avon and an American tour, these factors crystallised into a desire to return to the live theatre. 'In the background I could hear all the theatre noises. Actors' chat and so on. And I thought, "That's what I've been missing and that's what I want. To be working with real people again."'

Through 1973 and 1974 Glenda sought out theatre work in London and, despite being listed in America's *Box Office* magazine as one of only eight actresses in the top twenty-five cinema moneymakers of the year, she deliberately refused films that were too commercial, or would take her away from home for too long. Beckett rescinded his offer of the part in *Not I*, but Glenda returned to the stage of the Duchess Theatre in April 1973 in a new comedy by John Mortimer, *Collaborators*, with Joss Ackland and John Wood. The play was successful enough to have a replacement cast when the original leads moved on. Glenda's reviews were warm but, so Joss Ackland recorded in his diary, the production was 'not a happy experience. John was far too demented and extrovert and Glenda and I were forced to lose balance and underplay . . . Each time we left the stage she and I would put a little tick on the wall as we approached the end of our three-month contracts.'[10]

Fortuitously the end of her *Collaborators* contract coincided with Dan's first school holidays, so she and Roy jumped at the opportunity to take him to Italy for July and August, working short days and weeks on the curious Damiano Damiani film *The Tempter* while staying in the Frascati region just south of Rome. In the film a classic, old-style Glenda played – with either arch or camp irony, depending on your assessment – a repressed and repressive sadistic mother superior in an obscure convent in Rome which acts as an unconventional spiritual refuge for an incongruous group of sinners: a revolutionary bishop; an incestuous noble who commits suicide; a guilt-obsessed young woman; and a priest who hires a writer to transcribe his sins of omission under the Nazis.

When the Hodges family returned from Italy Glenda was supposed to be working on a production of Jean Rhys' *Good Morning, Goodnight*, but this was cancelled at the last moment. Instead she spent the rest of the year happily gardening and housekeeping – and picking up a French Film Academy Etoile de Cristal and an *Evening News* readers' best actress award – while *A Touch of Class* was released. If 1973 was quiet by the standards of an international Oscar-winning film star, 1974 was not much busier, and the two ventures that filled her year proved no happier or more artistically fruitful. First there was a fraught production of *The Maids* at the Greenwich Theatre, which could not have been more convenient for the Blackheath housewife. The cast was interesting – Vivien Merchant and Susannah York – but personal animosities between Jackson and Merchant made for a fractious time which was further compounded when Merchant was offered a part in the film in which Glenda was about to lead, Joseph Losey's *The Romantic Englishwoman*, and then had the offer withdrawn. Moreover, Glenda proved a tough colleague for Susannah York, who found that

> Glenda doesn't pull her punches and we had our share of arguments . . . on the other hand we had a very healthy respect for each other's talents and personality – at least I had for hers. Trying to look at it objectively – and she might not agree with this – I would tend to think that perhaps tact is slightly more natural to me than it is to her. I suppose we circled around each other for a while

at the beginning, but I think we were supported by this tremendous respect and actual affection – certainly on my part – for I really *liked* Glenda ... And I never like anyone if I cannot respect them. I actually felt a warm, sisterly affection for her. But I quarrel with my sisters and Glenda and I were also playing sisters and that rather conditioned our feelings towards each other.[11]

The Maids ran for a month and was subsequently swiftly filmed – for £250,000 – by Robert Enders in an adaptation by Christopher Miles in two weeks. All three actresses were paid on a percentage of the profits, so when Enders sold the film to Ely Landau's American Film Theatre for half a million dollars later that year they probably made more money than had ever been achieved before by anyone in a Greenwich Theatre production, even before the film was shown.

Glenda next embarked on filming for *The Romantic Englishwoman*. Joseph Losey, its respected American director, had fallen foul of McCarthyism and moved to the UK, where he had made the much-admired film *The Servant* with Dirk Bogarde and, more recently, *The Go-Between*. Losey was a complex man who had a remarkable knack of falling out with his closest friends, thanks to an acerbic tongue and an even more lacerating pen. Glenda had wanted to work with Losey for some time, as he was a professional whose work was always acknowledged to be serious in its intent, even if it often lacked something in the execution, but unfortunately this was the wrong movie to have chosen. Losey himself had doubts about the novel on which it was based, telling Alain Delon back in 1972 that it was 'not of sufficient quality for you and me', and he brought Tom Stoppard in to redraft the screenplay. Afterwards he stated, 'I have no reason to be ashamed of it as a craftsman, although I think it is a piece of junk.'[12]

Moreover he had difficulty casting the film. He wanted Dirk Bogarde to play the writer Lewis Fielding. Bogarde was scathing, declaring that 'it sounds like a Georgette Heyer novel', and that Glenda in the main role of Elizabeth Fielding would be 'about as romantic as a games mistress with an off accent'.[13] Losey had first wanted Julie Christie in the role of Elizabeth Fielding, who complained about Losey's next suggestion of Alan Bates for Fielding and was so noncommittal that he wrote to withdraw the offer and tell her to improve her 'communications'. He wanted Harold Pinter, Vivien Merchant's husband, to play the doctor, a minor role. Pinter declined, while Losey toyed with casting Vivien Merchant, who was incensed when he wrote to tell her that the producer had refused to let her play Isabel, a friend of the Fieldings, because she was 'the wrong generation'.

The final cast, Michael Caine (as Lewis Fielding), Helmut Berger (Elizabeth Fielding's lover) and Glenda, was, nevertheless, impressive and had the potential to make a fine film. Sadly the problems did not end with casting. Losey and his wife Patricia were extremely melancholy throughout the shooting, which began in Surrey on 21 October 1974. He was both quarrelsome with most of the cast and luxuriant in his lifestyle when they went abroad, neither of which endeared him to Glenda. Most disturbingly, Stoppard's reworking of the original text gave the film so many layers of possible meaning that what was intended as ironic ambiguity came across as no more than indecisive cinematic cleverness – or confusion.

The biggest problem for Glenda, though, lay with Berger, the son of a wealthy Salzburg hotelier and restaurateur. Berger could certainly act. He had been impressive in Visconti's *The Damned*, but he was regularly late, and one morning in Baden Baden he announced that he had tried to drown himself at 2 a.m., but had not carried it through because the water was too cold. His behaviour was sufficient on its own to incense Glenda, but in addition it was evident to others on the set that Berger took an instant dislike to her, and continually showed his contempt for her or tried to wind her into a rage.

Finally Glenda was disappointed in Losey himself, whom she found 'very much anti-female, there was something very misogynistic about him. Of course, he was terribly plagued with asthma, but he loved difficulties, particularly when they came from his stars, because it gave him that sense of being in control.' This does not accord with Losey's own assessment:

> A lot of people, of course, couldn't stand her, and she
> behaved extremely badly on occasion with folk who, as

far as their status on the set was concerned, were her social inferiors. We almost didn't get the film going because of that kind of difference on one occasion. People were afraid of her, because once in a while she would make a crack – and the cracks could be very nasty.[14]

It is difficult at this distance to judge the rights and wrongs of Losey's accusations. Her co-star Michael Caine has always maintained a discreet silence on the subject of Glenda, except to note that he thinks her 'the best film actress I ever worked with'. Over the years, in contrast, most of Glenda's colleagues have commented on the fact that she is, if anything, more pleasant to supporting actors and to stage crew than she is to her co-stars and directors, of whom she always expects rigorous professionalism. It is undoubtedly true that Glenda was very unhappy. She felt offended by Berger's attitude, and blamed Losey for not taming him. She was also disappointed by a film that had promised well, and she resented working away from home and from Dan.

Glenda won another round of warm reviews, even though the film as a whole suffered at the hands of the critics, and despite the fact that Losey, when he saw the first answer print, noted that 'when Glenda [is] too light, as she frequently is, [she] shows skin defects and bad teeth'. David Caute makes the perceptive point that Glenda brought with her to *The Romantic Englishwoman* 'the same "everywoman" combination of common sense, emotional longing, domestic acuity' that had so marked her performance in *Sunday, Bloody Sunday* 'but the script and Losey's direction cornered her in elaborate levels of non-reality and substituted artificially contrived confrontations for *Sunday*'s deadly innocence'.[15] The working environment had not been one in which Glenda could thrive. At one point she even managed to overdose on caffeine and was frighteningly ill. It is little surprise that the closest friendship she established in the film was with the cinematographer, Gerry Fisher, or that she refused to attend the Cannes filming and later wrote, with characteristic understatement 'my experiences of working with Losey were not particularly happy, or, from my point of view, fruitful'.[16]

By the end of 1974 Glenda had had a frustrating three years, with three weak films in a row to her name. The one film she had enjoyed and in which she took pride, *The Triple Echo*, had achieved only a low-key release in the UK, and although she had won her second Oscar, her career was in an uncertain state. Even her recent stage appearances had been only half-hearted successes. More importantly, she had not been involved in a completely enjoyable piece of work since *A Touch of Class*.

All of which left her a fractious and vulnerable woman – even if she was not prepared to show it.

CHAPTER SEVEN

─────※─────

A Passionate Affair

WHEN HEDDA GABLER RETIRES to an inner room at the end of Ibsen's drama her husband Tesman, Mrs Elvsted and Judge Brack continue chatting. It feels as if the curtain will come down on yet another evening of suffocating bourgeois ennui for Hedda until suddenly a shot rings out. Hedda is found lying lifeless, stretched out on a sofa, having shot herself in the temple. With heavy irony Ibsen gives Brack the final words of the play: 'One doesn't *do* that kind of thing!'

If there were ever a play that a woman prone to boredom in a troubled marriage should not undertake, it is *Hedda Gabler*. Yet on 1 January 1975 Glenda started rehearsals not just for a production of the play, but for a three-month world tour, a London season and a film.

By now Glenda's marriage was in a mess. She and Roy had always rowed, and Glenda had occasionally thrown things at her husband – 'anything that came to hand', he told me. But both of them considered this a sign of a healthily robust marriage, and in the early days of weekly rep they had been inseparable companions. At parties in the sixties, when Roy was more consistently employed than Glenda, they would often be seen sitting quite happily alone in a corner, scarcely bothering to make friends, and in many ways Roy was an ideal companion for Glenda. According to Pauline Devaney, 'Roy is very relaxed and a bit wicked – an anarchist and very theatrical, with a nice laid-back way with famous people. And Glenda has always adored wicked people, because she's not one herself.'

But Glenda's success had made their relationship tense. When her first few breaks came – *Alfie*, the RSC and *Women in Love* – and they cruelly coincided with a barren spell in Roy's career, he was an almost shockingly devoted follower. While Glenda was appearing as Ophelia Joyce Marlow recalls seeing Roy one night simply sitting in the corner of her dressing room as a stream of glamorous people passed through. Joyce was even more surprised when Glenda announced that Joyce and she were going to dinner, without even a suggestion that he might care to join them, and Glenda betrayed her ambivalence towards him by letting everyone know that 'Roy's producing again . . . at Butlins'.

As Glenda became a star Roy played the supporting role impeccably. In New York for *Marat/Sade* he, not Glenda, had congratulated Brenda Vaccaro and invited her to Glenda's party, which he was organising. Back in London he, not Glenda, had organised a starry party in Blackheath in honour of Brenda and her partner Michael Douglas. (Although it was Glenda who dealt with an unpleasant moment at the party when a drunken interloper started to abuse Brenda. Recalling 'the wimpo' Michael Douglas with evident horror Brenda said that 'not a hair on his arm, not a hair on his ass moved, but Glenda – Glenda grandly, beautifully and succinctly demanded that he leave and showed him the door'.)

Roy was also a very public film star's husband, regularly giving journalists interviews, and occasionally giving them some of their best copy on Glenda. When the Press asked how he could live with the actress who played Nina in *The Music Lovers* and rolled, naked, in orgasmic pleasure on the floor of a train, he acknowledged a sense of queasiness, but batted off their queries with a discreet 'Glenda on the screen is not Glenda at home. On the screen she is much more powerful than in real life. She's powerful because she's a great actress. I don't care what she does in a film. She's too good not to do it well.'[1] This was Roy on-message as far as Glenda's agent and her distributors were concerned, Roy as Glenda's number-one fan, but he could also be waspish. His oft-quoted comment on Glenda's ruthless workaholism was deliberate in its imagery:

> Of course, we have rows and sometimes, in the middle
> of them, when I'm telling her to push off, I realise it's
> all hers, the house and everything. Funnily enough it

never occurs to her to say it to me. She has no sense of material possessions at all. She moves through life like natural royalty – never carries any money. She thrives on work. If she'd gone into politics, she'd have become Prime Minister, if she'd gone into crime, she would have been Jack the Ripper.[2]

Yet, in Brenda Vaccaro's words, 'Roy was absolutely devoted to her', and he would admit quite openly both to his reliance on her and their rows, telling one journalist in 1972:

The worst thing, the one thing I really fear is loneliness, but, thank God, there's not much danger of that because Glenda and I enjoy each other's company – though sometimes it looks as if our relationship won't last much longer because we're normal enough to scream and throw things at each other occasionally. Not very often, luckily.[3]

Throughout their marriage he maintained that he was simply delighted in Glenda's achievements: 'I'm not jealous of her in any way,' he candidly told the *Evening Standard* in 1972, 'because she's far better than I was. She's a bloody good actress. If I thought I'd had more to offer and yet she had achieved the success then I would be jealous. But the fact is that she runs rings round me.'[4]

Nevertheless Roy's difficulty in finding theatre work and Glenda's meteoric rise created an imbalance in the relationship. At first he had genuinely enjoyed her success. Indeed, he felt that he had enjoyed it more than Glenda. 'After all, I enjoy spending money and Glenda doesn't,' he quips. But as time went by and Glenda became ever more successful, Roy felt left behind. 'I was one of Britain's first house-husbands, and I have to tell you that it doesn't work. It's just not possible. It takes away all your manliness.' In Roy's case this was particularly true because from the beginning he had done all the things that Glenda was not interested in: sorting out the money, paying the bills and arranging the mortgage. Even when her career started to take off he was still in charge of the household accounts and took charge of hiring staff, not least because, he believes, 'Glenda could never handle staff. She had to be friends with them all.' He could maintain his sense of masculinity because he managed the money, even if he did not earn it. When real success came, though, Glenda had to employ accountants, and suddenly Roy even lost control over the household chequebook, which left him only the little dignity he could muster from his own independent efforts. When it became increasingly clear that Roy attracted attention only as a proxy for Glenda, it was almost inevitable that any small cracks in their relationship would develop into irreparable splits.

Although Roy spent a large part of the late sixties and early seventies following in Glenda's footsteps, he had been inventive in his attempts to revive his own career. Partly thanks to Glenda's munificence (and partly on the recommendation of her tax advisers[5]) he set up a small art gallery in Greenwich and for a brief period this thrived, selling paintings to Glenda's more affluent colleagues like John Schlesinger. Roy only charged the artists he exhibited in kind, so the commission was a single painting. In many ways the arrangement was ideal – the gallery was so close to home that Roy could not only see Daniel safely stored with the child-minder, but could even pick up Pauline Devaney and Edwin Apps' son Barnaby as well. Unfortunately the gallery soon folded, and by the time Glenda had won her second Oscar he was back in the theatre, having assembled his own small company performing a mixed bag of classics and musicals at minor fringe venues in London, including an eight-person *Romeo and Juliet* at the Hoxton Music Hall. As with many companies of its kind On Stage relied on actors who were prepared to work for nothing but expenses, but even so box-office returns were minimal. Among other projects Roy persuaded the barefoot singer Sandie Shaw to play both Ophelia and George Bernard Shaw's Saint Joan for £8 a night; he staged *Antony and Cleopatra* starring Philip Madoc and Jill Gascoine; and for nearly two years he ran seasons at the Duthy Theatre in Southwark.

Meanwhile, despite often being separated from Dan Glenda grew ever closer to him, and would even sacrifice work for him, something she later declared she would never do for a man. 'I cannot conceive of a situation where I'd put the man first. If a man asked me to chose between him and my work I'd probably leave him anyway.'[6] But Glenda would accept a film during Dan's summer holiday if it offered a decent venue for Dan, and she would regularly turn down lengthy stints away from London so as to be with him.

Through the early seventies the Hodgeses' marriage went steadily further awry, and the rows grew in frequency and in strength. The beginning of the end, however, came when Glenda received her second Oscar for *A Touch of Class*, in 1974. That night, as soon as he heard the result, Roy rang Pauline Devaney and confessed, 'That's all we need. It's over. It's finished.' As he described, 'The first Oscar was sheer joy. But now I was being drowned by her success and I must have been feeling very jealous. I would really admire any man who can do it, but the only way I've seen it work is where the man becomes his wife's manager. And I wasn't prepared to do that.' At the same time Roy was finding Glenda's obsessive relationship with her family difficult. Not only would Christmas be spent up at Hoylake, but members of the Jackson clan, most regularly Joan and Lynne, would often set up camp in Hervey Road, or come as holiday companions with the Hodges, leaving Glenda and Roy remarkably little time to themselves. Others might have enjoyed this extended family, but Roy grew to resent it. 'You have to remember that I left home when I was sixteen, so I found it very difficult to understand,' Roy explained, 'but if you love Glenda you have to love her completely – there's no room for anyone else. And the only place she's ever got that sort of love is from her family.' With such jealousies in existence it is not surprising that Glenda and Roy's relationship was troubled.

It was a measure of Glenda's unhappiness with Roy that she agreed to the *Hedda Gabler* tour, overriding her natural hatred of leaving Dan behind. Glenda later admitted that 'if our marriage had been wonderful, I wouldn't have voluntarily left Europe for fourteen weeks'.[7] She was depressed and anxious when she turned up for the rehearsals on 1 January 1975. Patrick Stewart, who played Ejlert Lövborg in the production, recalled watching Glenda make her way down the street that first morning:

> She was striding towards the rehearsal room and every-
> thing about the way she was moving was determined and
> purposeful; but her head was *so* low down. It could have
> been, on the one hand, the human version of a charging

bull, or it could have been somebody who was going somewhere they didn't want to go to.[8]

Initially rehearsals went well, although the composition of the cast was likely to be volatile. On the one hand there was Glenda, unhappy in her marriage and not well disposed either to men generally or, after Jarrott, Cellan Jones and Losey, to male directors in particular. In her corner were Jennie Linden, her old accomplice from *Women in Love*, and a small bevy of women – Pam St Clement, Barbara Penny, Fidelis Morgan and Celia Imrie – all of whom shared a strong feminism and several of whom were lesbians. On the other hand was Trevor Nunn, Peter Hall's triumphant successor at the RSC, himself passing through a rough patch in his emotional life. Nunn was a great admirer of Glenda's, but like everybody else in the theatre he had heard of Glenda's exacting standards, and he was keen to impress upon her his own understanding of the play. In his corner was Patrick Stewart, who had appeared in Trevor's *Revenger's Tragedy* and all four of his productions of Shakespeare's Roman plays and had become a close friend; and Oz Clarke, now the wine writer, then the male understudy. On the sidelines were Peter Eyre and Timothy West, who had played in Glenda's early RSC shows.

By now Glenda had a clear idea of what made a good director.

> With a really good director the relationship is so interdependent, because really good directors are not brilliant generals who simply marshal their forces; good directors utilise the energies and the abilities round them in such a way as to show themselves what they're doing as much as to make demands on their actors ... The bad ones are wanting constantly to interfere and manoeuvre, whereas the good ones tend to wait ... It's the bad directors who have your performance in their heads in advance, it's impossible to try and reproduce that. At any rate, it is for me. I can't get into that at all. In which case I'm absolutely on my own. And it's very lonely.[9]

From early on Glenda found Nunn too directive for her liking. She balked at his suggestions and fundamentally disagreed about the character of the play. Timothy West says that 'It wasn't that she was foul to him; it's just that she questioned every single thing that he said and everyone then shrank away in embarrassment.' When Nunn pressed for his interpretation she dug her heels in and took it out on other members of the cast, especially Stewart, whom she referred to in the third person even when he was present. At the time Stewart felt confused, aggrieved and angry, not least because he preferred Nunn's system of early blocking and distrusted Glenda's method of working. When Glenda started to tell him how he should play Lövborg he became defensive and sulky, and when Glenda disagreed with Trevor Nunn he automatically took the director's side. Stewart is more understanding of Glenda now and admits that

> It's possible that during the *Hedda Gabler* rehearsals I permitted myself to feel intimidated because I was nervous of confrontation. I didn't know how to confront, or how to demand a fair share of the rehearsal time, or how to work with a person who was as self-obsessed and aggressive as Glenda and I have a feeling that I could have made a difference.

He is even prepared to explain away Glenda's self-obsession:

> You have to allow for the fact that she was playing the lead and every scene focuses on her. I know now what that does to you. In the work that goes into delivering a complex leading role it's necessary that you become obsessed. I didn't then know that you must hold nothing back, you must give all of your intelligence in the hope that you will lose yourself in the role.

Trevor Nunn, apparently the most assaulted of the company, always remained loyally taciturn on the subject of Glenda's behaviour, ambiguously stating that

> In a sense to work with her is the same as to meet her. She's direct, uncomplicated, honest, very alive. She's absolutely without machination or ulterior motives. She can be fun. She often is. But of all the actors I've worked with she has a capacity for work that's phenomenal.

There's immense power of concentration, a great deal of attack, thrust, determination. She searches hard. It's quite ruthless.[10]

The result of these personal clashes was a miserable rehearsal period in London, but the company managed to survive intact and gave a week of performances in Richmond before flying to Australia. Glenda was now experiencing emotional turbulence every bit as violent as Hedda's. She later revealed that her marriage to Roy had been very unhappy for almost four years and that it was only because she was too scared to make the break, and because of Dan, that she had not forced the issue earlier. She was especially miserable when she boarded the flight to Australia. Not only was she terrified of flying, but she had been complaining to friends like Joyce Marlow, who came to the first night in Richmond, that Roy was being a 'complete shit' and was showing no sympathy for her phobia. Her solution was to drink herself into a more carefree attitude. Once on the plane she also felt acutely guilty at being sequestered alone in the first-class cabin, so early in the flight she made her way to see the rest of the cast in economy.

With them was the lighting director for the production, a short, squat, boiler of a man, Andy Phillips, who had worked extensively at the Royal Court Theatre and was renowned in the industry for his use of white light instead of coloured tints, and his tendency to leave large patches of the stage in atmospheric darkness (hence Glenda's later nickname for him, 'The Prince of Darkness'). Andy had first come across Glenda when he was a humble electrician on the set of *Marat/Sade*. On the flight to Australia, as was his wont, he had been drinking, and when Glenda appeared in economy he launched into a ferocious assault on her performance as Hedda, accusing her of failing to understand the play and of playing it with no subtlety. The rest of the cast were shocked and feared an instant and virulent reprisal from Glenda, or at least a snarled put-down. In fact, Glenda merely rose to the challenge with her own caustic remarks about the lighting. By the end of the flight it was clear that Mr Phillips and Mrs Hodges were engaging in a savage bout of verbal foreplay.

Australia presented a whole new series of difficulties for the troubled company. There were problems with the management. The first-night party in Melbourne was mistakenly given in a seedy club and the assembled guests failed to applaud the actors when they arrived. Glenda and her crew sat in a corner for half an hour bemoaning the venue and occasionally sending Peter Eyre out to mingle with the public on their behalf before fleeing to Glenda's hotel room, where they proceeded to get heavily drunk. In Sydney the theatre, the Elizabethan, was actually scheduled for demolition, the carpets had already been removed and there was a great hole in the roof. According to Timothy West it was like

> a huge tropical railway station to play in and you have to yell above the noise of the trains and the sweet traffic and the fidgeting of people stuck to their seats in the intolerable heat. There's no air conditioning so they leave the lantern in the roof open and those huge flying black beetles come in and swoop down on to the stage. They have a particular fondness for Glenda's wig and want to nest in it – she's wonderful, never bats an eyelid.[11]

Equally irritating to Glenda was the fact that Trevor Nunn did not join the company in time to reblock the play for the much larger theatre and one of the actors, Timothy West, had to take the director's place – another lapse from Glenda's professional ideal.

Some things did improve, though. The relationship with Patrick Stewart had not gone well in rehearsal, but in performance he found Glenda a very different person, generous on stage, helpful and charming. At the start of the tour he resolved not to go on stage nursing grievances about the way she had treated him in London, but to make a determined effort to get closer to her. Every night he would knock on her dressing-room door between the half- and the quarter-hour call and he would spend ten minutes chatting with her as she prepared – to the extremely loud accompaniment, every night, of Joni Mitchell. 'Then I found Glenda alone was a very different person from the Glenda in the rehearsal room, quiet, thoughtful, amusing, sweet, interested in the other person – we could talk about the play and things that weren't working.' These nightly chats changed Stewart's perception of Glenda and he confesses that 'It was then that my crush developed because when she was not on the front foot swinging punches I found her a warm, fun and very sexy person.' One of the scenes in the play involved Hedda and Lövborg looking through a photo album and surreptitiously flirting while Tesman and Jude Brack are talking in the background, and every night Stewart now found himself 'literally turned on by playing that scene with her because her whole openness was tremendously arousing and because she made herself so vulnerable. It was probably the most erotic scene I have ever played in my life.'

By this time Glenda had fallen heavily for Andy, although the relationship was not to be consummated until later in the tour. Throughout the rest of the Australian leg of the tour she rang him for an hour at his lunchtime every day; and wrote him a daily letter, pouring out her heart, complaining about Nunn (who had apparently compounded his sins of omission by making a pass at her and then promptly being sick over a wall), about Roy, and about the appalling management. He returned to England once the lights were set, and in his absence Glenda was lonely and spent her time almost exclusively with the other women in the cast, despite the fact that she has always claimed to find 'the unadulterated company of women tedious beyond belief'.[12] Jennie Linden had her husband and son Rupert with her for most of the tour, but Barbara Penny, Fidelis Morgan, Pam St Clement and Celia Imrie spent so much time with Glenda that they had 'The Jackson Five' T-shirts printed, thereby further alienating several of the men. This was made even worse when Fabergé, who were, through George Barrie and Brut Productions, putting up the money for the film of *Hedda*, lent Glenda a private jet with an on-board chef and Glenda only took the girls on board.

One final source of offence was the incessant round of expatriate parties to which the company was invited. Glenda tended to decline the invitations unless they were to more intimate occasions. But Timothy West thought that 'When you're on tour you are an ambassador for Britain, and Glenda could have been a little more sociable with the constant round of real ambassadors. But she took the attitude that it was bound to be a bore and because she did it with so little grace it did cause offence.' At one point Glenda, Pam St Clement and Peter Eyre, an occasional honorary member of the

Jackson Five, were invited to Sunday lunch, in Sydney, which Glenda presumed would be a small, informal family meal. Instead it turned out to be a major social occasion organised by a rather grand society lady who was determined to show off her starry guest. Glenda had not even made the minimum of sartorial effort and wore jeans, a T-shirt and no make-up, which rather disconcerted her hostess, who was inebriated even before Glenda appeared. When the hostess tried to make conversation with a comment about how 'bloody tired' the queen had looked in a photograph in the Sydney papers that day, Glenda haughtily replied, 'So would you if you had to visit the colonies every year.'

After Australia the tour moved on to Los Angeles. By now there had been so many instances of appalling organisation that Glenda was ready for a row. When it transpired that the management had booked the company to play the very day they arrived, in Peter Eyre's words, 'she went ballistic'. When they then insisted that, having cancelled that first performance, the cast would have to make it up by working through the weekend – effectively thirteen performances in a row – Glenda hit the roof in a memorable scene in one of the dressing rooms, which had mirrors on all four walls. Peter Eyre recalls thinking that this would look magnificent in a film as the furious actress was repeated in an endless stream of reflections.

Despite Glenda's rages – Peter Eyre says that 'she was a monster, frankly, and everything you would imagine a prima donna or a diva to do she did' – the audiences for the production were phenomenal, and Glenda was greeted with adulation wherever she went. In Australia literally hundreds of fans had besieged the stage door after matinées, all demanding to meet Glenda. In Los Angeles every actor in Hollywood who could get tickets was in the audience and the first-night party featured not just friends like George Segal, but Greer Garson, Valentina Cortese, Francis Ford Coppola and James Stewart. Timothy West even recalls Bette Davis calling Glenda and asking for tickets – 'just put me anywhere at all – two in the sixth or seventh row stalls, on the aisle, will be just dandy' – despite the fact that the show had been fully booked for months.

The tour had arrived in Los Angeles, to play at the Huntington Theater, just in time for the Oscar ceremony. Glenda, having failed to appear for any of the three Oscar ceremonies at which she was nominated for best actress, nor having appeared to present the award for best actor the year after winning for *Women in Love* (as convention determined), this time presented the award for best actor to her one-time colleague Art Carney. It was a fraught night. Bert Schneider read a telegram from the delegation of the Viet Cong at the Paris peace talks. Ingrid Bergman unctuously apologised from the stage to Valentina Cortese for denying her the best supporting actress award. Bob Hope wrote an instant Academy disclaimer to the Schneider telegram and forced Frank Sinatra to recite it, which he did, to boos from the audience. Sinatra then tried to get out of singing 'That's Entertainment', the show's finale, with Hope, Sammy Davis Junior and Liza Minnelli. When it was all over Brenda Vaccaro, who presented the best short films award with Roddy McDowall, attacked the show's producer Howard W. Koch for the Academy disclaimer. It is scarcely surprising that Glenda was openly contemptuous of the Hollywood system, and came on stage without a smile, only allowing the barest mention of her two Oscars to cross her lips: 'Thank you. Thank you twice in fact.' It was an attitude she shared with Walter Matthau, who that night explained to Ellen Burstyn what an Oscar really meant: 'When you die, the newspaper will say, "The Academy Award-winning actress Ellen Burstyn died today."' Glenda's disdain meant that the following year she was not even able to vote for herself as she let her membership of the Academy lapse.

Andy was not with Glenda on the night of the Oscars, as Roy had come over specially. After Andy's arrival in LA to set the lights, he and Glenda had finally made love, much to the disconcertion of the hotel bell-boy, who was perplexed to see Andy leave the star's room.

Few of Glenda's friends could understand what she saw in Andy. Pauline Devaney called him 'a bar-room lothario', Bridget Armstrong 'a two-timing so-and-so'. Brenda Vaccaro says that he

> was shabby business [but] he opened a door for Glenda that had not been opened for years – passion. And she was taken aback by the sexuality of it all because it was just time to have this magnificent passionate relationship.

So she fell in love with Andy and that was that. It was a great tumultuous affair and she was compelled. Most men are scared to death of her. You have to be strong. She's a very difficult woman to play. His way was to knock her around a bit, verbally.

Other members of the cast did not take to him either. Timothy West could not understand what either of them got out of the relationship.

I remember Glenda coming off stage one day and demanding 'Why isn't there any light on me in that scene, Andy?' Andy, true to form, replied, 'Because you're doing such an awful job and there's no point in lighting it.' To which Glenda acidly replied, 'You wouldn't even know how to light a cigarette.' That's how it was every day. Yet they would be in each other's arms by the end of the day.

Peter Eyre thought Andy was 'profoundly disruptive', and when Glenda's sister Lynne met Andy she similarly took an instant dislike to him, although it took five glasses of wine before she would let anyone know about it.

All of this was irrelevant. Glenda had needed something rude to shock her out of what she herself referred to as 'living a sham', or, in Roy's words, to 'cut short her procrastination'. Glenda always respected people who stood up to her and Andy, who readily admits he is no saint, was assertive enough to make her realise 'there was no longer any point in carrying on with a marriage that was dead'.[13] As Pauline Devaney describes it: 'Andy always told Glenda the truth and that was a relief after all those sycophants. But in the end the affair with Andy was more of a release than a real love – it was more to do with her relationship with Roy than with her relationship with Andy.'

After Los Angeles came Washington (where Glenda had to fight the local unions to enable Andy to light the show). Then, from the fifth to the twenty-fourth of May, came a run at the Royal Alexandra Theatre in Toronto where Joan, Roy and Dan all joined Glenda (and where, incidentally, the production, because it was part of a subscription series, was simply advertised as '5–24 May: Glenda Jackson', without any mention of the RSC, the title of the play or the director). By now Glenda and Andy were enjoying a fully fledged affair, and it would have been difficult for them to have kept it secret from Roy, not least since most of the cast were fully aware of what was going on.

In addition, both Peter Crouch and Peter Bromilow, who accompanied Glenda for part of the tour, had told Roy, 'You'll laugh at this, but they say that Glenda is getting involved with Andy Phillips.' So when Roy met up with Glenda in Toronto he was already worried. When he and Glenda went out to dinner with Peter Bromilow before a birthday party that she had asked him to organise for her, he confronted her: 'They say that you're having an affair.' Throughout their marriage Glenda and Roy had always replied to any such accusation with a private joke: 'Who are these "they"?' The very fact that Glenda replied instead with an evasive 'They would say that wouldn't they?' put Roy on the alert. At Glenda's party later that night her behaviour seemed extraordinary. 'She was playing an unusual role – all frail and clinging – which is unusual for Glenda by any standards.' Roy now felt sure that something was going on. When Andy came up to the bar in search of a drink and Roy told him to help himself Andy's smirk finally gave the game away. He already *had* helped himself. There was a brief altercation and within minutes Roy had left the party and fled to the hotel suite that he and Glenda were sharing, and where Joan and Dan were already asleep. Later Glenda appeared and started hammering at the door, demanding that Roy let her in, which he refused to do until the hotel management came, whereupon he resolved to escape back to England. He rang the airport and ascertained that the next flight to London was at 8.30 the next morning. Retrieving his passport from Joan's handbag he walked out of the hotel and took a taxi to the airport. Only then did he realise that the flight was going to London, Canada not London, England and he would have to waste a miserable twenty-four hours with next to no money in Toronto airport.

Glenda did not get back to Britain for another three weeks, eventually arriving at Hervey Road with Joan and Dan very early in the morning. Roy got out of bed, and while Glenda was having a bath came across a bundle of letters tied up with ribbon that had fallen out of Glenda's handbag. He instantly realised what they were – the correspondence between Glenda and Andy. Thoroughly aware of their value in any ensuing court case he took them with him as he went for a walk on the heath. When he returned Glenda was incensed that he had read her letters, and he was equally furious to read 'Dear Andy, I have a terrible fear of flying, but when we are together I'm not afraid.' The battle ended with Glenda going to Hoylake with Joan and Dan, and Roy telling all to the Press.

Meanwhile Glenda had to complete both the London season of *Hedda Gabler* and then the film of the play. Patrick Stewart noted how much her performance changed during the tour, and Peter Eyre often caught her on stage re-rehearsing scenes on her own, but when it came to the film, her performance had to go through yet another transformation. The gestures, vocal range and style of playing appropriate for theatre were not right for the camera, especially under the careful cinematography of Dougie Slocombe.

Although Glenda had intended to do the film from the beginning it was not a foregone conclusion, not least because of the personal friction between Glenda and her director. Nunn presumed that he had a right to direct the film, as his RSC had mounted the tour, and he had been her employer for the play, but Glenda worried about Nunn's lack of cinematic experience and angled for a different director. When members of the cast caught wind of this a petition was drawn up demanding that Nunn direct the film. All bar Glenda signed it.

Glenda was in a strong position as the film was to be produced jointly between Brut Productions, a subsidiary of the perfumiers Fabergé, run by George Barrie, and Bowden Productions, which the American Robert Enders had set up with Glenda to film *The Maids*. This meant that for the film Glenda was employing Nunn, and the change in the balance of power made for an even rougher ride. Star and director hardly spoke to each other throughout the whole hasty production period. The final showdown came at the end of the fourth week of filming. The cast were delighted to see sandwiches and drinks appear mid-Friday afternoon, but were horrified to learn that Enders and Barrie had decided that there was no time left for filming. Two uncompleted scenes would have to be omitted. In the end Nunn himself paid for an extra day of shooting. There were other differences between cast and producers. At the time Stewart thought he was appropriately tempering this, his first film performance, to the new medium, but was later horrified to see the overdone results and now admits, 'I think I looked brooding because I had no idea what I was doing.' George Barrie would have gone further, thinking he was 'execrable' and trying to get Lövborg completely excised from the production.

Glenda's performance itself received mixed notices. On the tour *Time* had been derisive:

> The world has not been waiting for, nor is it long likely to cherish, Glenda Jackson's bizarre offering: a comic Hedda Gabler . . . She has apparently decided that Noël Coward is really the author of the play. Her performance will certainly rank high in the annals of dramatic travesty. She trivialises every major scene in the play.[14]

The *Los Angeles Times* agreed: 'We might almost be in a situation comedy about an absent-minded professor and his long-suffering wife. Oh, George, not again! When, one wonders as the curtain zips down, does the tragedy start?'[15] In Britain the play was again badly received by the critics. Herbert Kretzmer in the *Daily Express* complained: 'Glenda Jackson brings an inexplicable lack of conviction to the celebrated role, diminishing its rage to a kind of small-town petulance that left me considerably under-whelmed. The role never catches fire, and her eventual suicide seems almost irrelevant.'[16] Eric Shorter in the *Telegraph* made the further point that the production 'is all too apt to mock the play itself by introducing such a naturally modern actress and updating much of the dialogue; so that the attempt to bring the play within Miss Jackson's reach only emphasises as she toys with Gabler's pistols that she herself lacks the guns for the part'.[17]

Nevertheless, the film earned Glenda another Academy Award nomination – her last, as it turned out – although if the distributors of *Stevie* had not opened it for two weeks in American cinemas in

1978 Glenda might well have been nominated in 1981, when she won the New York Film Critics' Award for best actress for her part in that film.

One of the other visitors to Toronto had been Richard Fleischer, the diminutive director of Hollywood blockbusters like *Tora! Tora! Tora!* and *Twenty Thousand Leagues Under the Sea*, murder mysteries like *The Boston Strangler* and *10 Rillington Place* and even *Doctor Dolittle*. Fleischer had been recruited by Helen Strauss of Readers' Digest to direct a script she had commissioned on the life of the French actress Sarah Bernhardt. Strauss had already signed Glenda up for the lead at Claridge's, the day after she won her second Oscar. The meeting in Canada provided an opportunity for the director and star to approve each other – or at least for Glenda to approve the director. All passed well, although when Fleischer suggested Timothy Dalton to play opposite her she refused to countenance him. Finally a cast was put together with Glenda's agreement, including virtually all the actors from the television series *Upstairs, Downstairs*, and as soon as *Hedda* was in the can shooting started on *The Incredible Sarah*. This remains one of Glenda's greatest mistakes. Peter Eyre, convinced that Glenda's puritanical streak makes guilt so potent a force in her that she feels she must always be working, believes that this drove her to agree to some work that she should never have touched, a category into which *The Incredible Sarah* indubitably falls. She was certainly happy with the director this time – their mutual admiration is intense. According to Fleischer:

> She is one of the great actresses of all time and she was then at the height of her form and popularity, and I'm a director whose first interest is in the actor rather than the technical aspects. So Glenda liked me and I think that's just about the greatest compliment I could get. She said, 'You're a much greater director than you think!' Mind you, she fooled me quite a while because the first take was so good that I would just accept it. But then I found by mistake that if you took her to a second or a third take, she would get even better.

Throughout filming in London Glenda and Andy would have dinner once a week with the Fleischers and a close relationship developed, but problems arose when Readers' Digest started to interfere in the screenplay, spoiling some of the few intriguing parts of a poor plotline. Sarah's wooden leg was nearly omitted, and the Crimean War passed off with scarcely a drop of blood. All references to drugs were excised, despite the fact that Bernhardt's closest confidant, her brother, was addicted to a cocktail of intravenously administered substances. The result was a film that enjoyed nobody's real respect. The reviews were acerbic: 'Glenda Jackson's short summations of some of La Bernhardt's famous parts, from Phaedre to Joan of Arc, are lessons in how not to show discomfiture when you must be feeling it. But elsewhere her attempts to humanise this ineffably tiresome lady are doomed to failure within the confines of a concoction manoeuvred this way and that by Mr Fleischer as if he were pulling strings marked Funny, Sad and Moving.'[18] Or again, 'Glenda goes very gamely through this silly script.'[19]

Roy and Glenda were, at this time, in the process of divorcing and Glenda was happily announcing to friends and colleagues that she was very much in love with Andy Phillips. Roy had moved out of the Blackheath house to stay with an actress friend, Anne Berry, for a couple of weeks, but he was soon staying in a £14,000 flat in the Isle of Dogs on the other side of the Thames. Summer and autumn passed, but the acrimony scarcely abated. When Roy sued Glenda for divorce in November on the grounds of her adultery with Andy the legal battle was fierce, with Roy retaining the Hodgeses' lawyer and Glenda opting for a 'film star lawyer'. Roy maintains that 'If it had been up to Glenda I would not have received a single penny and if she had had to cut my throat to get to Andy Phillips she would have done.' Andy, by contrast, believes that there was talk in Glenda's camp of a counter-suit on the grounds that Roy was gay, talk that Glenda refused to entertain, again in Andy's words, 'because of the way she was brought up'. Many of Andy's ideas are dismissed by Glenda as fanciful (including his belief that 'all the dykey dames that surrounded Glenda wanted to make love to me as a surrogate for having Glenda herself', and that while he and Fidelis Morgan were in Morgan's Hollywood apartment watching Glenda give out the Oscar she was effectively offering herself to him). But when I asked Roy about the talk of his sexuality he admitted:

> Let's face it: I would follow a pretty arse of any kind a mile down the road. But in the eighteen years I was with Glenda I never followed an arse of any kind. Now that I'm aged seventy-one I'd jump into bed with anyone who'd have me. I'd take it as a compliment. And I do. But it was never an issue when I was with Glenda. I'd put all my baskets in one egg [sic] and that egg was Glenda. Of course I wondered a bit about the fact that we were having less sex, but I just supposed that was what happened after eighteen years. I think there was only one occasion when she ever referred to anything like that, when she told someone 'Oh forget it, you'll never get him to admit it.'[20]

Throughout 1975 Glenda's affair with Andy Phillips and the Hodgeses' impending divorce were splattered across the front pages of the national newspapers, and the Hervey Road house regularly had a minor encampment of journalists outside it. It was almost a relief when, in a brief two-minute hearing in early 1976, Andy was named as the co-respondent in the declaration of the decree nisi, joint custody of Daniel was granted and Roy was set to receive 2 per cent of Glenda's gross earnings in alimony. Roy delighted in telling me both that Glenda's alimony was paying for him to study English Literature and British Theatrical History at Warwick University, and that she still signs her cheques G. M. Hodges.

Although the courtroom legalities were swiftly dealt with, complex emotional problems remained. Glenda seemed very much in love with Andy and apparently relished her new freedom, but she felt so intensely guilty that she had left Dan behind with Roy so much while she worked that she was determined to remain on good terms with Roy. She even appeared to make attempts at getting back with Roy, which included insisting that Roy accompany her on a trip to Canada, the United States, Martinique and the Georges V Hotel in Paris, while she undertook a punishing round of interviews. Roy, however, was inconsolable. 'I think Glenda thought we could put it back together. But I thought that the only thing that kept our contract together was our fidelity to each other, and once that was gone there was nothing left.'

By the time the divorce came through Glenda was already midway through her next venture, a film based on Muriel Spark's novella *The Abbess of Crewe* and set in a convent. In it the election of a successor to the mother superior is fixed, and a new authoritarian regime is ushered in under Sister Alexandra, played by Glenda who, with a small group of allies, enjoys the high life while spying on the other nuns and trying to undermine the popular alternative candidate for mother superior, who offers the convent a regime of sexual fulfilment. The whole concept of the film – 'Watergate in wimples' – appealed to Glenda enormously. It would mean an almost entirely female cast and she would get to play comedy again, this time in a political satire. Filming began in early January, with some shooting in Philadelphia, the supposed location for the convent, but the vast majority of the scenes were shot at the All Saints Pastoral Centre, a Gothic convent in London Colney. There are some extraordinarily funny moments: Edith Evans dies well; the Greek actress Melina Mercouri (who herself became a successful socialist politician, claiming the Elgin Marbles in her role as Minister for Culture) manages an impressive satire on both Henry Kissinger as a roving nun, and on herself; and Sandy Dennis does a hilarious impersonation of James Dean. There were also some better scenes, notably one in which Glenda emasculates three bishops with deadpan irony without them even realising it. It was one of the scenes that the director Michael Lindsay-Hogg (reputedly the illegitimate son of Orson Welles) was forced to omit when the Roman Catholic Church, who felt they had been conned into allowing the film to be made at London Colney, raised major objections.

In a different era *Nasty Habits* might have been a hit, along the lines of *Sister Act*, but for all its topical originality (as she leaves the abbey Glenda, Nixon-like, tells the reporters, 'Well, you won't have Sister Alexandra to kick around any more') the film hovered too precariously on the borders of satire to reach a mass audience.

CHAPTER EIGHT

Back to the Stage

In May 1976 Glenda celebrated her fortieth birthday with a party at the Café Royal. This is an ominous moment in the life of many actresses. For men the parts continue to roll in. As a young man you can play Hamlet, as an old man, King Lear. But for women the options seem to grow fewer and fewer and, as Jennie Linden puts it 'ingenues are put out to grass at forty'. Glenda had been told by John Fernald that she would not work until she was forty, and although she had proved him wrong, she now had no intention of succumbing to the accepted wisdom that forty-year-old women cannot play romantic leads. In addition, she was not fully content. The constant process of accepting work that she was not fully convinced by had started to wear her down. As Juliet Stevenson describes:

> Being an actor is sort of humiliating. In every other career you have far more choice but in the theatre you have to decide for yourself whether you really want to just keep on recycling. And I have never been in anything where I felt that the production met its *full* potential. Acting doesn't meet all of you and the powerlessness is so frustrating. And success can be stultifying for a creative person.

This left Glenda, as it left so many of her colleagues, two choices: change profession; or try to guarantee the professional quality of the work you do. At this stage Glenda only toyed with the former, but she resolutely sought to do the latter. She had already tried several means of determining the quality of the work in which she appeared. She would rarely do something because of the money – Hollywood producers laughed their way to the bank when they found out how little she was prepared to work for if the script was right – and she did not insist on the accoutrements of stardom. Instead she sought a good script and a director in whom she had confidence. Increasingly she also started to have a say, which she frequently exercised, over the rest of the cast. She became a director of Bowden Productions, partly for tax reasons, but also as a means of avoiding the powerlessness that so often attends acting.

Around the time of her birthday she and Andy began to conceive of a theatrical production company that would put on classical plays in the West End. At first the idea was to join forces with people like Bill Gaskill at the Royal Court and the playwright David Hare, but as plans progressed the idea crystallised into a co-operative theatre company to be led by Glenda and Robert Enders, with about twenty actors. Salaries would not be high – £250 a week would be the highest, £75 the lowest – but they would be just better than the subsidised companies could afford, and the company, Bullfinch, would attempt to draw in some of the best directors available.

The choice of the two opening productions was certainly not commercial. John Webster's *The White Devil* and *The Duchess of Malfi* are both notoriously difficult Jacobean tragedies in the grand manner, with tortuous plots and a superfluity of corpses. In the end *The Duchess of Malfi* was never staged, but *The White Devil* gave Glenda a starring part as the murderous Vittoria Corombona. It also brought together an intelligent cast – Frances de la Tour, Jack Shepherd, Jonathan Pryce, James Villiers, Miriam Margolyes and Patrick Magee – under the direction of Michael Lindsay-Hogg and the lighting of Andy Phillips.

Jack Shepherd, who had been in *The Three Sisters* with Glenda at the Royal Court, and recalled her haranguing the Press for not giving any attention to any of the actors other than Marianne Faithfull, found her much easier this time round, and although there were last-minute problems which led to Frances de la Tour and Miriam Margolyes demanding that the first night be delayed, the company was generally happy when the play opened at the Old Vic on 12 July. It was not, however, an easily understood

production. Michael Lindsay-Hogg, thanks to his personal obsession with hotels, had unconvincingly and incomprehensibly set the
play in a thirties hotel, which made the improbabilities of the drama
all the less credible. Brenda Vaccaro, who came to the first night,
hated the production and told Glenda so. She even joked, 'I can't
wait to see the musical next year,' to which Glenda replied, 'We're
doing it on ice actually.'

The reviews were mixed, and a large part of the £30,000 budget
was not recouped, thanks to an impossibly hot summer during
which even the pubs started to run out of beer. Few tourists fancied
a gruelling evening in the oven-like heat of the Old Vic. Bullfinch
folded, and its proposed productions were abandoned.

The fact that Bullfinch did not survive its first production must
have been all the more galling for Glenda because while she was
in New York to discuss with Joseph Papp the possibility of her
playing Hamlet (something Sarah Bernhardt and Frances de la
Tour have done), a vitriolic article appeared in *The New York Times*
charging her with being a poor custodian of her own career. 'It's
time to hold Miss Jackson accountable,' wrote Vincent Canby.

> She isn't having a run of bad luck. She's accepting roles
> in junk movies that can't even be rationalised for meeting
> some popular taste. The movies are duds. Something is
> happening to her touch. Is it dire financial need, greed,
> a woeful lack of judgement? Unless she pulls herself
> together, a serious career could be heading for the rocks
> . . . I, for one, am tired of toting a lot of high expectations
> to a Jackson film, only to wind up having to make excuses
> for her. She, her agent, her best friend, her hairdresser,
> someone, should suggest that she slow down, read a script
> before signing a commitment, and make bloody sure that
> she can trust the talent around her. Otherwise curtains.

It was Robert Enders who relayed the piece to Glenda and he
received half an hour of abuse by way of thanks.

As luck would have it, Glenda had a relatively light workload in
1976, and after *The White Devil* there was only a brief radio play
with Rudolf Nureyev before the end of the year. She returned to
work only in February 1977, this time on a new play by Hugh

Whitemore about the eccentric Palmers Green poetess Stevie Smith, which was being directed by Clifford Williams at the Vaudeville. Glenda had met Stevie Smith back in 1964, when she had seen her perform her laconic poem 'Not waving but drowning' and described seeing

> this extraordinary woman with an enormous grin standing dead straight in front of me. And I mean straight – there wasn't a protective curve in her body. She was tiny and had a long skirt with ankle socks and sandals, and a little girl haircut with a straight fringe, and an immensely penetrating gaze . . . I thought, 'There's something amazing about you, lady.'

Certainly Clifford Williams felt that 'something in that funny little woman must have chimed with Glenda' because despite the fact that Williams had expected Glenda to be difficult the atmosphere of the production was immensely enjoyable and Glenda behaved impeccably. Hugh Whitemore was open to new suggestions and Glenda worked with him on reconstructing parts of the play. Mona Washbourne ('a daft but experienced funny little old lady actress', according to Williams) worked easily with Glenda and gave an expertly quixotic performance as Stevie's maiden aunt. Peter Eyre, who had turned down Andy Phillips' offer of a place in the Bullfinch company, played the male parts in the play with an eye for suitable understatement. There were try-out performances at the Riverside Theatre and when it opened at the Vaudeville *Stevie* was an unexpected hit. Glenda received rave reviews from both the critics and even Stevie Smith's old friends, who had been deeply sceptical about anyone playing their friend, let alone Glenda.

So successful was the production that the whole company was signed up to go to Broadway and a film was made with a slightly altered cast – at one point Andy had been mooted as producer, but Robert Enders eventually filled this role. The film was a minor success – Trevor Howard believed it was the script he and Glenda had been waiting to do together since *Mary Queen of Scots* – but in the process of putting it together Glenda inadvertently put several noses out of joint thanks to what one friend called 'her inability to tell people difficult things face to face' and her tendency to procrastination. Clifford Williams had directed every one of Hugh Whitemore's plays, but when it came to the film he was passed over in favour of Robert Enders, making his directorial debut. At the same time Peter Eyre's parts were split in two, and he was replaced by Alec McCowen and Trevor Howard. Peter was never actually informed about this by Glenda, despite the fact that they were still appearing together every night, and when he was told by the *Evening Standard* that he was not to be in the production he bitched that it was because he looked too young to be filmed opposite Glenda. Glenda compounded this lapse when the planned Broadway production was cancelled at the last minute, ostensibly because she was unhappy with the Schubert Theater. Literally two minutes later Peter Eyre heard from Peter Crouch that Glenda was in fact going to do a sequel to *A Touch of Class*. As Peter now says, without rancour, 'It seemed a bit odd in such a small cast to hear from Glenda's agent rather than direct from Glenda.'

The success of *Stevie* breathed new life into Glenda's career, and 1977 saw a rush of offers: the new film with Frank would see her playing opposite George Segal, although *Lost and Found* would not strictly speaking be a sequel to *A Touch of Class*; Howard Zieff wanted her to play opposite Walter Matthau; and Peter Brook was finally thinking of putting on the *Antony and Cleopatra* he had been promising Glenda for some time (although he was also thinking of casting Jeanne Moreau). Glenda and Peter Crouch and her agent in the US, Bill Robinson, found it difficult to juggle all these promising commitments. *Stevie* ended up being filmed very swiftly, and it was fortunate, as Alec McCowen noted, that Glenda never fluffed a single line and that most of the film was shot with a single take. Trevor Howard added:

> It was a film that had to be shot quickly . . . so it was all a bit rushed, which is OK if you're not aiming for something special, but I think we all felt this was. But because the play itself was so good and Glenda such a professional and excellent actress, it all worked exceptionally well and I felt very proud to be in it. Mind you, it was a bit abstract for me. I never really knew quite what I was supposed to be doing.[1]

Throughout this period Glenda was not only juggling offers of films and plays, however. Whenever she was filming away from home someone had to look after Dan, and even while she was appearing in the West End he had to be picked up from school on matinée days, fed and put to bed. Andy Phillips was unlikely to play the role of surrogate father very well and Roy was free, so often Roy looked after Dan. This was unbearable for Andy. 'Roy never let go of the boy,' he complains, 'which meant that it was like having another person in the room all the time – and if we were abroad and it was holiday time Dan would appear, followed by Roy.' Glenda's devotion to Dan was so deep that Andy felt that 'no other relationship with Glenda was possible'. Such jealousies led to regular bickering, and even on the first night of *The White Devil* there were rumours that Andy, who only ever felt like a lodger in Hervey Road, had been thrown out. By the end of the year they were back together, but it was an emotionally cautious Glenda who let her friends know that she had no intention of marrying him. Even talk of buying a new home so that Andy and Glenda could start afresh faded.

Interestingly, Andy maintains that when they were together Glenda was immensely naïve.

> She did live in an ivory tower, you know. She didn't have many friends who came round and she was like a little girl, like an American who didn't know that Vietnam had happened. Half the time she didn't even know what day it was. But she had a very carefully constructed public image, so her interviews would always have been exactly the same.

This construction of a public image was something that others had noticed from the earliest days. For Timothy West it was a question of the persona Glenda created for Peter Brook; for Pauline Devaney it was the rigour with which Glenda set about changing her appearance once she had realised that she needed to appear glamorous, in some sense of the term, if she was to get work. 'Glenda's a very hard worker and she worked very hard on her image. There's a very practical person in there, because if you are a film star you have to spend time on your image.' The genius of her public persona lay in the fact that it was one of a very dismissive, defiant young woman who cared little for stardom. Roy says that 'Glenda gave this impression that she didn't give a fuck for all those Hollywood people – and they all loved that.' Her stance was immensely popular. As Charles Marowitz describes it:

> Glenda Jackson personifies a kind of anti-sentimental candour, which, in our finest moments, enables us to reject the pap, kitsch and schlock that stultify our daily lives. It is the hip, knowing, genuinely sophisticated response to the hard sell and the superlatively mounted snow job. It persuades us that there is no amount of camouflaged mendacity that cannot be discerned and destroyed if our sensibility is sharp enough and our courage is intact. Perhaps that is why, initially, Jackson was the darling of the intellectuals and has now become something of a popular institution. That kind of withering directness is an essential antidote to the fraudulence of our times. It is not a coterie predilection, but a national hunger.

Through her assertiveness, her forthright views, her deliberate insouciance about nudity (which she was far from carefree about), and her apparent refusal to 'doll myself up' (while she was actually very careful about her appearance when 'on show'), she gave off an air of such acute truthfulness that few journalists or colleagues chose to probe any further. Control of her image became an additional method of defending her privacy from early on – and it worked, even if it frustrated friends and lovers.

Jealousy and frustration eventually led Glenda and Andy to row in earnest, without the almost self-conscious theatricality of her supposedly 'full throttle' rows with Roy. (Although even the mild-mannered Roy recalls hitting Glenda during one exchange when she kept on demanding 'And what am I meant to get out of this relationship?' 'She was knocking me to the ground with the viciousness of her tongue,' he told me, 'and I knocked her to the ground because I simply couldn't match her verbally.') From the outside it seemed to friends as if, with Andy, the verbal violence was incessant – both Timothy West and Brenda Vaccaro had commented on this from the beginning. A very few friends also knew that on at least one occasion Andy had hit Glenda hard in the face. Andy admitted as much to me, declaring, 'It was one of those eyeball-to-eyeball moments. She was almost daring me. She would always take a dare. She loved it. She flaunted it, although she said she had walked into a door.' When I asked Glenda about this her response was an unnerving mixture of sarcasm and insouciance: 'But I've never known a man who didn't raise his hand to me.' Such vulnerability is shocking in Glenda. Her outward demeanour, her ardent feminism, her matriarchal family all suggest a woman who would never countenance such male brutality, let alone implicitly expect it. Yet Glenda's life has taught her to deal with hard blows by anticipating them and rolling with the punches. For Glenda the best defence has always been defiance. It has made her a thick-skinned politician, but it also enabled her to radiate a bruised warmth in her acting, even in the coldest of parts.

Friends often wish that more of her vulnerable side shone through. Jennie Linden asked, 'I wonder whether anyone has ever had an intimate relationship with Glenda? She's too protected – and then again, why not?' Timothy West agrees. 'There are an awful lot of things that Glenda hates or that trouble her, and if only she'd say so one would put one's arm around her and give her a great big hug. Instead she just shrinks away and rasps occasionally.' Brenda Vaccaro, a friend who has got closer than most, told me, though, that she gave Glenda a crystal, onyx and diamond necklace on a very thin chain because she thought it suited her. 'It was very fragile, very feminine and very delicate, just like Glenda.'

Despite the tempestuous nature of their relationship, Andy was Glenda's companion, on and off, for nearly six and a half years. The first big test for the Jackson/Phillips/Hodges arrangement was a protracted period in Hollywood which Glenda had contrived to coincide with Dan's summer holiday. *House Calls* was to be Glenda's first true Hollywood movie, filmed, financed and produced in the sunshine state, with a Hollywood star (Walter Matthau) and a Hollywood director (Howard Zieff). Glenda decided to stay in the Beverley Hills Hotel and to rent a beach house in Malibu, just up the coast from Los Angeles, for Dan and Roy. Roy enjoyed himself, spending time with Dan, and catching up with Peter Bromilow, now a resident Californian, and Brenda Vaccaro. Andy, meanwhile, had to remain in London, working.

The Matthau movie could easily have been a disaster. Glenda was not enamoured of the star system and Universal Pictures showered her with the paraphernalia of stardom. There was an on-set mobile home that was 'a damn sight grander than my home in Blackheath', and when Matthau first met her he thought she was one of the electricians. 'The next time I thought she was the queen. That's the style of the woman.'

Instead Matthau and Glenda soon established one of the most enjoyable working relationships of both their careers. Matthau believes they are very similar people, comparing Glenda's austere side to his own 'Depression baby syndrome', which makes him wander round his Pacific Palisades house switching off lights to save electricity. 'My wife', he moans, 'could spend as much in half an hour as Glenda spends in a year.' Even their politics are similar. Matthau had been a Communist, serving briefly as a member of the Communist Youth League and signing the Stockholm Peace Pledge which landed so many actors in the McCarthy era on the dole. It was only the fact that his signature was illegible ('perhaps by design', he told me) and that he has kept quiet about his Communism until now that his Hollywood career was not harmed. Matthau also came from a poor immigrant family, and had been schooled in the politics of racism when he was hit on the nose at school and called a 'Jew-bastard', a phrase his mother, herself of Jewish Ukrainian birth, had to explain to him.

Matthau declares that 'I got happy every morning when I saw her. She always looked ready for trouble,' and they soon formed a formidable double act, conspiring against the director, whom they both thought was a schmuck. When Matthau bawled Zieff out one day Glenda instantly sprang to his aid. When they were filming a scene in which Glenda had to defend state medicine they ended up discussing the rights and wrongs of Soviet Communism. Unusually for Glenda she spent a fair amount of her time socialising with her leading man.

The plot-line of the film was classic Hollywood: recently widowed surgeon decides to make up for his thirty-one years of marital fidelity with a regular diet of philandering, but meets a not-all-that-gay divorcee who, having just left an unfaithful husband, is not prepared to share him with other women. The personal relationship between Glenda and Matthau made *House Calls* a success, and there were other witty performances, most notably Art Carney as the dangerously incompetent chief of surgery. A light romantic comedy which allowed plenty of room for the wry humour that both Glenda and Matthau do well, it did good business, easily beating Matthau's other 1977 movie, *Casey's Shadow*, which was released on the same day. The two stars resolved to work together again.

Glenda was not so lucky with her next two films, shot respectively in Bethnal Green at the end of 1977 and in Canada in early 1978. *The Class of Miss McMichael*, in which Glenda again shared the honours with Oliver Reed, was half black comedy and half gritty realism. It now reads as an offbeat lesson in seventies educational policy, with Glenda playing a liberal teacher in a battle-weary school and Reed as her hypocritical, authoritarian head. The director, Silvio Narizzano, had little money to make the film and it shows. The shortage of funds meant that Glenda was nearly killed in the most exhilarating scene in the film, when she systematically destroys the head's office around him. Instead of sugar glass the bookcase she pulled down on top of her still had real glass in it, which splintered and shattered over her head. Yet again Glenda vented her spleen on a hapless director.

Lost and Found similarly suffered from an uncertain style. The distributors resolutely packaged it as the return of the Segal/Jackson sparring team, a sequel to *A Touch of Class*, but Melvin Frank intended it to be a very different kind of film, based, as it was, on a desolate real-life battle between two professors in an American university for life tenure – a battle that ended with one of the two trying to take his own life. This was scarcely a story-line one could play for laughs, but Glenda was intrigued by the film's attempt 'to deal with an extremely painful subject in a way that was funny', and she had enjoyed working with both Segal and Frank, so despite having to leave Dan behind with Roy and her sister Lynne, Glenda set off for fourteen weeks with Andy in a freezing-cold Canada. Despite Anthea Disney's belief that Glenda and Segal were barely speaking to each other, they still enjoyed working together, and despite the film's misfortunes, they remained friends. Segal recalls going to the Hollywood opening and one of the famous Epstein brothers coming up to him to congratulate him on 'one of the ten best movies on life tenure I've ever seen'.

The real challenge of 1978, however, was Glenda's return, after fourteen years, to Stratford-upon-Avon, for Peter Brook's production of *Antony and Cleopatra*, in which she was to star alongside the powerful American actor Stacy Keach. It was a long-awaited production. Brook was rumoured to have told Glenda not to play the Egyptian queen for anyone else more than a decade earlier; Glenda had been trying to engineer an opportunity to work with Keach for several years; and the theatrical establishment always anticipated any new Brook production with eager excitement. The RSC company at Stratford that year was also exceptionally strong, and other productions of the year had been particularly successful. All the company were keen to audition for Brook, and he saw everyone before assembling a final cast that included Jonathan Pryce, Patrick Stewart and David Suchet.

One name that appears further down the cast list is that of Juliet Stevenson, who was still a newcomer to the RSC. Her arrival at Stratford had been rather sudden, having been summoned at 10.00 a.m., auditioned in London at 11.00, put on a 'play as cast' contract at noon and propelled on stage in Stratford-upon-Avon in the middle of the final dress rehearsal of *The Tempest* that same afternoon. 'When someone pushes you, you bounce on stage,' she was told, 'and when the girl in front of you barks, you bark.' As it turned out 'the girl in front' was Ruby Wax, another RSC neophyte, and it was with Ruby that an apprehensive Juliet went to audition for the part of Iras in *Antony and Cleopatra*. 'Peter Brook was my idol. I'd read everything he'd written,' Juliet says. Because Juliet arrived early for the audition she found herself alone with Glenda and in her own words she 'evaporated with terror'. When Brook then arrived and set up an improvisation based on Iras serving Cleopatra's every need, terror nearly petrified the young actress. 'I'd have been less surprised to be an astronaut than being there with this incredible powerhouse of an actress – who has absolutely no small-talk – and my theatrical idol. I don't think I could even hear what Peter Brook was saying, I was so transfixed.'

Despite her fears Juliet landed the part of Iras and found herself near to the inner core of the company. In the meantime Stacy Keach had had to pull out of the production and after considerable hesitation Alan Howard, then also playing Coriolanus, was persuaded to play Antony. This was undoubtedly a major disappointment to Glenda and to Brook, who had hoped for an actor who could rough Glenda up a bit and spark her into a really daring performance. Few people thought that Howard would achieve that.

Nearly ten weeks of rehearsals began in late July, although at first only the principals – Howard, Jackson, Pryce, Stewart and Paola Dionisotti – gathered together in the Methodist Church Hall in Stratford. Stewart, who has the clearest of memories of these four weeks of rehearsal, and wrote a record of the proceedings every day until the last night, recalls these as 'the grandest weeks of my career because the level of stimulation each and every day was as high as in any day in my life'. There were games to establish trust, to play with the text, and to explore new ways of representing Rome and Egypt without processions of actors in togas and head-dresses. Stewart also recalls that the day before the rest of the cast joined them featured a normal morning of rehearsals in the Church Hall. After lunch a rectangle of carpet and a few cushions had been laid out on the floor. Brook wanted the small cast to do a complete run-through of the play, with everyone picking up the smaller parts as and when felt natural. The only rule was that whenever you were on the carpet you were part of the action. 'It went like an express train because of the respect and confidence we had built up . . . and it was both fast and funny. By far the best rehearsal we ever did, and much better than any of the performances.'

Juliet Stevenson, who, as Iras, spent one day with the principals before the rest of the company appeared, found the rehearsals extremely hierarchical (something Glenda refutes), and Stewart agrees that one of the problems was that the core conviction behind the production was that *Antony and Cleopatra* was really a chamber piece, so that when played with a full cast the 'production began to dissolve and then dissipate'. Certainly, Brook believed in reducing the play to its personal tragedy: '*Antony and Cleopatra* has been smothered by images superimposed by the Victorian era and by the cinema. It is forty-five short scenes of intimate behaviour. There is no pageantry. Everything concerns personal relationships.'[2] It was a belief that Glenda shared, and she wished that the production could have been staged in a more intimate theatre, where the intensity of the private passions could have been retained, rather than the barn-like Royal Shakespeare Theatre in Stratford.

There were also other problems. Most of the company as a whole had been working together at Stratford for the best part of a year, and when Brook announced on the first day of full rehearsals that 'this company doesn't work well together' some of the actors took umbrage. When he then insisted on his usual working environment – no newspapers, no coffee, no bridge in the green room and all actors to be present throughout all remaining rehearsals – there was a silent, internal revolt. The situation was exacerbated by the fact that there were writers observing all the rehearsals for academic purposes. Richard Griffiths felt that 'it was as if all the world was going to look down the microscope at this show', and John Bowe thought the rehearsal room 'was like a prison'. Juliet Stevenson, who recalls witnessing Brook painfully peel away all the layers of resistance in a couple of actors (including Alan Rickman), says, 'There wasn't a moment in that room that I was not clenched up with terror. My muscles would scream with pain at the end of the day. But still I learnt more in that room than I have ever learnt anywhere else. It was the acting lesson of a lifetime.'

When the production opened, on 4 October, the expectations of the theatrical establishment were instantly demolished. Some blamed Brook. Richard Griffiths, who played the clown, felt that Brook had failed to notice the sea change in British theatre, and that he scarcely knew how to work with younger actors, but lays the lion's share of the blame on the design. One of his costumes was a 'tube dress made out of deck chair material with a pound of butter muslin dyed blue on my head, which looked shit whatever way I wore it'. Certainly the set, a semi-circle of connecting glass screens which was designed to limit the size of the vast Stratford theatre, made the production feel cold and passionless, and last-minute changes to the costumes, to render them more Egyptian or Roman, both disconcerted the actors and made for a bizarrely eclectic mix. Clifford Williams, who caught wind of the problems in rehearsal, blamed the arrogance of the cast: 'I was horrified to find this young company taking an incredibly antagonistic, who-are-you-anyway, attitude to Brook. They behaved like young morons. They were very defensive.'

The critics tended to blame the leads. Successive critics had described Cleopatras of the past as 'Lady Bracknell cruelly starved of cucumber sandwiches' (Edith Evans); 'a ravenous famine victim' (Peggy Ashcroft); 'a neurotic society hostess zonked out on tranquillisers and Martinis' (Margaret Leighton); and a 'half-crazed flapper' (Vanessa Redgrave). Glenda fared no better. Irving Wardle complained that 'direct human affection of the Roman kind is the one thing [Peter Brook] cannot get from Glenda Jackson's inexhaustibly various Cleopatra'. Even those closest to Brook complained that 'with a mis-cast Antony and a hyper-sensitive Cleopatra who had little going between them the scene [after the first defeat at sea] appeared to be a demonstration of petulance. They had not opened themselves up to each other, so there was no underbelly to the agony, no vulnerability and life to the suffering.'[3] Brook even felt obliged to defend Glenda in *The Times*, although he later confessed to me that 'it wasn't a happy experience', before philosophically adding, 'There are projects where everything falls into place. And there are others where it always falls apart.'

It certainly was not a happy production. Juliet Stevenson cannot recall a production where so many people fell ill, and quite a few members of the cast abandoned it before it transferred to London the following summer. John Bowe says:

> It used to break my heart. [Brook] used to make us go into the conference hall immediately after every single performance, and once we were all seated cross-legged on the floor he would tell us where we had gone wrong. The production was sold out and yet the packed audience was going out every night saying, 'Wasn't that boring'.

With such an unhappy company it was virtually inevitable that there were minor problems almost nightly. Paola and Juliet, who had been finding it difficult as Cleopatra's maids to find ways of being essential to her because Glenda was 'so very, very self-sufficient', destroyed all the confidence they felt they had

established with her one night by appearing late for their cue in
Act I scene iv, when Cleopatra demands that Charmian give her
mandragora to drink 'that I may sleep out this great gap of time/
My Antony is away'. By the time they appeared, panting, from either
side of the wings, Glenda had excised the scene and improvised a
soliloquy. On the Press night Juliet suffered again. The monument
where Cleopatra receives the dying Antony, and then takes her own
life, was represented by a carpet that was flown in upright to hit
the flat of the stage. Brook was not content to have the heavily
lead-weighted carpet descend and then for the actors to come in
front of it to start the scene. It would be more dramatic if Glenda,
Paola and Juliet could run from the back of the stage and appear
in front of the carpet just as it crashed into place. That way Cleopatra's 'O Charmian, I will never go from hence' would ring with
a more authentic determination. Thanks to the tiniest lapse of
timing Juliet was struck very heavily on the back of the neck by
the carpet and found herself flat on the floor at Cleopatra's feet.
Glenda arched an eyebrow and carried on as Charmian cast the
line 'be comforted, dear madam' more in the direction of the
beleaguered Iras than her mistress.

There were successes in the production. Stewart won an award
for this, his second portrayal of Enobarbus, and although many
people felt that Glenda's performance missed the mercurial
elements of Cleopatra, she excelled in the final act and a half.
Perhaps the most successful scene of all was the appearance of the
clown who brings Cleopatra the asp with which she takes her life.
Dressed almost formally in a clown's red nose Richard Griffiths
tentatively shuffled towards the semi-circle in the centre of the
stage. He had tricks up his sleeve: the asps were not in the basket;
it was empty; instead they appeared out of thin air. When he left
he made a series of hilarious false exits, finally returning for an
afterthought – 'I wish you joy of the worm.' Albert Hunt noted
that '[Cleopatra] seemed to establish a relationship with [the clown],
paradoxically as she had not with anyone else, including Antony;
she seemed genuinely interested in what he had to say. And far
from imperilling the death scene, by playing up the humour it
intensified it by contrast.'[4]

Acting with Brook again was rewarding for Glenda. She

constantly maintained the fiery, flirtatious intellectual teasing and he furiously kept her working, demanding something more honest, less mannered. On one occasion he spent a good fifteen minutes calmly dismembering her performance in front of the whole company. Patrick Stewart, mindful of the scenes with Trevor Nunn, awaited a ferocious response with bated breath. Instead, after an apparently interminable silence, there came a heavily ironic 'My God, Peter, you're not going to *cry* are you?' At the time Glenda felt that the rest of the company had not worked hard enough for Brook, partly because they had to perform in other shows in the season at the same time, but she now simply regrets that they were never able to perform it in a more intimate theatre. Either way, it was a depressing return to Stratford.

CHAPTER NINE

---※---

Thatcherism and Theatre

BY THE TIME Glenda had clasped the last asp to her breast, after five years of dwindling majorities, a change of leader and a no-confidence motion in which the SNP sided with the Conservatives, the Labour Party had lost power to the Conservatives. On Friday 4 May 1979 Britain had a new prime minister, Mrs Margaret Thatcher. Slowly but perceptibly Thatcher, a 'conviction politician', set about disparaging the post-war consensus that had produced the National Health Service, social housing and comprehensive education, as 'wishy-washy'.

So far Glenda had not regarded herself as a political actress. She had left that to the likes of Vanessa Redgrave and Jane Fonda, both of whom took direct action in pursuit of their political beliefs. As the film critic Alexander Walker described: 'unlike Vanessa Redgrave [Glenda's] politics were a sort of diffused feminism, militant up to a point, but not calculated to frighten the bankers in their counting-houses'.[1] Glenda was, if anything, slightly dismissive of the Redgrave agenda, announcing at one Hollywood lunch at which she was the special guest that there was something obscene about Vanessa's support for the PLO, especially when she did not even live in Palestine or Jerusalem. On another occasion when Glenda and Vanessa were both shooting different films at Pinewood, and Vanessa telephoned Glenda early in the morning (while she was still in the make-up room), trying to gain Glenda's support for one of her pet causes, Glenda listened attentively to the lengthy tirade, but astutely ended the phone call without committing herself. A perplexed Simon Williams, who overheard the conversation, said, 'I'm a bit surprised. I always thought your politics were of the left.'

'Yes,' Glenda declared, 'but not before my early-morning bacon butty, for goodness' sake'.

Glenda had long been a member of the Labour Party, but she had rarely played a forthright role in party politics, preferring to give time and energy to single-issue campaigns. The issues she chose were varied, from Third World poverty and homelessness to human rights. She campaigned for Oxfam, lending her name and face in the seventies to an advertisement with the slogan 'The day Glenda Jackson helped build an irrigation dam'. She sat on the executive of the National Association of Voluntary Hostels, which proudly housed about 10,000 people every year, and spoke at Shelter rallies. She joined a demonstration outside the gates of the Indonesian Embassy to protest against the detention of political prisoners. Children's charities were important to her: she was President of the Toy Libraries Association; she narrated a series of programmes for UNICEF; and she devoted time and gave money to a home for emotionally disturbed children in Berkshire that was run by the former actress Coral Atkins.

Glenda was also a vigorous supporter of the National Abortion Campaign, for which she organised a benefit evening at the Cambridge Theatre, raising more than £3,000. It was – and still is – an issue that makes her blood boil:

> I really don't see how anyone has the right to make a woman have a child against her will. It should be possible for her to go and have an abortion on the National Health Service without being made to feel criminal or inhuman. I think this Society for the Protection of the Unborn Child is the biggest load of rubbish. They are monstrous, all these middle-aged ladies, well past child-bearing age, and all those bloody men, all drooling over babies. Babies grow up; these people are not willing to look after them when they're sixteen and start throwing bricks through windows, are they? ... Why can't you say 'yes' to sex and 'no' to pregnancy? Because childbirth is allied to sex, if you have your cake you have to pay for it and if you get pregnant, that's your punishment. If you don't want it, tough bunny, kid. You've had the fun ... the fact that

All that glisters is not gold. Glenda failed to turn up in Hollywood for either of her Oscars for best actress. The first, for *Women in Love*, was delivered to her at the Dorchester in London by Hal B. Wallis, her future producer on *Mary, Queen of Scots*.

Right The first leaflet in Glenda's first general election campaign.

Glenda won 'Stunt of the day' in the *Guardian* for this photo opportunity with Glenys Kinnock in the 1992 election campaign. Rumours that the wall was only built for the photo and was subsequently dismantled were half true as it was part of a building training centre in Hampstead.

MEET
GLENDA JACKSON
Your Labour Candidate

Glenda woos British voters in Benidorm, 1996.

All five women candidates for Hampstead and Highgate in 1997. The only other MP to have four female opponents was Anne Widdecombe.

Only a week into Government and after two days as the Parliamentary-under-Secretary for Transport in Labour's first Government since 1979, Glenda helps launch the 'bike for breakthrough' charity cycle ride outside the House of Commons.

Glenda Jackson MP looking out over London from Hampstead Heath.

a great many people get pregnant because they observe the law of obeying their husbands, nobody thinks of that ... How dare they condemn a child to be born to a mother who doesn't want it? How dare they take that upon themselves?[2]

At the start of the seventies she had been nettled that people objected to her nude appearances on screen on 'moral' grounds. 'If there was a true morality in the world it would be marvellous,' she argued. 'But morals in Britain seem to limit themselves to the sexual habits of people. I heard there were homes where children in prams still get bitten by rats. That's immorality as far as I'm concerned.'[3] She had begun to think of what she herself could do to improve the world in which she lived, even in 1972 declaring that 'The Welfare State seems to me to step in too late and I think if you disagree, as I do very strongly, with the way it is organised and run, then you have to put yourself in the front line and see if you could do it any better.'[4] Very occasionally this would take her into the realm of electoral politics. In 1974 she supported Dr Una Kroll, who stood for Parliament in Sutton and Cheam for the Women's Rights Campaign, and an imaginative local Labour Party in Bristol approached her about standing in the 1979 general election. 'I'd like to have a crack at it but I'm probably too old and too under-educated,' she stated. As she told the *Daily Mirror* in 1979, 'the truth is I'd like to channel my energies to help the disadvantaged before my brain loses its capacity to learn anything but lines. One day I know I will.'[5] Her disappointment with the schism-rent seventies Labour Party had prevented her from getting more closely involved in party politics.

The environment in which she worked was one of unspoken socialism. Many of the directors for whom she had worked shared a set of left-leaning philosophical and ethical assumptions, and as long as Glenda felt she was able, through her work, to take steps towards exposing 'man's inhumanity to man', she felt she had done her bit. She was proud to pay taxes, even if that meant that almost two-thirds of her earnings (after her agent had taken his slice) went to the Inland Revenue.

Within her own profession she sought to be true to her principles.

This was not just about turning down work that she did not respect, even if there were enormous sums on the table – she was rumoured to have rejected $1,500,000 for a third Segal movie. It also meant trying to ensure that the acting profession itself was equitable and fair. When the right-wing caucus on Actors' Equity, led by André Morell and Nigel Davenport, managed to get Equity to disaffiliate from the TUC, she joined the group led by Hugh Manning and Miriam Karlin (one of Glenda's recruits for the Cambridge Theatre NAC benefit), who were lobbying for a return to the TUC fold. With Michael Croft, Vanessa Redgrave, Marius Goring and Miriam she was also involved in the campaign to deregulate entry into the profession, arguing against the ludicrous catch-22 whereby you could only act in the professional theatre if you had an Equity card, and you could only get an Equity card if you were acting in the professional theatre. Glenda sat on the Equity Council for several years, as part of both the soft-left Centre Forward group and its successor, the precariously named Campaign for Reaffiliation and Progress within Equity – CRAPE. Miriam remembers Glenda then as 'embryonically an MP', full of well-formed opinions, but strategic in the way she deployed them. 'She would remain very silent, listening to everything, weighing it all up, and then she would put up her hand. When she spoke she would be very concise, with none of the waffle that we would all indulge in.'

This involvement in 'soft politics', and several appearances on Radio Four's *Any Questions*, gave Glenda the appearance of being far more outspoken than the majority of her acting colleagues. It was almost inevitable that she became – at Peggy Ashcroft's suggestion – an early recruit to Arts for Labour, which sought to find prominent Labour Party supporters in the arts and give prominence within the Labour Party to arts policies.

Two events brought Glenda's politics even more evidently into prominence at the turn of the eighties: Maggie Thatcher's arrival at Downing Street; and the battle for the leadership of the Labour Party in 1980. Her socialism was robustly pragmatic. She explained that:

> I am a committed Socialist, but I don't go as far as Wedgwood Benn. If he ever gets the leadership we will have

a Tory government ad infinitum. I don't believe the country is that left-wing. You have to be practical, have to know what will work. It's absurd to get stuck on abstract philosophies which may work in the best of all possible worlds but which bear no relation to people's lives today. If they go on like this they will lose so many votes. It's dreadful.[6]

Glenda was clearly politically aligned, but from the start of 1979 her energies had been devoted to an extremely rigorous work regime which saw her complete two films, two radio plays and two long West End runs in the space of two years. Ironically, the first of these two films, Robert Altman's disastrous *Health*, saw Glenda playing a candidate for election as president of a health convention. She had such enormous respect for the quixotic Altman and his work, especially *M*A*S*H*, that she agreed to do the film without seeing a script. If this had been released in time for the US Presidential elections in 1980 it might have made more of a topical mark, but it was only given a limited release a few years later. The film as a whole feels too chaotically surreal to be readily watchable. It is also, incidentally, poorly served by an appallingly inaudible soundtrack. The cast was impressive: Lauren Bacall as the alternative, catatonic, candidate for president; Carol Burnett as a bumbling White House representative; James Garner. Despite the film's imperfections there are some inspired moments: security guards dressed as vegetables and fruits; Glenda's treatise on modern politics ('the idea that you can merchandise candidates for high office like breakfast cereals is I think the ultimate affront to the dignity of the democratic process . . .'); Bacall's one arm aloft narcoleptic spasms. Even the concept of Glenda playing a candidate for president of a health convention was deeply ironic. After all, her personal health regime meant overdosing on coffee and cigarettes (verging on thirty a day). 'Between nervous shaking from the caffeine and coughing from the nicotine, I'll have as thorough a work-out as if I've jogged for seventeen blocks,'[7] she proudly announced. The filming was at least enjoyable, involving two months away from the English winter in St Petersburg, Florida.

Similar reasons to those for working on *Health* brought her together with Matthau the following year. Matthau was to appear in a comedy sleuth movie set in Continental Europe, the US and Britain, but he had enjoyed working with Glenda so much that he insisted he would not make the film unless she was in it. When the producer complained that there was no female part for her to play in *Hopscotch*, Matthau announced that he would write the part himself, which he did, before ringing her with some 'cock-and-bull story about needing someone he could rely on over in Europe'. Glenda was dismissive of the part – 'let's be honest, this film is not what you might call a major acting challenge. My character is a cypher, she's there to prove the hero is not homosexual. Walter asked me to do it, we had great fun on *House Calls* and I said "Yes" instantly'[8] – but it meant two pleasant weeks filming in Germany, and an opportunity to spend time with Matthau again. Matthau enjoyed this film every bit as much as the one before. 'She's just beautiful, the way she thinks, the way she talks, her looks, everything,' he told everyone, delighting in playing Scrabble with his leading lady and being entertained by her at a splendid fish restaurant in London. He also recalls inviting Glenda to dinner with a Tory MP who had wanted to meet him, during which she 'demolished the man's whole Conservative argument more effectively than any politician I have ever heard'. As Glenda escorted Matthau back to his hotel that night Matthau urged her to make politics a serious career – 'you're so goddamn good at it'. Meanwhile Matthau, as a Ukrainian Jew who had served in the Second World War, found filming in Germany a deeply disturbing experience, 'because of what the ordinary Germans did as willing conspirators during the war'. His response was simple – on his first day of filming in Munich he got so drunk that he had to sleep the whole afternoon.

Neither of these films did much to enhance Glenda's career. Although *Hopscotch* is a reasonably good romp, its best scenes were those shared by Matthau and Jackson, and outside these the action feels tame. And *Health*, despite good intentions, has few redeeming features.

Glenda next found success in the theatre, when in 1980, just as the Bristol riots began, she took to the stage at the Duke of York's Theatre in a new play by Andrew Davies about a Midlands school-teacher, *Rose*. This sardonic comedy of modern manners was a big enough hit for Glenda to betray her principles and agree to a longer run than her usual three months, and it ran to nearly full houses from February to September. Glenda had asked Davies to strengthen the other characters in the play so that it was less of a one-hander, but she still received the vast majority of the critics' praise. The *Evening Standard* declared 'she is really funny outlining to an astonished male all the seduction techniques she expects him to try before he has laid a finger on her'. And the *Evening News* rhapsodised, 'One day Glenda Jackson will give a bad performance, and on that dire date there will be a total eclipse of the sun, fountains will run blood, and terrible will be the cries of anguish. This extraordinary actress so lights up the stage that once again she is going to dim the brightest adjectives in my armoury.'

So successful was the six-month run – at a time when London had more theatres dark than at any other period since the war – that a Broadway production with Glenda and Jessica Tandy was planned for the following year. Broadway is a far more savage theatrical market than the West End, however. James Hazeldine even recalls seeing the signs go up for a George Segal and John Lithgow play, *Requiem for a Heavyweight*, and come down again in a single day. When *Rose* opened at the Cort Theater in March 1981 there was a derisively critical comment to match every eulogy the play had received in London. Davies recalls the savaging: 'Frank Rich, "The butcher of Broadway", went something like "It is always a pleasure to welcome Miss Glenda Jackson back to our shores, but what is she doing in this pile of garbage by somebody called Andrew Davies?"'[9] *Newsweek* sneered: 'It's too bad that an actress of Jackson's stature has to cross the Atlantic to reap the embarrassment of chilly reviews and audience indifference towards a work that earned her plaudits in her own country. Some plays simply don't – and shouldn't – travel.' A very few of the New York critics enjoyed her performance, however. One described her as 'a raw-boned, close-cropped mass of contradictions: masculine and feminine, arrogant and vulnerable, repellent and appealing, in one of the year's strongest performances'.[10] Even though a planned three-month run was cut short by a month she was nominated for a Tony award, which, in a British year on Broadway, she lost to Jane Lapotaire in *Piaf*, while Ian McKellen won the best actor award for his Salieri in *Amadeus*. Glenda's reaction to the critical mauling was equanimous. The morning the reviews came out she rang Davies and took him out to lunch, regaling him with all the appalling notices she had received in her time, and announcing that the critics never really know what they're talking about.

The two productions of *Rose* were lit by Andy Phillips, who was still an occasional fixture at Hervey Road, although the rows continued. Andy now recalls a regular pattern: a fight would develop; either he would storm out or she would throw him out; a fortnight would pass in which he would stay with a friend and she would refuse to take his calls; suddenly she would ring late at night and demand that he return; after remonstrating with her for refusing to answer his calls, he would pack up and return. It was a wearying existence and many of Glenda's friends worried about Andy's formidable drinking habit and his potential for violence. There were occasional discussions about getting married, but Glenda continued to tell her friends and the public that marriage was not really for her any more. Andy, of course, had his own complaints. He says that Glenda was 'incredibly jealous', that she had 'a devastating tongue', that she is 'very competitive' and that 'she was so moral it was painful, as she would use it as a way of kicking everyone else in the shins'. He even blamed his drinking on Glenda: 'You had to have something to protect you. Otherwise you just became a servant.'

Despite these deep-seated problems their stop-start relationship continued for six and a half years, but by the summer of 1981 even this had run its course, and one day Glenda took all Andy's clothes from the house and left them with his mother. Andy tried to ring her but got no answer. A few weeks passed before late one night, ringing from Dublin, he managed to get through. 'Hi, what do you want?' Glenda asked. 'Nothing,' Andy gruffly replied. 'So why ring?' Glenda answered as she put the phone down. *Rose* was to be the last Glenda show Andy lit, and to date Andy has remained the last man in Glenda's life, a fact that saddens several of Glenda's friends, but which fails to disconcert Glenda. Even in 1976 she told the *News of the World*, 'I don't think I like men really. I always think it's one heck of a lot of layout for a very small return with most of them.'[11] She still admits that 'I hope I can still get my heart broken. I don't look for grand passion now, but I want to be capable of the feelings. I'd hate to lose that capacity. Not having sex any more doesn't bother me and I'm not afraid of being alone, not even in old age, as long as I can take care of myself.'

The truncated Broadway production of *Rose* at least made another project possible for Glenda at the turn of 1981. Glenda had been approached about the possibility of playing the part of Patricia Neal in a television film. Patricia had been a well-known actress who won an Academy Award in 1963 for her performance as the housekeeper whom Paul Newman rapes in *Hud*, but only a couple of years later she suffered a series of massive strokes while three months pregnant, leaving her almost completely paralysed and with very severely impaired speech. After bullying and encouragement from her husband she eventually acted again, in the film *The Subject was Roses*, and the new film was to be a chronicle of that fight back to health. She was American, but her husband was the British writer Roald Dahl, so there were scenes to be filmed in both Britain and in Los Angeles. The original script by Barry Farrell, entitled *Pat and Roald*, had been cinematic in its scope, although intended for television, and it was with the possibility of a film in mind that Glenda and Dirk Bogarde had made their way to Hollywood in early 1981. Bogarde, who was to play his friend Roald after twelve years away from Hollywood, was nervous about the whole venture, and when it was suddenly discovered that the script was too long because it would not fit into the advertising breaks on US television, he was terrified of endless rows.

Thanks to a gap before the Broadway opening of *Rose* Glenda was free to play Patricia Neal, although she was delayed in England. Micky had suddenly died of emphysema (to be followed only two weeks later by Aunt Esther), and Glenda had taken Dan up to Hoylake for the funeral before catching a flight from Birmingham to Los Angeles. It was a worn and weary Glenda that arrived in Los Angeles. 'When Glenda eventually arrived she was far too exhausted to say anything,' Bogarde relates.

> She came down to my suite the night she arrived in a pink candle-wick house-coat; she said it was a dressing gown and did I mind? I didn't; and perhaps it was. Her

face was white with fatigue, her eyes pulled through to the very back of her head like upholstery buttons, but all her faculties were splendidly intact. It was our first meeting – we had never even spoken on a telephone together – and it was a miraculous, instant joining. My failing courage soared; with this person at my side I'd be able to fight all the bloody sponsors, producers and script girls. I thought that I passed muster as well, for as she was walking down the hotel corridor with her small entourage after a happy, and even relaxing, hour in the suite I heard her say: 'Well, he seems all right, doesn't he?' I felt braver than a lion.[12]

There were endless traumas with the filming of the US scenes of what eventually became *The Patricia Neal Story*: Patricia Neal's daughter Tessa was distressed both that the film was being made at all, and that Glenda was to play her mother; the television companies made daily changes to the script; the British director, Anthony Harvey, who was intent on making a movie rather than a television programme, shot scenes in a dark, grainy style, which the producers complained would be unwatchable on television. In Bogarde's words 'it was a battle for banality against quality, and it raged unabated. People were frequently fired, removed from the set by physical force in the very middle of shooting a scene . . . and the crew, with good reason, grew more nervous and despondent.'[13] Glenda – who had to spend much of the filming bandaged in bed with tubes up her nostrils – was kept going only by the 'miraculous joining' with Bogarde, with whom she formed the kind of close and lasting relationship that she had really enjoyed only with Matthau. Instead of 'harbouring her energy' and sitting alone on set Glenda would spend all day chatting with Bogarde, and they even dined together at the end of the day's shooting.

When the American scenes were finished Glenda and Bogarde went their separate ways – Glenda to New York for *Rose* and Bogarde to his olive grove in France – and it was not until June that the remaining scenes were filmed back in England, where Anthony Page, who had directed Glenda at Dundee in 1961, took over the direction.

The outcome was a startling success. Glenda's performance was distressingly accurate, from her carefully constructed speech – comprehensible but still suggesting the inarticulacy of a stroke victim – to her slow transformation from denial and anger through to ferocious acceptance. Although there was great sadness during the filming, and the Dahls' twenty-nine-year marriage came to an end just as the film was about to be screened, their daughter Tessa was so impressed she rang Bogarde to tell him, 'I didn't want her to play my mother, I didn't think *she* was beautiful enough, but she is. She is my mother.' There were rave reviews for both the stars when it was first shown on US television in December, and there was talk of Emmy awards and a film release. Sadly the fact that it was up against *Hart to Hart* only a few days after its star Robert Wagner's wife Natalie Wood had drowned, meant that it lost out in the US ratings war and all such ideas were dropped, just as other plans – for a Ken Russell film with Anthony Hopkins and Jodie Foster, a film of *Rose* with Angie Dickinson and a musical with Carol Burnett – similarly sank without trace.

The one scheme of this period that came to fruition was the subtle Alan Bridges film, *The Return of the Soldier*, in which Glenda played opposite Julie Christie, Alan Bates, Ann-Margret, Frank Finlay and Ian Holm. Based on a novel by Rebecca West, it tells the story of a patrician First World War captain (Bates) and his return from the trenches to his Palladian country seat and, finally, his senses. His memory of the past two decades has been expunged. He fails to recognise his wife (Christie), and all he can recall is his youthful passion for a middle-class girl (Glenda) without whom, he declares, he will die, despite the fact that she is now married to a schoolteacher (Finlay). Neither marriage is idyllic. Christie is a haughty, superficial snob, and Finlay's character suggests a marriage without passion. Bates' adoring cousin (Ann-Margret) tries to restore his memory by encouraging the relationship with Jackson and bringing in a psychiatrist (Holm), who eventually manages to get both Glenda and Bates to discover the emotions they had forgotten – both of them having lost five-year-old children.

Life off-screen during the filming of *Return* was almost as complicated as that on-screen, thanks to a tiny budget and the involvement of the three unpredictable star actresses who shared nothing so

much as their independence of mind. Because much of the filming was done at Firle Place in East Sussex, within striking distance
of Blackheath, Glenda commuted back to Dan every night, but
Julie Christie and Ann-Margret both took up local residence. Julie
Christie, who confesses to an appalling memory, says that 'as far
as I can recall we really kept ourselves to ourselves and the moment
we had finished filming we would each disappear to our caravans'.
Simon Relph, one of the producers, believes this was no accident:

> Julie is shy, Glenda has always been a recluse, and Ann-
> Margret is shyer than shy – the Ann-Margret in the
> night-club act is a character she plays. Julie and Ann-
> Margret got on very well. Glenda and Ann-Margret got
> on very well. Julie and Glenda got on, but just. Basically,
> they challenge one another. Julie thinks Glenda is more
> of an actress than she is, and Glenda thinks Julie is
> more of a star than she is. They admire those qualities
> in each other, but it's still a bridge to cross.

The ever-congenial Alan Bates was left to act as the uniting force
between the women.

For all the underlying tensions, this, like her part in *The Triple
Echo*, was to be one of Glenda's best and most underrated appearances. Although it did well at the box office, some critics found the
film too slow and reacted against the 'costume drama' setting, and
so failed to note not just Alan Bates' superbly mercurial performance, but also Julie Christie's adept portrayal of a profoundly needy
yet unpleasant woman, and one of Glenda's warmest performances.
Glenda's tearful collapse as she stands in the patrician nursery
recalling the death of her child is one of her most affecting film
moments. (It is also intriguing to see early cameos from both
Pauline Quirke and Kevin Whately.)

Glenda celebrated her forty-fifth birthday in New York in May
1981 – yet another landmark in the passage towards the twilight
zone of an actress's career, when she is just too old to play the lead
romantic interest in a movie, but is reluctant to succumb to playing
batty old women and other people's mothers. As a good feminist
Glenda had regularly inveighed against the paucity of parts available

for actresses, even in modern plays, haranguing James Cameron-Wilson in 1977 with:

> Where are the new women's films? The fact that films have women in them doesn't necessarily mean that they are good parts for women ... I do find it absolutely extraordinary that good writers have not found the emergence of the women's movement worthy of examination, that they are so nervous of it, they'd sooner dismiss it as being a lot of hysterical, probably lesbian, women not getting their fair dues.[14]

This was Glenda fighting on behalf of all women, but when it became apparent that there was a definite pattern in the changing nature of the parts being offered to Glenda herself, her general political concern became a specifically personal worry. With the death of her father she knew the time was soon coming when she would have to work ever harder to stay in the game.

There were still great parts to play in the theatrical canon – both classical and modern – but the competition was intense. Moreover, many of the mature parts that Glenda would want were in plays for which it would not be easy to find an audience, even if her name guaranteed good publicity. Some actresses faced with the same dilemma had found refuge in the permanent companies – the RSC or the National – and it was certainly possible to put together a couple of seasons' worth of leading classical roles, but Glenda was never a 'company' actress, detesting the internal politics of Stratford and the South Bank, and she preferred to remain a freelance leading actress. It is no small credit to Glenda that in ten years between 1982 and 1992 she managed to make some of the most challenging plays commercially viable, bringing Brecht, Lorca, O'Neill, Racine, Howard Barker and even Botho Strauss to the West End without the support of either of the subsidised national theatre companies.

Four of these productions were to come out of the innovative Glasgow Citizens Theatre stable, including Robert David Mac-Donald's *Summit Conference*. This had originally been conceived as a cheap play (i.e. a small cast with a single set) to complement a luxuriant Glasgow production of Coward's *Semi-Monde*, and had played in the Glasgow season in 1978 with Ann Mitchell and Julia Blalock as Eva Braun and Clara Petacci, respectively Hitler and Mussolini's mistresses. Philip Prowse, who had designed Glenda's leather costumes for *Fanghorn* many years earlier, and directed the first Citizens production, managed to persuade both Glenda and the languorously voiced Georgina Hale to take the play into the Lyric in 1982, with the part of the guard whom the two mistresses humiliate to be taken by the then unknown Gary Oldman.

The play was not welcomed by London's critics. Michael Coveney at the *Financial Times* applauded the Citizens for suddenly bursting 'excitingly upon a dour and defeatist West End [with this] wonderful political comedy', but others were more critical. Benedict Nightingale damned the production in the *New Statesman*, complaining that

> Georgina Hale's Clara minces and teeters about, adenoidally bleating from inside a little black frock; and together they turn on the third member of the cast, a forlorn boy-soldier played by Gary Oldman. They get him drunk, yank down his trousers, inspect his penis, daub him with rouge, mocking him first as a woman, then as a Jew. It is nasty, very nasty; but it is also, of course, pretty meretricious stuff.

Robert Cushman in the *Observer* wrote: 'Mr MacDonald says nothing new, and says it aridly.' Only Michael Billington really rejoiced in Glenda's performance, commenting in the *Guardian*, 'it is a fine piece of acting in which rigidity of soul is contrasted with skittishly feminine appearance, all garden party talk and billowing white tulle'.

Despite the mauling – which Georgina thought meant it would have to close in a fortnight – the play had a long run. Audiences relished the off-beat irreverence of the play and its violent excavation of political extremism, even if there were occasional demonstrations – both interval departures and more intrusive declamations halfway through the performance, both from irate Nazi followers and anti-Nazis. Glenda especially relished the play's examination of Fascism at the time of the Malvinas war – and she delighted in her line that whereas Caesar came, saw and conquered, Mussolini only came when he saw someone else had conquered.

Besides giving Glenda work through to the end of 1983, *Summit Conference* also established a close personal relationship between Glenda and Georgina Hale which was to last some ten years. Georgina is a very self-effacing actress who radiates vulnerability, both on and off stage, and this evident sensitivity was deeply attractive to Glenda, who adopted her as a protégée. The fact that Georgina had disastrous taste in men and had suffered a turbulent first marriage was something that Glenda could identify with, especially now that Andy Phillips had finally passed out of her life. When Georgina missed the dress rehearsal of a subsequent production they both starred in, Racine's *Phedra* (as the author of the new translation, MacDonald, insisted on titling it), because she was in an emotional state, Glenda was the most compassionate of friends. Glenda's immense desire to protect others, especially those who seem most vulnerable, is not often commented on, but moments of magnanimity, that would shock many of her colleagues who had seen her shout, cajole and complain, appear throughout her career.

A couple of years later one young actor just out of drama school, who had a short scene with Glenda in the film of *Strange Interlude*, and was immensely impressed to be working with her, saw her push everyone in the company away, especially anyone who was too sycophantic. But when he fell into the river during their scene it was Glenda who ran off to get blankets and took him into her caravan dressing room, where they nattered for hours about everything from the occult to psychiatry. They bumped into one another in a restaurant a few years later, and he was amazed not only that Glenda instantly remembered him but that she was 'immensely lovely' to his mother, and when he later asked her to drop a Christmas card to his ailing grandmother, whom she had never met, he was even more surprised to find that she was more than happy to do so. Similarly, the night before Glenda was to open in *Strange Interlude* in New York, one of her co-stars, James Hazeldine, discovered that one of his sisters had just died. Glenda noticed something was wrong during the dress rehearsal and when he told her, offered not only to cancel the first night, but also to pretend that it was all her fault. Glenda was also immensely generous to Peter Bromilow, even buying him the tiny Hollywood bungalow that he had fitted out with a red and black dungeon, fully equipped with ropes, pulleys and handcuffs.

This generosity and ability to recall names was something Georgina had noted early on. They had first met in 1967, on the set of *Which of These Two Ladies is He Married To?* When they next met, on the set of *The Boy Friend*, Georgina was amazed that Glenda instantly recognised her. It was not, however, until quite late in the run of *Summit Conference*, when Prowse came round to the dressing rooms and gave them both harsh notes in their twenty-third week, that Glenda and Georgina became close friends. The next two nights Glenda completely changed her performance, throwing Georgina off balance. Disconcerted, Georgina stormed around backstage before pouring out her heart to the wardrobe mistress, Bobby Fox. Bobby's advice was simple – 'overcome your fears and confront Glenda'. Glenda immediately met her halfway, moulding her new performance to Georgina's. This event cemented a friendship that was to see Glenda put Georgina up in a hotel in New York when she was performing *Strange Interlude* and in Los Angeles when she was in *Who's Afraid of Virginia Woolf?* Backstage it had not been an untroubled production. George Segal relates that Gary Oldman thought that Glenda was 'a nightmare' in rehearsal, and Prowse and Hale both thought that Oldman behaved like 'an attention-seeking diva'.

Glenda had planned a West End production of Brecht's *Mother Courage* for 1983, but when *Summit Conference* was over she found herself unemployed thanks to a rights dispute with the RSC, who were planning to stage it the following year, and refused to allow any other productions that might attract their prospective audience. She did not work again until the summer, when rehearsals started for the impenetrable play by Botho Strauss, *Great and Small*, which was to tour before arriving at the Vaudeville in August. In common with many of Strauss' other plays for the Berliner Schaubuhne, *Great and Small* is an esoteric work in which elements of surreal farce battle with periods of remorseful melancholy. It is a challenging play, and it was as adventurous for Duncan Weldon to finance the production as it was for Glenda to appear in it, even if it did have two old companions in the cast: Barry Stanton and Brian Deacon. Jack Tinker, who hated the play, cynically thought he understood why Glenda had agreed to do it: 'What star could resist a role which not only shows her as an object of pity, but also allows her high-flown expressionist monologues, screams and tantrums, funny walks, the chance not only to go off her trolley, but to push all her worldly goods around in one – and a comic turn in an over-large crash helmet?'

Barry Stanton recalls that Glenda was not easy to work with at this stage of her career because she would bring a whole village with her to a production – a make-up artist, a dresser, even an occasional publicist – and she insisted on participating in choosing the people she would work with. She had more or less chosen the director for *Great and Small*, 'probably the most difficult director in the world', Keith Hack, and she insisted on cutting whole tranches of the play. Even with the cuts audiences found the play too long and incomprehensible, and upwards of a hundred members of the audience would flee every night during the interval – a figure that reached 500 one night at the Palace in Manchester, where one critic condemned it as 'a wildly episodic faintly absurd piece, full of assorted, barely identifiable nutters parading their stream of consciousness ravings in front of one another'. In London a third of the audience failed to return for the second half and even warm reviews in the *New Statesman* ('Glenda Jackson's performance is one of the surest and most varied I have seen from her; she gets right to the heart of Lotte's nervy, naive and desperate character') and the *Guardian* ('An astonishing performance: crop-haired, long-necked, deliciously nosy, she has the blithe fixity of purpose of a comic character yet at other times the frightening ability of a Beckett heroine to stare into the abyss') were not enough to guarantee more than a brief run. Milton Shulman in the *Evening Standard* left the theatre 'with the sad feeling that Miss Jackson may grow to know what real loneliness is before the play is gone and forgotten'.

Undeterred by such a response to challenging theatre, Duncan Weldon and Glenda returned to the West End the following year with another Keith Hack production, the five-hour-long 1928 Pulitzer Prize-winning American play by Eugene O'Neill, *Strange Interlude*. This time the critics were unanimous in their praise. Even though Jack Tinker disliked the play and the production, which he thought was 'little more than *Dynasty* dressed up as art', he acknowledged that 'You have to hand it to her: Glenda Jackson is nothing if not game.'[15]

Strange Interlude is not light entertainment, not least because of its length (people jested that you did not so much buy tickets as enlist), but this production triumphed not only in the strong cast, which included Edward Petherbridge, Brian Cox and James Hazeldine, but also in the sureness of touch with which it played up the comedy without harming the tragic grandeur of the protagonist's passage through several decades, haunted by the loss of her father and her lover. Glenda's performance was magisterial. Sheridan Morley's review in *Punch* was typical:

> Whether playing this turbanned old matriarch with all the icy grandeur of Joan Crawford at her best, or starting the evening as a gauche and lovelorn widow of the First War determined to surround herself with obsessional men, Glenda Jackson gives a performance of towering strength and fascinating variety, so that even after five hours and thirty-six years in her company I would happily have started with her on Act Ten.[16]

So successful was the London production – a sell-out for three months from April to July – that there were immediate plans to take it to Broadway, but this was not possible until American Equity relaxed its objections and allowed most of the British cast to transfer over. Here too the production was a stunning success, and the Nederlander Theater was sold out, despite charging $50 a ticket for the first time on Broadway. The two young American producers from St Austin in Texas were so pleased and so determined to appear generous to their star that they offered her anything she wanted for the opening-night party. Glenda, outraged by such 'pretentious showbiz bullshit', defied them to produce an elephant. Needless to say, an elephant was produced and forty tables of guests were packed for a vast clambake. Sadly nobody had thought to wait for the cast, so there was no table for Glenda and her colleagues, but Glenda was convinced that this was no more than fair – after all, she had got her elephant.

Hazeldine believes that *Strange Interlude* could have run for several months longer, but both Edward Petherbridge and Brian Cox had other commitments in England, and Glenda was keen to get back to London and to Dan, who was now sixteen and had to face his GCSE exams in the summer. In May 1985 Glenda returned to London, in time for a revival of another Citizens production, which she had undertaken at the Old Vic the previous November, Racine's reworking of Aeschylus: *Phedra*.

Recently years have seen several productions of *Phèdre* (most notably Diana Rigg's), but partly thanks to a general British distaste for French drama, and partly due to the difficulty of translating French Alexandrines into anything other than bathetic rhyming couplets, the story of the wife of Theseus, regarded as the crown of classical French drama, is rarely performed. Philip Prowse had talked with Glenda about the possibility of doing *Phedra* during the run of *Summit Conference*, and when both she and Georgina jumped at the suggestion, MacDonald had set about writing a new translation, which was ready in time to start rehearsals in October 1984 for a limited run at the Old Vic.

Michael Coveney says in his history of the Citizens that 'Prowse and MacDonald went for baroque broke, matching where possible Racine's metre, that extended rhythmical tread which is almost invariably rendered in English as pantomimic pentametrical, with a stage composition of swagged curtains, tarnished gold, standing pillars and burning urns.' At the end of the play Prowse created a characteristic *coup de théâtre* – it felt as if the whole stage was about to collapse, providing a suitably grand backdrop for Phedra's suicide. Coveney felt Glenda's performance 'was the Cleopatra she never delivered at Stratford-upon-Avon ... It was tragic on the grand scale, using every part of her voice – its hard, cackling timbre and mellifluous dulcitude, its fishwife flare and soft embrace. She painted an entranced portrait of a woman, and mother, who was on the rack.'[17] John Barber, in the *Daily Telegraph*, praised the same versatility: 'the actress finds a voice to tear buried feelings out of herself as jagged and as hoarse as her torment. She moves from a scratching bitterness to a totally unlooked-for tenderness when she speaks of the love her man has shared with another woman.'[18]

Within the French theatre *Phèdre* is seen as a touchstone for the great actresses. It was one of Bernhardt's *tours de force*, and the film of Edwige Feuillère in the role is still used in French drama schools, so it was a notable achievement for Glenda that when the seventy-seven-year-old Feuillère came to the production she was shocked that Glenda could actually manage eight performances a week, including two days with two performances running back to back. Much to everyone's relief and surprise, *Phedra* sold out its month-long run at the Old Vic in December 1984, and a second run was booked for the Aldwych in 1985 – which also sold out. It had been a significant commercial success.

These two productions, *Strange Interlude* and *Phedra*, re-established Glenda as one of Britain's greatest stage actresses, but the full finery of a mature Glenda Jackson stage appearance was revealed only in her next performance. *The House of Bernarda Alba*, Federico Garcia Lorca's play about honour, fidelity, guilt, sexual yearning and self-oppression, is one of the most Spanish of plays, and the Lyric Hammersmith commissioned the Spanish director Nuria Espert and Strehler's designer at Milan, Ezio Frigerio, for a six-week run. The translation was again by MacDonald, and again there was an impressive cast with Joan Plowright as the maid Poncia, Glenda as Bernarda Alba, Patricia Hayes as her mother, and Gillian Hanna, Amanda Root, Deborah Findlay and Julie Legrand as her daughters. Rehearsals were not particularly happy, thanks to disagreements between Glenda and Joan Plowright, who in Philip Prowse's opinion came waddling on as a duchess when she was meant to be playing the housemaid. Despite this it was a startlingly realistic production. Frigerio's rigid, whitewashed set, thrust to the apron of the stage, shone harshly under strong white lights, and it did not take much to imagine the Spanish midday heat. Some critics thought Glenda too young for the part, but Michael Ratcliffe in the *Observer* eulogised: 'with her unsleeping cat's face, Miss Jackson . . . chisels every syllable with fastidious contempt and describes the territory of her dictatorship with the cutting swathe of a stick'.[19] When the production was revived for four months at the Globe Theatre early the following year Michael Billington, writing for the *Guardian*, thought 'Glenda Jackson's Bernarda Alba is even better than before in that she makes you feel a certain pity for this blind, stupid, tyrannous old matriarch: there is also a genuine passion as she pronounces the last rites over her dead husband.'[20]

By the time of Mrs Thatcher's third successive election victory on 11 June 1987 – the first election in which Kinnock fought as Labour leader, Bryan Gould led the campaign team and when Peter Mandelson was still the Labour Party's Director of Communications – Glenda had, then, appeared in three successive theatrical hits, all of plays considered difficult, and none of them produced in the subsidised theatre. There had also been a lighter new play with Nigel Hawthorne at the start of 1986, *Across from the Garden of Allah*. She had appeared in some films: in 1983 she had made *Sakharov* with Jack Gold; in 1985 *Turtle Diary*; and in 1986 a second feature for Robert Altman, *Beyond Therapy*; but none of these was a major Hollywood production. *Sakharov*, which was filmed without make-up and with the active support of the Sakharov family in a *cinéma vérité* style, hit its mark as a docu-drama, but was never as demanding as Glenda's earlier work. *Turtle Diary*, in which Glenda shared the honours with Ben Kingsley, was a pleasant sentimental drama, but it scarcely achieved distribution outside the UK. While it was a delight to work with Altman again, especially in a cast that included Tom Conti and Jeff Goldblum, the results were no more impressive than on their first outing together. The film's surrealism is so uncertain as to render the whole film irritating rather than witty.

Glenda's later films also suffered from problems. Ken Russell's wildly epicurean *Salome's Last Dance*, which featured a performance of Wilde's play *Salome* in an actual brothel that Wilde had visited, and in which Glenda played Herodias, succumbed to an almost pornographic self-indulgence. (It was described by one of the cast, Douglas Hodge, as emanating from 'Russell's seriously mad period'.) In 1988 Glenda appeared again for Russell in the slightly better film *The Rainbow*, in which Russell tried to return to form with a long-anticipated adaptation of D. H. Lawrence's precursor to *Women in Love*. This time Glenda played the mother of the character she had played twenty years earlier, but although Russell's dissipation was more effectively reined in this time, even Glenda felt that 'it simply didn't work, not least because Russell had focused on the wrong part of the Lawrence novel'.

Turtle Diary had been Glenda's first contribution to a new venture she had initiated with Albert Finney, Diana Rigg, Richard Johnson, Maggie Smith and John Hurt: United British Artists. The idea, based on the 1919 formation of Hollywood's United Artists by Charlie Chaplin, Douglas Fairbanks and Mary Pickford, was to give the group of British actors real control over their work. There would be eight-week West End runs, which would then be adapted and filmed for distribution by Lord Grade and his Embassy Communications, and there would be commercial films, the first of which was *Champions*, with John Hurt. This was not the first time that Glenda had tried to seize control of her career: there had been the short-lived Bullfinch season; an attempt to take a lease on the Garrick Theatre for a Women's Playhouse Project; and Bowden Productions, of which Glenda remained a director. This entrepreneurial spirit had enabled her to do a lot of work that was in her own eyes 'respectable': complex, subtle plays and well-written films. But the desire to control her working environment, which many people noted in Glenda, started to prevent her from developing any further. And one specific production proved that being in almost sole control of a production was not good for her.

In 1988 the usually superstitious Glenda engaged in one of the rashest commitments of her career: playing Lady Macbeth opposite the Canadian actor Christopher Plummer in an American production that had no real director. The original idea for the production had come from Glenda. When she was playing *Rose* in New York she urged her dresser, Melinda Howard, who had also dressed Plummer, to do something other than just dressing. Melinda then completed a course in directing, and started to put together a production of *Macbeth*, which was to start in Canada and transfer to Broadway.

The troubles began immediately. Melinda never got to start the rehearsals, as the producer Garth Drabinsky insisted on bringing in Kenneth Fraenkel as director. He too was replaced, when things started to go wrong early on, by Drabinsky's second choice – the Briton Robin Phillips, who ran the Shakespeare Festival at Stratford, Ontario. When new problems arose he also left the production, to be succeeded by Zoe Caldwell.

These difficulties were compounded by problems with the

original grass-covered set (Glenda called it a 'bloody Cheddar Gorge'), which meant all the actors kept skidding off stage. Plummer suffered a twisted knee and a torn ligament, and lost a tooth one night when he slipped into one of the murderers. When Fraenkel went the designer Tony Walton and lighting designer Paul Cello followed. By the time the production arrived in New York, after taking in Baltimore and Boston, it had got through three directors, five Mac-duffs, six cast changes, two set designers, two lighting designers and a plague of flu. It is not surprising that Glenda had been reported by one Boston critic as being 'alternately rude, irascible, cryptic, sly, dangerous, supercilious and briskly condescending'.[21]

The resulting *Macbeth* was greeted with derision in New York: every critic commented on the lack of coherence in the production. Plummer and Jackson were slated, while the rest of the company was described as 'a servile supporting cast [from] the antique days of stock'. For some British critics there were memories of Glenda's Ophelia. W. J. Weatherby wrote in the *Guardian*,

> Glenda Jackson's Lady Macbeth is an unusually sensuous, almost girlish portrayal that loses some of the Machiavel-lian quality in the early scenes to squeeze the last drop of feeling from the final breakdown. A great director might have drawn a truly great performance from her, but we are too aware of a dominating actress often left to her own resources and occasionally forced to resort to standard, heavily mannered, Shakespearean solos.[22]

Robert Cushman added:

> The leads are marooned in the star-conscious Fifties . . . Plummer . . . is just blandly speaking lines and even his competence tells against him. One begins to wish that he and Jackson were real Hollywood people, with no idea how to speak verse; the occasion might have a raw blood-sport excitement about it, or at least be good for a laugh.[23]

Given the play's reputation Glenda might have hidden behind superstition to excuse herself. Characteristically she takes the blame fully: 'The mistakes that were made have absolutely nothing to do with the dark forces and absolutely everything to do with human fallibility.' The mistake, of course, had been to proceed without a director. Glenda had been fussy about directors ever since Brook and Russell, and her best performances had always been given when there was someone effective in charge to help channel her energies. It was not a mistake she would make again, and she subsequently worked for directors she already knew (Russell and Prowse twice more, Hugh MacDiarmid once more).

The only exception was a three-month run in Los Angeles at the end of 1989, when she appeared as Martha in *Who's Afraid of Virginia Woolf?* Here the director could scarcely be considered a risk as he was also the author, Edward Albee, yet this meant little to Glenda and this was scarcely the happiest of working relationships for either of them. Glenda was again apart from Dan, spending September through to December in a fifth-floor flat in Granville Towers in Hollywood. Although the play gave Glenda another chance to catch up with Daniel's godparents Peter Bromilow and Brenda Vaccaro, she felt suffocated by Hollywood's immense expectations for this production, which almost matched those for *Antony and Cleopatra*. In addition, Albee had not himself directed since the seventies. George was played by John Lithgow, the actor then best known in Britain for *Harry and the Hendersons* and now for *Third Rock from the Sun*.

Despite backstage disagreements Hollywood was not disappointed. Charles Marowitz, now theatre correspondent for the local *Herald Examiner*, noted that:

> Jackson's sarcasm, like an excoriating flame-thrower, defoliates everything with which it comes into contact. Her primeval bray and annihilating boredom combine to produce a poisonous gas against which all protective masks are futile . . . The chemistry between Glenda Jackson and John Lithgow is of the sort that produces proliferating combustions. This George and Martha are a well-sustained double act that wreaks more laughter than Albee's play has probably ever provoked before.[24]

Only two critics had negative comments to make. Bruce Feld felt that

Glenda Jackson, one of the finest actresses in the world, is not at the moment a great Martha. She postures, she snarls, she articulates with the thrust of a director, her Mussolini lips tugged firmly down at the corners as she strides the stage. Yes, the accent is American and technically fine. But the arc of her performance is not. She offers very little emotional growth in the play, and her movement from braggart to bathos is more reminiscent of a circumflex on a page than the mighty Golden Gate bridge, which is what it ought to suggest.[25]

Dan Sullivan worried that 'Jackson's enormous self-sufficiency as an actress keeps us from feeling that there's anything under Martha's scorn but more scorn', but even he felt that 'no actors have done the George and Martha show with more style'.[26]

By the time Glenda had set out for Los Angeles in September 1989 she had already organised commitments for most of the following year. There was to be a month-long production of a Howard Barker play she had recorded in 1984 for Hugh MacDiarmid at the Almeida, followed by *Mother Courage* at the Glasgow Citizens in May, and then the transfer of *Who's Afraid* to London in July.

Or at least that was the plan.

CHAPTER TEN

The Celebrity Candidate

LEADING ACTRESSES of a 'certain age' are almost inevitably analysed by critics who set themselves the task of answering the question 'Is she really one of the greats?' Glenda is no exception. Indeed, her subsequent change of career has given piquancy to these analyses. Snide comments along the lines of 'she was never really any good anyway', or 'the parts were drying up, you know', or even 'she was always the same, dour, drab, dull', are not uncommon among both the acting fraternity and hostile backbench MPs who want to explain Glenda's transition from actress to minister as the flight from a failed career. Even some of Glenda's friends think that by the mid-eighties she had gone as far as she could with her acting. Joyce Marlow feels that Glenda was 'just not prepared to go the extra mile' in her later performances, and the spark of energy that had characterised her early work had been extinguished. Barry Stanton puts a different gloss on this, believing that by the mid-eighties Glenda was so difficult to work with, so dictatorial in the rehearsal room and so demanding of directors that she was running out of people with whom she could work. Elizabeth Spriggs, who has managed the transition from ingénue to character actress relatively easily, goes even further, maintaining that Glenda was only ever a technically proficient actress and that her inspiration simply dried up along with the parts.

So was (is) Glenda a great actress? She is undoubtedly a phenomenally disciplined and proficient technical actress. Even in the YMCA Players her Scottish accent was impressive, and she was impeccably American in both *Who's Afraid of Virginia Woolf?* and three O'Neill productions. Her portrayal of Patricia Neal was affecting because of its medical accuracy, and she was equally convincing as Elizabeth the frightened child and Elizabeth the crabbed autocrat. Actor after actor has told me how adept 'one take Glenda' is at learning her lines, finding her light on stage, spotting the camera and standing stock-still. Glenda says that at RADA she had learnt simply that 'you are your own instrument' and that 'it's up to you to keep that instrument in as good trim as possible – physically and mentally. It's your voice and *you* are all you have to express anything with, and you have to keep it alert, alive and capable of expressing.'[1] It is certainly true that one of the most remarkable aspects of Glenda's work is her cracked bell of a voice. She can flit between octaves, pouring honey or spilling razor blades. She can whisper with precision across vast empty halls and fill them with expansive warm tones. And she knows how to make herself beautiful.

Moreover, something that is often forgotten about Glenda is her ability as a comic actress – able equally to dance with Morecambe and Wise and the Muppets, and to bring a light touch to the most serious of classical roles. This often disconcerted critics, but in *Hedda Gabler*, *Strange Interlude*, *Who's Afraid*, even in *Antony and Cleopatra*, she demonstrated her extraordinary ability to exploit the humour of a situation without being gratuitously comical. Her technical strengths made her a witty comic actress and she could often use seemingly incongruous timing to devastating effect. Glenda tends to be dismissive of her comic talent, but after successes like *A Touch of Class* it is not surprising that when Hollywood called for Glenda it was just as often for a comedy as for a tragedy.

Glenda has all the technical attributes that Ken Tynan believed a great actor required: 'complete physical relaxation, powerful physical magnetism, commanding eyes that are visible at the back of the gallery, a commanding voice that is audible *without effort* at the back of the gallery, superb timing, which includes the ability to make verse swing'.[2] These aptitudes were not inherited by some felicity of birth, but acquired through long, hard work. Peter Brook remembers her intense concentration from her early days with him: 'The image I carry most vividly from all the work we have done together is not of her in performance – it is of Glenda watching. For hours on end, starting with the first Theatre of Cruelty, I see Glenda, huddled in a corner, motionless, silent, critical, missing nothing.'[3]

Some of Glenda's critics argue that this technical mastery only shows an immensely disciplined and proficient actress, and that it is not really acting, not the courageous process of submerging oneself in another character, and assuming another personality, and they point to her later performances to show that she was always 'very Glenda'. She hotly denies this interpretation of acting: instead she sees it as being about stripping oneself bare, finding the part inside oneself that matches the emotional make-up of the character, and then conveying the truth of the character as one's own truth. Jack Shepherd explains the same phenomenon: 'If you are playing a lawyer you cannot just pretend to be a lawyer, you have to ask yourself "If I were a lawyer, how would I behave? Can I find the lawyer inside me, and if so how can I relate that lawyer to the lawyer in the text?"' It is precisely this process that Barry Stanton noticed in Glenda: 'She would never play a character – she stands miles away from a character and drags it towards her and forces it on to her.'

Always resentful of the fact that many people think of acting as frivolous, she told the actor Clive Swift:

> I never regarded it as a glamorous profession; to me the interest was always the difficulty of it. It's very difficult to act well. It's very difficult to really, truthfully, present to an audience – in a way that the audience is not aware that you're presenting – what the author wants them to feel or think. You are, in a way, simply a channel between the author and the audience and that's very difficult. I can't emphasise enough that it is a profession that requires a great deal of discipline. It's *not* a lot of people playing games. It's not particularly fun, it's not particularly amusing – I'm talking now about if you take it seriously, which is not the same as taking *yourself* seriously. It demands a great deal of you and you have to be disciplined, you have to be healthy and you have to be ready to work when the opportunity presents itself to you.[4]

This disciplined, rigorous, demanding understanding of acting often made Glenda a disturbing actress to watch, although it was not her technical abilities that made her a great actress, but another personal attribute that Ken Tynan recognised as essential to greatness: '*chutzpah* – the untranslatable Jewish word that means cool nerve and outrageous effrontery combined, and the ability to convey a sense of danger'. Glenda's Charlotte Corday was remarkable not for its verisimilitude, but because you genuinely feared what she might do next. The intensity with which she drew Mrs Elvsted to her as Hedda felt electric with danger. The bewildered fury she showed in *The Triple Echo* reeked of instability. Her collapse in *The Return of the Soldier* was all the more affecting for its complete unpredictability, and the sense of disciplined abandonment that she achieved in *Women in Love* remains devastatingly entrancing. Time after time she shocked her audiences, whether playing *Who's Afraid* or *Hedda Gabler* for laughs, throwing herself off a fifteen-foot ladder or writhing around on a train floor. Charles Marowitz says that 'It was always the sense of being close to elemental forces that accounted for Glenda's fascination; the knowledge that she is capable of manifesting those potent inner states, that in most of us remain contained or suppressed.'

Glenda's greatness lay as much in her ability to make a part her own as in an ability to pretend to be someone else, and her best performances were always those that combined technical brio with startling audacity. This capacity was completely undiminished by the nineties. In the last full five years of her full-time career, from 1985 to 1989, she appeared in three immensely successful transferred productions (*Strange Interlude*, *Phedra* and *The House of Bernarda Alba*), two of which were filmed for television; she made five other films (admittedly of varying quality); she appeared in both New York (twice) and Los Angeles theatre productions; and she premièred two plays in London.

Moreover she was still in steady demand. There was talk of ludicrous sums of money for a Hollywood soap opera, of Matthau and Glenda doing a film of Edward Bond's play *Sweeney Todd* (although Matthau balked at the idea of doing a Dick Van Dyke cockney accent), and mention of pairing Glenda with Dirk Bogarde again in a film adaptation of Arnold Bennett's novel *Buried Alive*.

All this came to nothing. Throughout this period one irrepressible emotion worked inside Glenda – her sense of guilt at the futility of much of her work in the face of the great issues of the day. She had long let it be known that she wanted one day to do something more useful than act, and deep inside she felt that she *ought* to be doing something that was socially valuable. She alluded to this conviction in an intriguing interview given to Laura Hitchcock for the programme notes for *Who's Afraid of Virginia Woolf?* Commenting on the character of George, and his failure to go into politics, she noted that 'many of our best people won't go into the political arena', before excusing herself for her own failure to take up social work as she had once promised. 'So many social workers wrote and told me not to do it,' she explained.

She had spent the early years of the eighties oscillating between politics, social science and acting. In 1979 she started a social science degree at the Open University, but dropped out a few months later when she started to fall behind with her essays. This in itself was a significant declaration of intent, especially at a time when 'mature students' were still rarities. In 1983 she was approached about the possibility of standing for the marginal Welsh seat of Bridgend. She turned this down because she had decided instead to pursue a humanities degree at Thames Polytechnic. Yet again she dropped out, this time even before she had started, thanks to a mixture of uncertainty about her own academic ability and offers of new work. Throughout this period she continued her single-issue campaigning, visiting Ethiopia, in 1986, to help Oxfam in its efforts to combat the famine. In June 1989 she even approached Voluntary Service Overseas (VSO) about the possibility of working in Africa for a couple of years.

None of these attempts at a new career took off, but the Thatcherite eighties saw Glenda grow increasingly frustrated by British politics. On the one side there was Thatcherism itself, with its rampant free market, its obsession with personal satisfaction and its emphasis on looking after yourself. Glenda abhorred these values even more than she detested Thatcher's poll tax, her privatisations and her autocratic style. 'It started with Margaret Thatcher,' she says:

> I would have done anything legal to get her out. I was so angry when I heard her 'no such thing as society' speech, I walked into my glass doors . . . What I found

most offensive about Thatcherism was seeing vices transformed into virtues. Greed became good. Traits I consider virtues were suddenly considered pusillanimous, a
cop out, a way of passing on responsibility.[5]

Glenda's appearances on political programmes became more vehe-
ment and more frequent. She found it incomprehensible that the
Government would not institute sanctions against the apartheid
state of South Africa, so she became involved in the ANC campaign, even chairing a United Nations committee on the cultural
boycott in September 1988. 'I've always felt', she declared, 'that
denying people the right to anything on the grounds of their race,
colour or creed is an abomination. To institutionalise it in the laws
of a country is a double abomination.'[6]

At the same time Glenda was distressed by the Labour Party's
failure to behave like an electable party, or cohere around a pragmatic programme. Certainly Glenda was as fired up by class-
consciousness as the next socialist. She often recalled with horror
sitting behind two old working-class ladies watching a post-war
Anna Neagle and Michael Wilding movie, during which Anna
Neagle refused to marry Wilding because she was of a lower class,
whereupon one of the two ladies turned to her friend to whisper, 'Of
course, she's quite right. You see, she's not a lady.' Such 'absolute
acceptance' of the class divide shocked Glenda deeply, but it produced in her not a demand that the working classes immediately
leap to the barricades, but that Britain become less class-obsessed,
less hidebound by tradition and more meritocratic; and that the
Labour Party 'bloody well get its act together'.

Throughout the early eighties Glenda was a die-hard opponent
of the extremist politics of both Arthur Scargill and Militant
Labour, which had infiltrated local Labour parties in many of the
major cities, most notably Liverpool. In essence she felt that their
political antics were playing to the gallery, while failing to realise
that the people in the gallery wanted something far more pragmatic
from the Labour Party. The politics of Militant Labour and Derek
Hatton were just 'self-indulgent crap'. When Neil Kinnock took
the opportunity of his Labour Party conference speech in October
1985 to condemn both Scargill and Militant in Liverpool, before

starting the process of expelling them from the party, Glenda was so delighted that she immediately sent him a congratulatory telegram. She was also vitriolically dismissive of British working-class posturing, finding the American political emphasis on 'the people' far more inspiring. She protests:

> The classic example for me happened when we were fighting a by-election in Greenwich, which was particularly ugly because there was internecine warfare in the Greenwich party at the time. And there was a sizeable number of young men who seemed to have just graduated from the London School of Economics, all of whom were wearing donkey jackets emblazoned on the back with Greenwich Borough Council. No member of the working class in my view, era and age, would have gone knocking on anybody's door in their work clothes unless it was an emergency of some kind. And that kind of impertinent presumption of what motivates the working class is something that I find intensely irritating and it permeates through every layer of national life and warrants being pulled out root and branch.

This combination of her hatred of Thatcherism and her distrust of left-wing gesture politics finally began to harden Glenda's resolve to do something other than act. As she said in 1989, 'We're living in a bloody slum. It looks like a bloody fire sale, everything's been so transfigured.'[7]

In December 1989 Glenda came her closest yet to escaping the theatre when two branches of the local Labour Party in Denis Healey's constituency of Leeds East were rumoured to have approached her about succeeding him as their Member of Parliament in the forthcoming election. Glenda was tempted, but told *The Times*: 'I am enormously flattered, but to follow Denis Healey's act you would have to be a genius.'[8] The advantages of representing Leeds East were manifest. It was a safe Labour seat and a cynical candidate would, once selected, barely have had to campaign in Leeds prior to the election itself. For an ordinary actress this would have been immensely useful, as it would have enabled her to continue working right up until Parliament was dissolved, and it would have virtually guaranteed an income for life from the day after the election. But Glenda has never been ordinary, and she turned down Leeds East because, far from enabling her to continue acting, it would make it impossible. She could not conceive of being an absentee candidate, and most acting work was going to be in London. That meant that if Glenda were to change career she would have to fight a London seat. Blackheath lay in a constituency that already had a Labour MP, so there was no opening there, and Kew, where she had lived while at RADA, was solidly Tory. It was ironic that the constituency Labour Party in the only other seat in London in which she had lived, Hampstead and Highgate, should, in the shape of two local members, Janet Guthrie and Penny Abrahams, contact her about the possibility of standing late in 1989.

Glenda senses many frustrations – that women are treated as second-class, that actors are presumed to be brainless – but one of her most heartfelt is that the inhabitants of Hampstead and Highgate constituency are stereotyped as wealthy and intellectual – in short, as the chattering classes. In fact, the seat for which she stood for Parliament (the boundaries have since been redrawn) is characterised more by endless blocks of council flats, poverty and unemployment, racial diversity and homelessness than by grand Parliament Hill mansions. Large swathes of the creative intelligentsia are camped out in the twin villages of Hampstead and Highgate,[9] but most of the constituency is covered by Kilburn, Swiss Cottage and West Hampstead, where Camden Council, the Post Office, the health service and the railways are the main employers, and acre after acre is covered with dilapidated estates.

The constituency had been represented by the Tories for most of the century, with the last brief Labour interlude in 1966, when the genial Ben Whitaker had been MP. The victor in the subsequent election was the Tory Sir Geoffrey Finsberg, who, incidentally, Glenda's friend Joyce Marlow recalls always smelling of stale urine at primary school. By the time Glenda had been approached about the seat Finsberg had already announced his retirement, and the Conservatives were also looking for a replacement.

Getting selected as the Labour Party candidate was never going to be easy. For a start, although she had famously appeared in a

Labour Party election broadcast and canvassed for many a candidate, Glenda had little understanding of the ins and outs of Labour Party democracy. She had never been to a ward Labour Party meeting. Indeed, at a Greenwich by-election, when an *Express* journalist demanded what her socialism really amounted to, she confessed as much before turning the journalist's cynicism to her own advantage. 'Well,' she said, 'I've been a member of the Labour Party for years, but if you're asking do I go to ward meetings – well there I have a little difficulty – you see, I *work* in the evenings.' Her sharpness impressed the regular theatre-goer Neil Kinnock, but when Glenda said to him that she was thinking of standing for Parliament he tried to dissuade her, arguing that she was far more useful to the party as a double Oscar-winning actress who supported Labour than as an MP. 'After all, there are dozens of perfectly decent people who can be half-decent MPs, but very few who can be an outstanding actress.' Once Glenda showed her determination, however, the Kinnock machine swung behind her.

What was to prove far more difficult, though, was the Hampstead and Highgate Labour Party, which has always been a recalcitrant and querulous local party, so proud of its independence that it had refused to accept the national Labour Party's offer of a full-time agent, in case their 'political control' of the local campaign should be compromised. It was unlikely that they would take Glenda just because she was famous, and any intervention from the national Labour Party or Neil Kinnock's office was likely to backfire. Glenda had to win people over one by one. That meant a round of private meetings in advance of the Labour Party branch meetings at which nominations would be considered, before a final hustings meeting and ballot of the constituency's General Management Committee. Even this would be difficult. Glenda was due to set off for Los Angeles to appear in *Who's Afraid of Virginia Woolf?*, and on her return would be appearing at the Almeida in Islington every night, just as local ward nomination meetings were going ahead, so she would have to rely on others to support her.

While Glenda's campaign was getting under weigh, others, including several of the local party officers, were campaigning for the adoption of a left-wing Camden councillor, Kate Allen, who also happened to be neighbouring MP Ken Livingstone's partner, and another group tried to present another local, Maureen Robinson, as the local unity candidate. From another neighbouring constituency, where Frank Dobson represented Holborn and St Pancras, there was warm but discreet support for Glenda's candidacy from both the right-wing chair of the party, Dianne Hayter, and from the full-time agent, Nick Smith. There was some scepticism at the Greater London Labour Party headquarters about an actress running an effective campaign in an extremely difficult seat, but there was an overwhelming impression that the rest of the London Labour Party wanted Hampstead and Highgate to select Glenda as their candidate. This inevitably made life more difficult, as did Glenda's staunch support for Neil Kinnock's attempts to moderate party policy. Hampstead and Highgate members wanted to make their own decision, and did not care for having Glenda foisted on them by either the party or the Press, who, the moment they heard that Glenda was thinking of standing, started salivating at the prospect of at least a year's 'actress turns politician' stories.

Every Labour Party selection battle is fraught, even more so if it is fought under the glare of international publicity. The labyrinthine procedures that the National Executive Committee had invented in the late eighties made the selection process even more complicated for an ordinary member to comprehend, than today, so activists tended to dominate the public debate. One of the Labour Party's more ludicrous rules was that no candidate was allowed to use the Press to advance their campaign or denigrate another's. In a regular constituency contest this was patent nonsense – an attempt, as Terry Ashton, the General Secretary of the London Labour Party, called it 'to take politics out of a political process'. In Glenda's case it made even less sense. The Press – in England, America, Japan, Spain, Chile, Iceland – were fascinated by the double Oscar-winner's great act of renunciation.

This was doubly helpful for Glenda, as she was not only able to seem present by appearing regularly in the papers, but Steve Taylor, the chair of the local party, who had no intention of voting for Glenda, managed to fuel Glenda's campaign by taking exception to the publicity she was receiving and firing off an angry letter to her, demanding that she desist from speaking to the Press forthwith. A couple of days after Glenda received his letter Neil and Glenys

Kinnock came to see *Scenes from an Execution* at the Almeida. At dinner afterwards Glenda asked the Labour leader what she should do. Neil, who had himself written the party rules on publicity for candidates, was jocular, encouraging her to reply to Taylor in robust terms along the lines of 'You must think I came down with the last shower. Pull the other one.' Neil had not, of course, expected Glenda to follow his advice word for word. He was amazed to see Press accounts the following week of Glenda's reply to Taylor, in which she had adopted his jocose tone and had even used 'pull the other one'. When he rang to say he had expected her to moderate his suggestion, she simply replied, 'In my book, if you are in a party, you follow your leader's advice.' In fact, Glenda's letter was a success, as she managed to convert what might have been a story about 'famous actress takes advantage of her position' into one about 'constituency chairman tries to silence Glenda'.

There were other problems though. One of the ward chairmen declared to all and sundry that 'no one will vote for that fucking slut'. Glenda missed two of the nomination meetings, in Kilburn and Highgate, and her opponents raised the question of why she had done an advert, with George Segal, for Lord Hanson, one of the Tories' principal donors. Glenda's rebuttal, that her fee had gone to charity, just like her fee for an advert for Boots, calmed her supporters' nerves, but when, rather late in the day, a new candidate, economic history lecturer Sarah Palmer, appeared, claiming the apparent backing of the national Labour Party, Glenda had to work hard to maintain momentum for her campaign.

Meanwhile, the subtle blandishments of the London and national Labour Party had helped persuade several of the key trade unions in the local party, the railwaymen and the communications workers, to back Glenda, and by the time of the ballot it seemed likely that she would win, but not without second preferences. She had originally intended to give a rabble-rousing political speech at the final hustings in the hope of appealing to the left-wing idealism of the activists, but the fact that she was clearly ahead convinced both her and her closest supporters that there was no need to risk alienating those who already intended to vote for her. Better by far to make a simple speech: attract the women's and feminist votes by applauding the constituency for having nominated three women;

flatter as many people as possible by remembering their names; attack the Tories; and let the others alienate their supporters. Hugh Manning recalls that Glenda's speech was extraordinarily apolitical.

Glenda has always admitted to being a nervous performer, even saying that as the years went by her confidence waned, and she would often stand backstage before a first night sweating with nerves, but she was more nervous than ever at the Aslef headquarters in Arkwright Road where the final results were to be declared on the evening of 28 March. Despite this evident frailty, Glenda won the Hampstead and Highgate nomination that evening by a wide margin, almost succeeding on the first ballot, which gave her 47.7 per cent of the constituency and affiliates' votes, to 24.8 per cent for Kate Allen, 17.8 per cent for Sarah Palmer and 7.7 per cent for Maureen Robinson. After two further rounds of 'exhaustive' balloting Mac Bull, the new chair of the constituency Labour Party, finally announced, 'Comrades, we have a result,' to a great roar of applause. Glenda had won with 59.2 per cent of the vote to Allen's 30.5.

Glenda found it genuinely difficult to express her pleasure that evening, telling the Press that this was 'a very curious sensation. This is one of the proudest and the most humbling moments of my life', far surpassing the accomplishments of the Oscars – after all, someone else really won the Oscars for you. This selection, she rather disingenuously announced, she had won for herself. In reality a good half a dozen people from both the left and the right wings of the local party had worked every bit as hard as Glenda in securing her nomination – but that evening nobody was going to detract from Glenda's evident delight, and Frank Dobson was happy to quip from the other Camden constituency, 'I look forward to being the least well-known MP in Camden.'[10]

Finally Glenda had also been helped in her campaign by another round of excellent reviews for her stage appearance in Howard Barker's *Scenes from an Execution*, which she had successfully recorded for radio in 1984 (when it won both the Society of Authors' Sony Award and a Prix Italia). The critics were unusually unanimous in their praise for her performance as the artist Galactia, with Michael Coveney declaring her to be 'in ebullient, uncompromising form',[11] and Michael Billington confessing a belief that

Glenda had slaved over the creation of her on-stage performance, and relishing her 'astonishing head-shaking canine growl at her lover when she tells him "I think you are marvellous at honouring yourself"'.[12] The *Financial Times* called it

> her most assured stage performance for years. Gone is the compulsively nodding, head-dipping nervous mannerism that marred even *Strange Interlude*. The technique is spare, confident, authoritative; and the vocal mastery is less of a show-off exercise than it was in *Phedra*. Here the throaty snarl, chesty baying and venomous quaver are in place, scoring emotional bull's-eyes every time.[13]

All of which underlined for the members of Hampstead and Highgate Labour Party the fact that one of Britain's greatest actresses was prepared to make an enormous sacrifice. The Conservative papers, the *Daily Mail* and the *Express*, bemoaned the fact that Glenda had expressed 'her disillusion with acting as worthwhile work for grown women',[14] and warned 'God save the male majority in the House of Commons'.[15]

Glenda's selection posed as many personal questions for her as it answered. The date of the election was to be decided by the prime minister, and Mrs Thatcher showed no sign of seeking a dissolution of Parliament, especially while the Labour Party was enjoying vertiginous opinion-poll leads following the imposition of the poll tax. This meant that Glenda found it increasingly difficult to make long-term acting commitments, just in case there should be a sudden general election. Hampstead and Highgate would be no pushover: the Tory majority was not large, a mere 2,221, but Glenda was certain that if Finsberg had been standing again it would have been impossible to wrest the seat from the Tories. The fact that he was standing down, and that in the same week as Glenda's selection the Conservatives had chosen Oliver Letwin, a young merchant banker who claimed to have invented the poll tax while working in the Downing Street Policy Unit, gave Labour a chance, but it would take a resolute, well-organised and intensely political campaign to win.

Glenda made some immediate decisions. There would be no more work overseas, so a possible film of Liz Taylor's book *Charades* fell through. Similarly, long runs were ruled out, so a planned London transfer of *Who's Afraid* never happened, and from the start of 1991 Glenda accepted work only if it was understood that she might have to drop everything at the last minute.

Early in 1991 Glenda's mother, Joan, had a sudden heart attack and died. Since Micky's death she had stayed in the Alderley Road house with Lynne, where she had delighted in welcoming Glenda and Dan for Christmas every year. When Dan went to college in the North West he became an even more regular visitor, normally encumbered by his washing. On one of these visits, however, Dan and Lynne arrived back at the house just as a burglar was rifling through the living room. Glenda's CBE and a few other awards were stolen. The loss was upsetting enough for Joan, but the sense of being violated and of not being safe in her own home disturbed her far more. From that moment, everyone, both in the family and in the village, noticed that she had lost her sense of self-assurance. She started to worry about things, about Dan's career, about Glenda's entry into the rough and tumble of politics. Lynne says that 'She really went into a decline, and within a year she died.' The funeral, on a freezing cold snow-covered day in Hoylake, saw the whole family together again, although a fierce family row ensued which has only recently been patched up.

Back in London Glenda got on with the campaign. Hampstead and Highgate had already appointed its own agent, an affable young journalist at the *New Scientist* named William Cullerne Bown, who, although he was not paid for his work as agent, spent virtually every spare hour in the next two years devoted to Glenda's election, and took the whole election campaign as unpaid leave. Thanks to the local party's intransigence there was no full-time agent, but Frank Dobson's daughter, Sally Dobson, was taken on part-time to act as Glenda's assistant and to help co-ordinate the campaign, and she was soon installed in the party's tiny office in Swain's Lane. Through 1990 the campaign team began to coalesce around William and Sally, with the original supporters who approached Glenda, Janet Guthrie and Penny Abrahams, playing an important role. It also included Deborah Townsend, who ended up in charge of the all-important poster boards, Nick Prior, a member of the campaign team, John Seynor, the computer officer (who had to make do with a bank of 386s) and Tim Walker, the campaign press officer.

Glenda also had to make some strategic decisions. Everyone in the campaign team was clear that while Glenda's fame was an advantage ('candidate recognition', in the jargon, was high), it could prove a double-edged sword. Glenda herself believed that ordinary voters would be less than convinced by an actress's qualifications for representing them, and argued that she would have to present herself as a fully-fledged politician. So whenever she was asked, she told people that if she were elected she would not be acting again because 'I believe that if you're going to do the job properly you can't be a part-time MP, and I know you can't be a part-time actor'. She also resolved to smarten up her appearance. For years Glenda's uniform for press conferences had been consistently casual – scrubbed face, jeans, T-shirt – and journalists had delighted in her evident disdain for her appearance. Even in July 1990 the *Daily Mail* was describing Glenda's apparel as 'a jumper with a faded wallpaper pattern, baggy jeans, floral socks and black trainers that bear a resemblance to hobnail boots'.[16] This was fine for an off-duty actress, but, so her campaign team argued, people expected parliamentary candidates to dress smartly. Glenda could no longer afford interviews that started in the vein of Jean Rafferty in 1989:

> she came scuttling in, head down, a slight pale figure wearing one of the worst garments I have ever seen on anyone. It was a large overshirt made of what looked like storm-bashed deckchair canvas, with broad stripes of faded yellow and off-white and a third colour that may have been green, or maybe grey.[17]

She had to smarten up her appearance, and began to sport efficient-looking, tailored black and red skirts from Jean Muir.

Glenda's immediate concern was to be seen in the constituency, and the Saturday after her selection she was out kissing babies, shaking hands and meeting people with her growing campaign team. It was a successful day, covered by London television as well as the local papers, but it was to be something of a one-off for some time. Glenda's work commitments were substantial. For much of the year she was unable to attend any evening meetings, although she found the time to campaign against the Royal Free Hospital becoming an NHS Trust, petitioned No. 10 Downing Street against fur imports into Europe, and cut the ribbon at a Highgate recording studio for women.

In the meantime Glenda was still earning a living, and following her selection as candidate she spent nearly five months in 1990 on the project she had essayed years earlier, only to be barred by the RSC: Brecht's *Mother Courage*. She told one journalist:

> It's physically and emotionally demanding but I've played roles which are more emotionally quicksilver. When I think about it I can see that Mother Courage is admirable but horrifying. She's what she has to be ... I remember reading an article that Helen Weigel [generally acclaimed as the greatest Courage] wrote having seen Ethel Merman in some musical like *Annie Get Your Gun* and saying how enormously impressed she was and saying she would be a wonderful Mother Courage. I found this very helpful – it wasn't that I tried to play Mother Courage like Ethel Merman but I kept in mind the size of her performance.[18]

The production opened at the Glasgow Citizens in May. Philip Prowse had allowed himself to break out of the Brechtian mould. Brecht's captions were removed, and the opening sequence featured a typically Prowsean *coup de théâtre*: peasant women drifted through a sunlit field, languidly harvesting ripe corn. Slowly, without menace, a group of soldiers gathered beside them. Then, abruptly, the silence was shattered as lights were flashed aggressively in the audience's eyes to the sound of an ear-splitting explosion, and the corn vanished.

This was Glenda's fourth production with Prowse, and he found her as easy as ever to work with, except, curiously, on one occasion when cameras were filming rehearsals as part of a programme on Glasgow in its year as City of Culture. 'Suddenly', he told me, 'she seemed to want to appear in charge of everything and everybody and she started making an issue out of something that was totally irrelevant.' Moreover, when the production was set to transfer to

London, Glenda refused to have Edward Woodward replace Gerald Murphy and objected to Paola Dionisotti.

Glenda's performance did not go down well. Clive Hirschhorn thought it was 'totally devoid of pathos',[19] and Benedict Nightingale complained that the

> quintessential Jackson sound, a rasping blend of snarl and caw, is much in evidence. Less happily, so is a sort of ironic crooning, which momentarily lifts the vowels two or three octaves. That can sound operatic, sometimes, even camp, as if Frankie Howerd were incongruously adding an 'ooh' to the ravening creatures assembled in Glenda Jackson's voicebox.[20]

And Nicholas de Jongh went even further: 'You could no more squeeze blood from a stone than you can extract a milligram of pathos from Jackson's Mother Courage.'[21] Only Paul Taylor was more ambivalent, commenting that

> the battleaxe voice alone makes you quail: a nasal Scouse whine which rises in arcs of sarcastic incredulity or dips into a chesty, contemptuous baritone. The odd 'well-spoken' vowel alerts you to how often, even in this squalor, Courage invokes the cramped ideal of the respectable – a keep-yourself-to-yourself mentality which is handy, as Jackson hilariously demonstrates, for brushing off those whom the war has ruined.[22]

Despite the critical mauling, Glenda's *Mother Courage* was sold out for both its Glasgow and its London run, in the Mermaid Theatre, and nobody could deny the bravery of the performance. In addition, most of the critics commented on the London run, which differed from the original, as Bill Kenright had bought the Citizens production and recruited his own extras. Much of the harsh precision of the Glasgow production was lost en route.[23]

The run ended on 22 September, just in time for Glenda to attend the Labour Party conference in Blackpool, but by then several members of the local Labour Party were getting impatient with their famous prospective candidate, who had failed to attend several ward meetings. October was an unhappy month for Glenda – she spent large parts of the Labour Party conference in bed with acute sinusitis – and when she returned to London she was faced with a ward resolution that condemned her for not spending more time with 'grass-roots supporters'. This was defeated at the monthly constituency meeting, but not without difficulty, and it was not to be the last clash with the Hampstead party, which, in 1991, took a pacifist line over the Gulf War, and later opposed the dropping of Clause IV. To this day some longstanding Hampstead activists find Glenda either too aloof or too right-wing.

The constituency meeting at which Glenda was criticised for not showing her face enough persuaded her that any further commitments would have to take second place to her role as candidate. Moreover, up until now Glenda had assumed that Mrs Thatcher would not call an election while the Labour Party was still 12 per cent in the lead in the opinion polls, so it was likely that the Government would run its full term and the election would be in 1992. On 22 November 1990, however, the seemingly unthinkable happened, and the Conservatives, through processes even more labyrinthine than those of a Labour Party selection, deposed the easily demonised Mrs Thatcher. Five days later the bland John Major assumed her mantle, and instantly committed himself to removing the least popular vestige of Thatcherism by abolishing the poll tax. By the end of the month the opinion polls had been reversed, and the received wisdom was that this would mean an early election, as Major would want to capitalise on his honeymoon with the electorate. At the start of 1991 Glenda started campaigning in earnest as an almost full-time candidate.

She launched an appeal for Bangladesh, walked for the Terrence Higgins Trust, called for electoral reform, campaigned for a new Greater London Authority, lobbied Camden Council to prevent developments in Belsize Park, argued for more public transport, welcomed the Kinnocks to see Miriam Margolyes in *Dickens' Women* at the Hampstead Theatre, opened the new Mandela Theatre at the Camden Education Institute and the Holborn Centre for the performing arts, lobbied the Government on behalf of the nearby National Youth Theatre, demanded action on homelessness in London, and week in week out she stood outside tube stations handing out leaflets, she visited old people's homes, schools and hospitals, knocked on doors, and wisecracked and cajoled people into voting Labour.

By the autumn of 1991 Glenda had been a PPC – Prospective Parliamentary Candidate – for a full eighteen months and the campaign team was well advanced in its plans, even having drawn up a complicated twinning arrangement with the next-door constituency party, Holborn and St Pancras, where Frank Dobson was assured of an easy victory (and where I had taken over as the full-time agent). Much of the constituency had already been canvassed in anticipation of the election, and many of the leaflets had already been written. Activists were still picking up resistance to Glenda as they went from house to house. Voters were saying she was still just an actress – how could she possibly represent them? It was around this time that Glenda and her team made a decision to put a stop to anything that might seem in the slightest bit artistic. From now on all invitations to arts-related events would be turned down. Glenda would campaign on 'hard' issues: housing, health and education. She kept to this resolution for the rest of her career, despite a daily post-bag of at least four or five such invites. Eschewing her celebrity status did not always win her friends, however. The national Labour Party wanted Glenda to do events outside the constituency. She wisely refused, arguing that her artistic status was actually her Achilles heel and that she had to establish herself as a true Hampstead and Highgate politician. Problems with the local Labour-run council also meant that Glenda was banned from appearing with any Labour councillors, especially the leader of the council, Julie Fitzgerald.

A key part of the strategy to get people to take Glenda seriously was her keynote speech at the autumn Labour Party conference, which in 1991 was to be held in Brighton. Mid-term party conferences can be dull, either dragged down by the weight of earnest opposition endeavour or stymied by the Government Press machine's desire to manage the news, but all Labour Party conferences have the capacity to spark off unexpected moments of passion and controversy. The Brighton conference of 1991 was no exception. Expectations were extremely high, as Labour had led the Tories in the polls for nearly three years and was now level pegging with them. Nearly everyone had convinced themselves that the long days of darkness were soon to end, and that Labour was bound to win the forthcoming election. Sally Dobson was even boldly declaring that, barring a catastrophe like Kinnock being revealed to be a child molester, Labour was bound to win. Others were not so sure. Kinnock was thought by some to be a liability, and it was being openly suggested that perhaps it would be better if Labour took a leaf out of the Tories' book and ditched him in favour of the reassuring John Smith. Still others felt that the problem was Smith himself, who failed to acknowledge that Labour's position on taxation and the economy was deeply unpopular with the electorate, and who manifestly failed to give unconditional backing to his leader. Perhaps Kinnock should sack his chancellor.

These mixed emotions swirled around the conference hall, so Kinnock's expertly rhetorical speech was received with delight and euphoric relief. The euphoria was so contagious that Kinnock ended up singing 'We Shall Overcome' a capella. It was a curiously dated moment of triumphalism matched only by Jim Parish, the Labour Party's events impresario, who presumptuously decided to play Queen's 'We are the Champions' at the end of the conference, despite the fact that Queen were one of the very few bands to have broken the South African arts embargo. Nevertheless the feeling was that everything had gone sparklingly well. When the Director of Public Prosecutions was found propositioning prostitutes in King's Cross on the day of the vote on nuclear weapons, Frank Dobson joked that he had arranged it specially to obliterate coverage of one of Labour's least popular policies.

In the midst of all this Sally and William had decided it was important that Glenda should give a speech on a 'hard' subject – in other words, anything other than the arts. In recent months Glenda had done several worthy speeches – on waiting lists at the Royal Free, on council-tax banding, on proportional representation – but the opportunity to address the Labour Party conference, not as an actress but as a politician, and to be reported not by the celebrity Press, but by political correspondents, was important in establishing her new image. She was not, however, the only Prospective Parliamentary Candidate who wanted to speak, and conference delegates were starting to get weary of PPCs having their three minutes of glory and getting in the way of the debate. Unlike most of her prospective colleagues, however, Glenda was virtually guaranteed to be called in the education debate. The Labour Party Press office had already released her speech, which had been written by Glenda herself, her son Dan and Sally. There had been endless rehearsals. Glenda had bought a smart new grey jacket which she wore over a red dress, and Sally had replaced Glenda's security badge with a red rose. At the last minute a section about John Major was added to the speech. Just as on the night of her selection, Glenda was extremely nervous. Even though she had performed before larger audiences before, this time she was saying her own words, not those of a playwright or a character – and she felt more exposed. She sat with Sally, Dan and myself – with Barbara Castle nearby – and waited patiently to be called. Despite being assured a spot, the debate was overrunning badly, and David Blunkett, who was chairing the session, had a long list of others to call. First Graham Lane, then Alison Lister, to move and second resolutions, were called, followed by a seemingly interminable list of delegates. Sally worried that all her work would be in vain because time was running out. But finally the blind David Blunkett called 'the woman in the red jumper and grey top', pretending he had no idea who he was calling, before asking 'Is she there? Come on Glenda, love.'

Finally Glenda walked up to the rostrum. For the first time in the week there were no boos when it was announced that she was a PPC and not a delegate. There was even a rustle of applause. 'I am a product of the welfare state,' she began.

> It was that socialist dream made reality by a socialist government that gave me all my opportunities. I was educated at a local school – a state school. That meant we had to pay to go there. My parents paid, so did their next-door neighbours and the people next to them. In fact, the whole of my street paid. They paid through their taxes. They paid for me to go to school. But they didn't just pay for me, they also paid for the children next door and the children next door to them and the children next door to them. And they did that because it wasn't just my school, it was our school, it was everybody's school. And thanks to that same welfare state I

was given a second educational opportunity via the Royal Academy of Dramatic Art. And forty years later I stand here addressing conference, yet without state education it's doubtful I'd be addressing envelopes.

The speech was a roaring success. Exceptionally, delegates took to their feet to applaud her. Frank Dobson announced that Glenda was 'magnificent', Kate Hoey ran over to congratulate her and the cameras flashed while David Blunkett tried to keep the debate going. The Labour Party chief Press officer, Colin Byrne, was delighted and Sally was over the moon. It felt as if Glenda the politician had been born.

With this new political status came an attack from the Conservative Press. The next day, while all the other newspapers were reporting Glenda's speech, the *Daily Mail* was relating that Brian Dance, headmaster of the fee-paying private school once attended by Roy Jenkins, St Dunstan's College in Catford, was lambasting Glenda for her hypocrisy. Despite her eulogy on state education, he maintained that she had tried to get Dan into his school in 1981, when Dan was eleven. According to Dance, Dan failed the exams in 1981, but following a second visit from Glenda to discuss her son's academic future, she entered him for the exams the next year. As it turned out, Dan had never attended a private school of any kind, but went to Kidbrooke Comprehensive in Greenwich before reading English at Lancaster University. Moreover, Glenda maintained that it was solely at Roy's insistence that they had explored the possibility of sending Dan to a private school, once they were divorced. 'My son has two parents,' she pointed out. 'His father insisted we look at private schools. I never wished my son to attend such a school, and my view prevailed.'

By now Glenda was getting used to issuing rapid rebuttals. There had been the row over publicity during her selection, the Hanson Trust dispute, and a steady stream of stories in the local papers about how party workers found Glenda remote. With so much publicity – far in excess of anything a normal PPC could expect – Glenda relied heavily on Sally Dobson to manage the news for her. One of Sally's first spin-doctoring sessions had involved responding to Glenda's speech to the Parliamentary Lobby Correspondents lunch in 1990. Glenda had started well, with some well-placed self-deprecatory humour:

> A second subject of annoyance [for me] is clothes. For male politicians, sartorial elegance is an option. I know, I've seen Ken Livingstone. But for women, the size and splendour of their wardrobe is of greater significance than the size of their majority. Everything they do or say is judged in relation to their attire . . . Personally, I have always thought that my choice of clothes struck a nice balance between the durable but elegantly practical. However my constituency party see me more as a cross between the old-fashioned and the anarchic. And according to Anne Robinson, 'casual is a kindly way of describing her appearance'. And Anne should know.

So far so good. Where Glenda slipped up, however, was by ending her speech with a string of Essex girl jokes: 'What's the similarity between Mikhail Gorbachev and Essex girls? They both get screwed by six men while on holiday.' The Press took delight in exposing Glenda as naive and it was more than Sally could rescue.

Many had naturally presumed that *Mother Courage* might be Glenda Jackson's last theatrical appearance. In fact this was to come in the spring of 1991, when Glenda returned to the Citizens for Eugene O'Neill's classically inspired *Mourning Becomes Electra* – or *Dynasty* meets *The Oresteia*, as one critic called it. This is four and a half hours long, and one of O'Neill's most difficult plays. The small cast is engaged in patricide and incest, leading to Christine Mannon, the matriarch played by Glenda, shooting herself, and her daughter Lavinia, played by Georgina Hale, condemning herself to a living entombment. Christine is one of the leads, but the real focus of the play rests on Lavinia, meaning that Glenda was not under the same intense pressure.

Glenda, fearful of a snap election, had been hesitant about committing herself to another Glasgow production, and had only agreed on the understanding that she would have to jump ship if John Major called the election. Philip Prowse believes that by this time Glenda had already emotionally left the theatre and her heart was not really in the work, but that she looked forward to working with Georgina again, who had not been in *Mother Courage* because of an operation on a cyst on one of her eyes.

As it turned out, the rehearsals were rather strained. Early on there was a discussion about one of Georgina's exits. Glenda felt quite strongly that she should do it in a particular way, and Georgina disagreed. Glenda didn't understand Lavinia's motivation, she argued, and it was Georgina's job, not Glenda's, to decide how she made an exit. The row escalated, and soon Georgina had boxed herself into a corner. Glenda told her that she was being dishonest – she couldn't possibly believe what she was saying. Finally, Georgina lost her temper and from then on, even though they were both staying in the same house in Glasgow, they scarcely spoke to each other, except to do business. 'We got through it the best we could,' Georgina admits, 'but it was like a love affair that had had a bad knock and I am terribly stubborn.' Sadly, they have scarcely met since then.

Mourning Becomes Electra ran for three weeks in April 1991 and received reviews every bit as mixed as those for *Mother Courage*. John Peter complained in *The Sunday Times*:

> I marvel at the obtuseness which allows a great theatre like the Citizens to put on such flabby, overblown stuff. Perhaps the temptation to have Glenda Jackson as Christine Mannon was too much. But the grand, resonant voice simply belts out the lines with a monotonous grandeur, occasionally rising to a harsh nasal passion. Impersonation, if I can call it that, alternates between a stony gaze and a sardonic snarl. 'Tell me you love me' sounds like a threat from an extortionist, or a particularly dismal weather forecast.[24]

And Benedict Nightingale, for *The Times*, cavilled that 'The potential member of Hampstead seems uncomfortable with love, either tender or obsessional, as she is at ease with power. Whatever this bodes for Parliament, it does not help O'Neill.'[25]

The two Michaels at the *Guardian* and the *Observer* were resolute in their praise for Glenda, though. Michael Billington thought this 'one of her best ever performances ... a hard, cruel, glittering woman in whom mockery and passion fight for supremacy',[26] and Michael Coveney lauded a performance in which 'Jackson slithers and writhes and finally expires in a blasted, blank, sobbing fit that may be the most terrifying thing that she has done since the *Marat/ Sade*'.[27]

Strictly speaking *Mourning* was not Glenda's last professional appearance. Later in 1991 she filmed a bio-pic on the life of Arnoldo Bax with Ken Russell, which appeared in November 1992, the BBC screened its film of the *Bernarda Alba* production in December 1991, and during the Glasgow run ITV had screened the third of their adaptations of John Le Carré's Smiley novels, *A Murder of Quality*, in which Glenda appeared opposite Denholm Elliott. There was also a cameo appearance in a final movie, *King of the Wind*, which was not released until 1993, but *Mourning* certainly felt like Glenda's final performance, and from May 1991 she was no longer an actress but a full-time politician.

CHAPTER ELEVEN

———✷———

A New Life

THE YEAR 1991 AND THE EARLY months of 1992 passed slowly for Glenda, impatient now to get on with what she hoped would be her new job. By the turn of the year her campaign was well advanced. There had been soft canvassing ('I'm calling as a member of Glenda Jackson's campaign team. Could you tell me, if there were a general election tomorrow, which party would you be most likely to vote for?') in every ward for more than a year, and the party had relatively accurate information on voting intentions from nearly four-fifths of the electorate. There had been street stalls and public meetings, and leaflets and letters explaining Labour Party policy. A campaign headquarters had been identified: the ballroom in Aslef's grand building in Arkwright Road, once Sir Thomas Beecham's home. 'Hit squads' from the neighbouring constituency party in Holborn and St Pancras had been organised, to blitz special areas of the constituency with leaflets and posters. Sites had been cleared for massive poster boards. Everything was ready. But John Major held off in the hope that his fortunes would rise, or that Labour would start to show signs of division or inexperience.

In the midst of this Glenda had to face one of the most upsetting periods of her life. When her son Dan left for college at Lancaster University to read English, she had taken the opportunity to move to another house in Blackheath, but after his three years he moved back home, and soon became part of the election team, working part-time with Sally Dobson in the Swains Lane office. Grateful of the help – Frank Dobson's two sons also ended up helping in the campaign – there was some uncertainty in the local Labour Party about Glenda's son playing such a role in the campaign, but all passed well until, one midnight in February Glenda was woken by the police. Dan had been out drinking with some friends at a karaoke party in the North Brook pub in Lee, and there had been a row. A seventeen-year-old, Jason Norris, had hit him in his right eye with a broken pint glass. Dan was taken to hospital in Lewisham, and then moved to the Greenwich General Hospital, where the eye had to be removed, as the eye muscle had been badly severed. Needless to say Glenda was distraught. Dan had been the most important person in her life for many years now, and she was a more than devoted mother. She dealt with the situation with courage, telling the Press that Dan was dealing with it 'very bravely and I am very proud of him. He knew within minutes of being glassed that he would never use that eye again.'[1] She even pointed out that Dan did at least have a role model as his uncle, Gill's husband Stan, had also lost his eye. When Jason Norris was eventually convicted and sentenced to five years, she was again understanding, telling the *Daily Telegraph* 'I feel terribly sorry for the mother of the boy. Five years is a long time in a young life. But, clearly, there needs to be a deterrent since this kind of incident seems to be on the increase.'[2] Glenda did not, however, leave it at that, and a couple of years later she and Dan were to be seen campaigning for the use of new specially strengthened plastic glasses in pubs.

Less than three weeks after Daniel's accident the general election campaign began in earnest, when John Major finally sought a dissolution of Parliament from the Queen on Wednesday 11 March. Polling day would be nearly a full month later on 9 April. Major's mid-morning visit to Buckingham Palace came as no surprise to the campaign team in Hampstead and Highgate. Even before he was back at No. 10 Downing Street, large Vote Labour poster boards started to appear along all the main roads in Camden. Labour Party members, who had been given Glenda Jackson posters months beforehand, started to put them up in their windows, and the first leaflet drop began. Glenda, though, was caught off guard, having slipped out to the shops when the announcement came. Her first reaction was to wash her hair, and that same evening she was to be seen outside Hampstead tube station, no longer a prospective candidate. The BBC's first reaction was to cancel a planned showing of *House Calls*.

From the outset it was clear that even though this was the twenty-sixth most marginal seat in Britain, key to a Labour victory, and therefore likely to receive more than its fair share of national attention, the media were set to focus to an unprecedented degree on Hampstead and Highgate. From Thursday morning the campaign office phone started to ring with requests for interviews from Japanese television, Australian radio and newspapers from across the globe. Glenda's agent, William Cullerne Brown, and Press officer, Tim Walker, later special adviser to Jack Cunningham, acerbically pointed out to the national Labour Party Press office in Millbank 'not one of these interviews will bring Glenda a single extra vote', but eventually they caved in and agreed to Glenda doing a single Press conference for the international media at national headquarters.

In the meantime Glenda set about trying to meet as many voters as possible. Thanks to the fact that the party had already spoken to so many voters in the constituency it was possible to identify groups of voters who each received personalised letters – the most sophisticated system of direct mail so far used in a UK election. Those who identified themselves as Liberal Democrats or floating voters were written to immediately, council tenants later. Strong Labour supporters received a letter just before election day reminding them to vote, and people who said they might vote Labour received a different letter urging them: 'Don't be put off by all the negative campaigning. Be positive and vote *for* an end to the recession, *for* a properly funded NHS, *for* more investment and higher standards in schools.' At the same time a phone bank was set up in the basement of John and Barbara Mills' house in Mornington Street, where floating voters were called every evening for the last ten days. So sophisticated was the campaign that people who intended to vote Green were phoned by Lord Stanley Clinton-Davies, a one-time European Commissioner of the Environment, offering to answer any questions on Labour Party environment policy.

Instead of the usual adoption meeting at which the local party formally appoints its candidate and agent, normally attended by only the most eager activists, the two Camden Labour Parties agreed to hold a joint adoption meeting for Frank Dobson and

Glenda in a studio theatre at Haverstock School, opposite Chalk Farm Station. Fifty, perhaps a hundred members of the party were expected. In the event more than fifty journalists turned up, including six television crews, and the tiny theatre was packed. Little Labour flags – not Union flags, as reported – were handed out, and 300 or so Labour Party members cheered Glenda and Frank to the rafters as they arrived to the strains of Holst's *Planets*. The euphoria was increased by the announcement that evening of the first poll of the election – Labour had a lead of 8 percent. The candidates were then nominated, in Glenda's case by a teacher and by the last Labour MP for the seat, Ben Whittaker, and Frank by a paediatrician and a health service manager, before a vote of acclamation for both candidates and then their addresses. Frank spoke first and, in typical fashion, moved half the audience to tears with his appeal for a better kind of society, taking a risk by using the tragic death of station officer Colin Townsley in the 1987 Kings Cross fire as an example of a more humane, socialist creed. Glenda's speech was less convincing, but she received a standing ovation for her concluding remarks: 'The people of this country, the people who are its lifeblood, find themselves under unrelenting attack from poverty, from crime, from unemployment; from all those things that in the year 1992 should be anathema to any civilised society.' As the two candidates went to a Press conference in another room (at which Glenda was asked by the *Wall Street Journal* why she didn't wear make-up), the party members remained to hear the comedian Harry Enfield, who lived in Camden, do a 'loadsamoney' fundraising appeal. Intriguingly, there was probably only one person at the rally who was more nervous than Glenda, and that was Harry, who turned up an hour and a half early and smoked the best part of a packet of cigarettes while he waited.

The campaign itself, rather than Glenda as an individual, started to get the attention of the national Press – partly because so many journalists lived in the constituency. The *Sunday Express*, much to the constituency poster officer Deborah Townsend's delight, declared in its leader that

> On the very day the General Election was announced, bright posters for Labour candidate Glenda Jackson went

up throughout the crucial marginal seat of Hampstead and Highgate. Tory campaigners fighting to defend a majority of only 2,221 were not issued with posters until last week. That small hiccup in Hampstead just about sums up a Conservative campaign which until this week-end has failed dismally to take off.[3]

Although the Conservative campaign took some time to get into gear, the battle lines were drawn up very early on. Almost from the moment the Etonian Oliver Letwin was selected, in 1990, Glenda started to remind everyone that he actually claimed credit for inventing the poll tax. It took Letwin some time to realise that he was not going to win this particular battle. The national protests about the poll tax were 'a song and dance about not much' he told local journalists, 'I was in at the beginning of the whole reorganisation of local government finance and it is something I feel extremely strongly about. It is a completely misunderstood phenomenon.'[4] It was not until a week into the campaign proper that he started to master the national Tory message, with two simple charges: John Smith's shadow budget would mean ordinary people would pay nearly £1,000 more in taxes every year; and people only had to see what Labour had done to Camden Council to see what a Labour Government would be like.

Glenda's strategy was equally simple. Always remind people that Letwin invented the poll tax, and try to squeeze the Liberal Democrat vote (8,744 at the previous election) by persuading them that only Labour could win. Part of the difficulty of the campaign was that these two messages were to some degree mutually exclusive. Liberal Democrats and floating voters were known to find negative campaigning distasteful. Indeed, the first hiccup in Glenda's campaign came when William Cullerne Bown had prepared a leaflet devoted to the issue of Letwin and the poll tax. Under the headline 'The true face of the Conservative Candidate', and a cartoon of Letwin by Trog, a special edition of 'Labour News' announced 'Oliver Letwin is the Conservative Candidate. He is also the man who invented the Poll Tax. Do you *really* want him as your MP?' It was straight knocking copy and it offended one of the cardinal rules of campaigning – never mention your opponent's name. When

Holborn and St Pancras members came to deliver the leaflet they refused to hand it out and there was a series of arguments between William and myself about the wisdom of mounting such a negative assault. Glenda finally pulled the leaflet.

In the midst of a general election it feels as if every day brings vital challenges that must be met for success. The truth, of course, is very different. The battle to win the daily – or in the case of the *Hampstead and Highgate Express* and the *Camden New Journal* weekly – Press headlines is intense, but by the time the election campaign itself starts most of the dice are already cast, and all the energy expended on damage limitation is wasted. Certainly this was the case in 1992. The underlying problems that had hampered Labour in 1987 had not yet been resolved. Kinnock was not fully trusted. The majority of the newspapers were opposed to a Labour victory, and were prepared to run vitriolic campaigns to bolster Major. Only the *Financial Times* proved a last-minute convert. Labour was perceived to be profligate, a party of tax and spend, still wedded to the unions and to unilateralism, whatever the leadership might say. People had been hurt by the recession, but they still believed that the Tories were the most trustworthy guardians of the public purse.

Additionally, the Labour Party had not yet acquired its ruthless campaigning discipline. To local Labour Party agents the idea of the Sheffield rally seemed folly when it was first mooted at a meeting with campaign co-ordinators in February. Surely Labour Party members would be better deployed knocking on people's doors than travelling hundreds of miles to attend a fancy event? When Mike Newell, the director of *Dance with a Stranger* and *Four Weddings and a Funeral*, produced a party election broadcast for the Labour Party in which a young girl was denied treatment for 'glue ear', the party's failure fully to research the case on which the story was based led to a week of headlines that portrayed the party as at best manipulative and at worst incompetent. The girl in question, Jennifer Bennett, had both a Tory mother and a Tory councillor grandfather.

In the last days of the campaign the Labour Party ran out of steam. Kinnock was jetting round the country in a mad show of youthful vigour, but most of the head office team was exhausted. Telephones were left unanswered, Conservative attacks were not rebutted and people took their eye off the ball. Paddy Ashdown, as leader of the Liberal Democrats, had been determined to get proportional representation on the agenda, and as the polls in the last week showed Labour and Conservatives neck and neck, he argued that in order to provide stability in the event of a hung Parliament, the Liberal Democrats should form a five-year agreement with one or other of the parties, in exchange for PR. The official Labour Party line had always been that Labour anticipated forming its own majority Government, but the Monday before the election Kinnock intimated that he might do a deal with the Liberal Democrats. It was a disastrous slip. It suggested uncertainty and lack of confidence.

On the doorsteps of Hampstead and Highgate these matters scarcely mattered. The issues were health and education – Labour won on these, as it did almost everywhere – and taxation, the economy and Neil Kinnock, where Labour lost badly, not least thanks to the vitriolic Tory campaign, which succeeded in persuading at least one unemployed man in Kilburn that he would pay an extra £1,000 a year in tax if John Smith ever became Chancellor of the Exchequer.

Contrary to popular conception, canvassing – as it was still called in 1992 – is not about persuading people to vote for you. All the evidence suggests that this is a fruitless exercise, as most voters will tell you anything to get rid of you. Instead, voter identification, as it is now called, is a matter of finding out who is intending to vote for you and making sure they actually vote, by keeping in touch with them, by giving them postal vote forms, by reminding them to vote on the day, and even by dragging them out of their bath and hauling them round to the polling station as 10 p.m. approaches, if necessary. Leaflets, letters, posters and street stalls help to get your message across, but actual contact with the candidate is most likely to encourage a potential supporter to vote. Pressing the flesh takes courage, but it is one of the political arts at which Glenda excels. Whether on the doorstep or outside the tube, Glenda manages to transfix people with an intensity that most candidates do not dare to assume. She listens, she remembers people, and she is endowed with phenomenal reserves of energy.

The writer Julian Barnes was one of the many thousands of

people canvassed by Glenda, a moment he described for the *New Yorker*.

> She [did not] try to stun me with glamour; her face was devoid of makeup, her hair was wind-battered, and the scarlet trousers that glared from beneath her long brown coat added a homely rather than a dashing touch. She listened attentively to my views, asked for my assistance, and after a couple of minutes – but it seemed longer, much longer – she departed with a friendly smile. I realized as I watched her go that *l'esprit de l'escalier* also strikes those standing at the top of the steps. My best quips and questions have gone unvoiced. But when Glenda Jackson comes to call, as a Labour candidate soliciting your vote in the general election, you do tend to get a bit tongue-tied.

At public meetings – a now antiquated form of campaigning that still reigns in Hampstead – Glenda was equally magnificent, if prone to generalisations and moral assertions. Barnes again: 'While the others speak Glenda Jackson sits with almost alarming stillness, perhaps a relaxation technique learned in the theatre. No anxious shuffling around, no couldn't disagree with you more scribbling on a pad in front of her ... her speaking style is equally crisp, and, needless to say, the microphone is unnecessary: "I'm not showing off, but if I can't be heard, who can?"'[5]

Glenda once described her feelings about speaking in public:

> I think we generate our own fears. And sometimes they can be useful and sometimes they can be crippling. I used to worry when I didn't get stage fright. You have a heightened awareness which you can trace to psychological things. But you have to be as ready as you can be. If you watch an athlete – I noticed this particularly in the Olympics, I found I could know who was going to win in the single events because the people who won, and we are talking about minuscule time differences between winning and coming second, but the person who a fraction of a second before the gun went off just let go. Some

inner voice, and that is a process I can relate to. It's not about becoming free of self-consciousness. It's just about, well, letting go. Harder to explain than to do.[6]

Meanwhile, Glenda's campaign team was leaving nothing to chance in the pursuit of weekly photo opportunities. Twins called Hannah and Jessica were identified who were turning eighteen and would be first-time Labour voters. Glenda Jackson boxing gloves were made for them for a 'Glenda's double whammy' photograph for the *Mirror* (which was spiked in favour of the news of Prince Andrew's impending divorce). When the Union of Jewish Students suggested that Glenda might take part in an anti-prejudice campaign featuring a photo opportunity with Clare Short and a small herd of goats on Abingdon Green, opposite the House of Commons, again Glenda was game for it. Sadly Mrs Thatcher had declared the day beforehand that she would not be contesting the second round of the Tory leadership ballot, and journalists had just trampled the green into a virtual mudbath. Yet another campaign idea failed to see the light. But there were successes, and Glenda managed to secure two 'stunt of the day' prizes in the *Guardian*.

Glenda did not receive universally favourable coverage during the campaign. The *Evening Standard*'s theatre critic, Nicholas de Jongh, never a Glenda groupie, reviewed her appearance at the Holly Lodge Community Centre a week into the campaign:

> How, I wondered, would this most aloof and supercilious of actresses fare in the down-to-earth business of electioneering. I have watched Glenda Jackson facing the public and the Press in the past. And on those occasions I concluded that I had never seen an actress, or an actor, exuding such boredom, such reluctance to engage in small talk with people. Now that she had gone into politics, would she put on a new face? She arrived, or rather she walked on . . . looking every inch an actress. Charisma cannot be lightly set aside. Miss Jackson moves with airs and graces.

De Jongh recognised that 'it takes real bravery, real daring at the age of 55 to sacrifice the rewards and glamour of an international career on stage and screen for Westminster's dogfight. She has just taken on the hardest and boldest role of her life.' Yet he felt that she never really engaged with any of the ordinary people she met. She looked 'impassive, miles away', listening to a social worker, her approach was 'rather impersonal, low-key and distant', and she reminded him of Kenneth Tynan's description of Edith Evans: 'her characteristic late manner, tranquillised benevolence cascading from a great height, like royalty opening a bazaar'.[7] Glenda's Press officer, Tim Walker, resolved never again to allow a newspaper to send a theatre or arts critic to do a profile of Glenda.

There were other problems. Labour councillors had voted in a new, punitive controlled-parking system for Hampstead village, and an £11 increase in council rents, which Glenda could not condemn without confusing Labour supporters, and which she could not openly support without drawing the wrath of prominent local residents like Boy George – who announced he would be voting against Glenda because of her vacillation. Some people complained that Glenda was not 'cuddly' enough, that she never thanked her campaign team for anything, that she was mean with her money. The vast Press entourage that attempted to follow Glenda around was also putting off ordinary voters, so Glenda not only acquired a minder, Simon MacDonald, but the media were deliberately sent on wild goose chases to give Glenda a chance to meet the public unencumbered. Through all this Glenda was both full of energy and exceedingly even-tempered, and although there were occasional rows over her timetable it was extraordinary that Glenda, who had a reputation as a difficult actress to direct, took the fact that a whole body of people had suddenly taken over her life in her stride. If anything, she seemed to relish the tight schedule, the need to think on her feet, the bossiness with which everyone minded her. It was a challenging campaign for Tim Walker, but he was happy at the end of it to write notes for any future Press officer: 'Glenda Jackson is her own woman and will be even more so by the time she has been an MP for five years. The better your relationship with her the easier it will be. However, if you arrange too much without her consent there will be trouble.'

Polling day is in equal measures tiring and frustrating for candidates. For the party faithful there are polling stations to staff, poll numbers to be collected, and last-minute reminder leaflets to be delivered (Hampstead and Highgate started receiving its last leaflet at 5.30 that morning). There are lifts to the poll to be organised, and there are complicated arithmetical calculations to be made to determine whether turnout in key areas is going well. There is not much to do for the candidate: only circling the polling stations and the key estates with a loudhailer, rallying, thanking, praising the troops and preparing yourself for the count.

In Glenda's case the count was to be held jointly with Holborn and St Pancras in Camden Council's tatty but large St Pancras Town Hall. As Frank Dobson's agent I recall leaving my home near Old Street just as the polls were closing to get to the count before the first of the ballot boxes, confident that Frank would have won – I guessed a majority of 10,000 – but uncertain whether he would be moving out of the Shadows and into a Government Ministry. As the cab turned the corner by King's Cross station I remember hearing the BBC's exit polls, which suggested that the Conservatives were likely to be the largest party. Labour had lost. My own calculations in Holborn and St Pancras suggested a 2.5 per cent swing to Labour, half what Labour needed to form a majority, but almost exactly what Glenda would need to win. As the two Camden Labour Parties had booked the Camden Palais, with a sixteen-foot-square back-projection screen, for the results party, my only hope now was that at least Glenda would win.

Election counts should be exciting. Invariably they are fractious and tedious and their moments of exhilaration are brief. When the result finally comes it is not even a surprise for any of the candidates and their agents, as they have been given a chance to challenge the figures and the contested ballot papers before the public announcement. In Glenda's case the tedium was exacerbated by the appalling inefficiency of the council officers. The result was expected at 1.00 a.m., but at 2.00 the ballot papers had not even been verified, and it was another hour and a quarter before the returning officer was ready to call the agents and candidates together to agree to the announcement. In the meantime the results had been drifting in. Chris Patten, the Conservative Party Chairman, had lost his Bath seat to the Liberals, but by midnight it was clear that John Major's removal company would not yet be required. When Glenda turned up at St Pancras Town Hall the Labour camp was in a weary and disconsolate mood. Sally Dobson was caught between two feelings – sadness that her father was evidently not on the eve of a ministerial career, and hope that Glenda might do better than the national average. The supporters in the Camden Palais had further worries. The fact that there was still no result at 2.30 a.m. suggested that it was too close to call, and that there might be a recount. In fact Camden Council was just being slow. In the hall, though, it looked as if Glenda had lost. Labour Party polling agents were convinced of it. Unofficial counts of the first ballot boxes seemed to give Letwin a three-to-two majority, but the Tory agents were just as convinced that Letwin was doomed because there were not enough crosses for David Wrede, the Liberal candidate. Liberal Democrats must have decided to back Glenda. As the papers started to be sorted into their piles and then clipped in bundles of 500 with red, blue and yellow hair grips, the Labour camp grew more desolate. Blue grips extended the whole length of the far distant table. Red ones scarcely made it into the corner. Frank Dobson suggested shunting some of his spare votes over – an unconventional brand of PR.

Finally the assistant returning officer summoned the agents and candidates, and there were suppressed smiles from William Cullerne Bown. It seemed that the counting agents had been piling the red grips on top of each other. Within moments the cameras – BBC, ITN, Canada, Japan, Italy, Spain, Australia, CNN – moved into position, and the agents and candidates were summoned on to the stage. Glenda had won, by 1,440 votes, a swing of twice the national average. William alternated between looking sheepish and smug. Letwin affected stoicism. And Glenda, dressed in a schoolish black and white, with two awkwardly posed roses on her left lapel, extended a grateful, slightly embarrassed, open-handed salute.

CHAPTER TWELVE

Power at Last

IN THE DAYS THAT FOLLOWED the 1992 general election Glenda struggled with mixed emotions. On the one hand she had fulfilled an ambition. She was ready to take on her new career, and she was filled with anticipation about signing on at the Palace of Westminster. After two years as a candidate, and almost as many decades of increasing theatrical restlessness, she would be able to take action, rather than just hold opinions. On the other hand she was bitterly disappointed that Labour had lost the election. Early on the morning of 10 April her friend Neil Kinnock had swiftly conceded defeat. His words could easily have been Glenda's:

> I naturally feel a strong sense of disappointment, not so much for myself, for I am fortunate, very fortunate in my personal life. But I feel dismay, sorrow, for so many people in our country who do not share this personal good fortune and who, as a result of further years of Tory Government, will experience further disadvantage. They deserve better than they got on April 9, 1992.[1]

Two days later he announced his resignation as leader of the Labour Party and made way for his shadow chancellor, John Smith.

Among others, Glenda blamed the national Labour Party for the defeat. Only days after the election she sounded off in her response to the official questionnaire about the national party's assistance: the key seats candidates unit at Millbank was 'totally useless – A WASTE OF TIME'; the national campaign posters were 'not brutal enough'; and the international Press was a 'pain in the ass'. It was only by virtue of the twinning arrangements with the next-door constituency party and by the valiant efforts of her campaign team that Hampstead and Highgate had managed to buck the trend. Glenda's sense of depression and frustration was intense. Her ability to 'do something more useful for people' was to be severely restricted by the fact that she was no more than an inexperienced backbench Opposition MP – Opposition offered scant opportunity to redress the injustices of the Tory years.

Experience – above all parliamentary experience – counted for much in a Parliament where remarkably few members were new. Knowing how the Commons worked, how to play the game, even how to find the Chamber, was important in a system still heavily dominated by old men. Glenda soon bemoaned the fact that there were scarcely any women's toilets in the building, and the complexity of its layout. 'I have already been lost three times,' she complained to her diary on 27 April, 'I do not know where I am supposed to be, never mind how to get there. And no matter where I do walk, I seem to end up next to a statue of Winston Churchill.' Three days later she was still losing her way:

> I am lost in faceless corridors. There is not a statue of Winston Churchill to be seen. Then suddenly a figure appears from a side door. For one terrible moment I think I have solved the mystery of Lord Lucan. Then I recognise the reassuring figure of Douglas Hurd. Following at a respectful distance I allow him to lead me to the Commons lobby and to safety. Later I reflect on my fortune at coming across the Foreign Secretary. Had it been the Secretary of State for Transport I would probably have been left wandering the corridors of power for ever.[2]

She told me that acquiring an office was an equally frustrating task:

> The actual business of becoming an MP was all just terribly mysterious. In theory it was just a matter of coming in, getting your pass and putting in a letter for an office. In practice, you knew you weren't going to get one for ages but you set about trying to organise an

office. It was nightmarish, even though I gather this was the first time all the political parties published little booklets on what to do as a new MP – because of course people have forgotten they know the things you really need to know, so it seems you're always asking daft questions.

She wrote of her troubles in the *Independent*:

People have said to me that your first week in the Commons is like your first week at school. My school was never like this. People told you what to do, they were less friendly, and there were more girls. I also had a desk. At the moment I am working out of a corridor. A phone is nothing more than a hopeless fancy; an office, the promised land.

That was Wednesday. On Thursday Glenda was at least in a temporary office, but again she was troubled: 'My researcher [her son Dan] and assistant [Sally Dobson] have phoned me to find where I am and I am unable to tell them. All I can say is that I am in faceless room 403. It is like something from *Nineteen Eighty-Four*.'[3]

Glenda was also less than impressed by the labyrinthine and anachronistic traditions of Westminster, which reminded her of nothing so much as a public-school debating society. 'My first week is nearly at an end. But my ignorance remains less than blissful,' she confessed with self-deprecatory humour. 'A fire alarm sounds and I make immediately for the nearest exit. Then someone kindly points out it is in fact the Division Bell and when it rings in future I should make for the Commons Chamber. I have not heard the real fire alarm yet but this seems likely a recipe for tragedy.' She found these minor eccentricities of the parliamentary system both amusing and irksome:

You see, it's all predicated on the British love for being as bloody-minded and as unhelpful as it is possible to be, dressed up in the guise of tradition, practice and being fair. It has nothing to do with any of those things. It seems to me to be part and parcel of what is still strong in Britain and something that has to be changed: the belief that amateurs are better than professionals. Well they're not.

From the start the inadequacy of Parliament, and Labour's failure to win power, created a strong emphasis on the one part of the job which truly was about achieving results and which most resembled her former intent to be a social worker – constituency casework. In itself this was a major new experience. Glenda said that: 'I was actually dealing with a constituency case the Sunday after the election and I'd never done that before in my life. Which highlights the absurdity of this place, namely that you *are* the Member of Parliament and there is absolutely nothing to support you in that from Westminster.' She takes a genuine pride in her constituency work, although she admits how little an MP can achieve:

> Sometimes you can do something for people and sometimes you can't. And what I've always found absolutely amazing is (a) how people are always grateful though in fact you're simply doing your job, and (b) how even when you don't get them the result they still say thank you. I find that very touching, because we are talking about people whose lives are shot to hell, and shot to hell because of political decisions.

This resolute commitment to dealing with individual problems has attracted Glenda almost universal commendation. When one constituent discovered I was writing a biography of Glenda he rang me to gush over the phone at inordinate length about the 'delightful' Glenda and 'everything she has done for me and my family'. Another told me, 'I expected Glenda to be very frightening, but she was brilliant at putting me at my ease. She explained it all to me and wrote I don't know how many letters.' Several have recounted how surprised they were that Glenda remembered their names and all their details several months after seeing them. As with the rest of Glenda's life, there is no fuss at her extremely regular surgeries. She is candid and matter of fact, she gives people time, she listens to them, and although she rarely provides them with the answer they were anticipating, she comes across as genuinely interested in the problems her constituents bring to her. The issues are immensely various: persuading the council that they should rehouse a young black couple suffering racial abuse from their neighbours; fighting immigration battles with the Home Office; righting mis-determination of Social Security benefits; even arbitrating in noisy-neighbour disputes.

As Glenda was preparing for her first surgery, though, her opponents in Hampstead and Highgate were trying to contest the result of the election on the basis of two elderly voters who had turned up at the polling station on election day only to be told that someone had already cast proxy votes for them. The Conservative agent accused Glenda of vote-rigging, demanded a rerun (despite Glenda's 1,440 majority), and reported the matter to the police, who proceeded to investigate. This was to take six months and, as is the case with most battles over the casting of proxy and postal votes, the result was inconclusive. The police found that there had been two minor cases of forgery – probably by one unidentified person – but that there had been no material breach of the Representation of the People Act (which governs elections), and that therefore the election itself was sound. Glenda herself was in no way incriminated. This did not stop the Hampstead and Highgate Conservative Association. 'This is a very grave and serious matter,' the new Conservative agent, Carl Gibson, expostulated. 'In view of the confirmation from Scotland Yard that offences have been committed, we are now considering applying to the High Court for a writ to overturn the result. We held this seat for more than twenty years and we cannot allow Glenda Jackson to remain in office while police have evidence that such offences took place.' Glenda was infuriated that she was effectively being accused of vote-rigging (the headlines ran 'Fake votes for Glenda Jackson' and 'Glenda Jackson in vote-rigging row'), but she eventually shrugged off the allegations as 'sour grapes'.

Despite Glenda's mixed feelings about the Commons' recondite way of doing business ('sheer awkwardness dressed up as quaint idiosyncrasy' as another MP who was new in 1992 described it), Glenda was quick off the mark with her maiden speech, rising to address the House of Commons for the first time only a month and two days after the election, two days after her fifty-sixth birthday.

The conventions governing maiden speeches are every bit as

rigid as those attending every other Westminster tradition. New MPs are expected to praise their predecessor, even if they fought a bitter campaign against them, and are expected to talk rhapsodically of their constituency and to adhere to non-contentious issues. In return for adhering to these conventions the House hears the new Member's speech in silence.

The content of Glenda's speech provided no surprises. She started with a warm tribute to her predecessor, Sir Geoffrey Finsberg, before moving on to an elegant if slightly sarcastic attempt to counter the general impression of the Hampstead and Highgate constituency:

> There is a popular myth regarding my constituency, one much loved by the Press, of a leafy suburb populated solely by millionaires whose only drink is champagne and whose only conversational exchange could be deemed to be chatter. The facts make a rather different picture. The largest single group in my constituency consists of pensioners, and the largest group within that group consists of those on some form of social benefit. This month, 5,000 of my constituents are unemployed. In the borough of which my constituency is part, 1,000 families have no home of their own.

She stretched the conventions banning maiden speech controversy sufficiently to have a dig at John Major's Government for its stance on immigration, on education, and on Third World Aid. She argued that:

> The Prime Minister has spoken of his wish to provide ladders of opportunity for our people. However, a ladder can be a dangerous place if it is not rooted on a solid foundation and leaning against an equally solid wall. If it is dangerous for the most able-bodied amongst us, how much more dangerous is it for the very old and the very young, the frail and the disabled? My constituents welcome the idea of greater opportunities being provided, but the opportunities must be available to all our people and they must be based on the solid building blocks of

education, training, health care free for all at the point
of delivery and, perhaps most important of all, decent
affordable social housing.

Glenda ended with a moment of genuine modesty. 'It is a great
privilege for any person to be called to the House as a Member. It is
a particular privilege for me to represent the people of Hampstead
and Highgate. I am grateful and deeply proud that I represent them.'
The words of the speech were conventional and the delivery was
straight. It was remarkable, though, especially to those who
expected that the double Oscar-winning actress would be an expert
speaker, that Glenda was visibly nervous. Glenda confesses as much:

I have never been as frightened in my life, and I know
the feeling of fear well. I still can't define why I should
have been so petrified. The house was by no means full.
I had sat, however, from 2.30 to 8.30 waiting to be called,
and I was frozen stiff. Then it suddenly hit me I was
actually the representative of more than 60,000 people.
And I was thinking all the time of all the magicians of
the English language who have lived in Hampstead. I
kept on thinking of Keats, bugger me, he would have
been one of mine. I shook, my knees were going and I
felt sick.[4]

Part of Glenda's fear undoubtedly sprang from the fact that the
moment she arrived in the Commons she was aware that others
had high expectations of her. She was not the only celebrity to be
elected in 1992: the Olympic gold-medallist Sebastian Coe was
the new Conservative MP for Falmouth and Camborne; and the
broadcaster and author Giles Brandreth, another Conservative, had
been elected for Chester. But Glenda was undoubtedly the darling
of the media and: 'When I came in everybody was waiting for me
to fall flat on my face.' A mixture of envy, faux contempt for success
and a genuine incomprehension of Glenda's motives made many
of her new colleagues, even in her own party, at least suspicious,
and at worst resentful, of her. In this context there was a very real
danger that the traits that had been Glenda's strengths in the theatre
– determination, a preference for work over sociability, intellectual

rigour – would prove to be weaknesses in her new metier. After all, politics requires a particular brand of amiability and interminable patience, without which a politician, especially an individualistic one, can appear aloof and arrogant.

Glenda's tactic was both astute and typically down to earth. Chris Smith, now Secretary of State for Culture, Media and Sport and a neighbouring London MP, says that,

> One of the best things about Glenda is that from the moment of arriving in the House of Commons she refused to play the *grande dame*. She was a figure with a big reputation, so amongst some members of the party there was something of an ambivalent attitude. In fact, some were a bit worried that the Labour Party was being hijacked by Glenda Jackson. But she managed especially well after being elected to scotch those concerns, because she went out of her way to say 'Yes, I had a past, but that's all over now. Now I am a politician and I'll earn my way just like anyone else.' She never once traded on her reputation, despite being deluged with requests to adorn the playbill for public meetings.

Indeed Glenda was only too aware of how negatively actors-turned-politicians can be viewed:

> The perception of the profession is based upon those whom people see regularly, and so actors are presumed (a) to be millionaires, which comes from America, and (b) to live outside what is deemed to be a real or ordinary life. And we're expected to be stupid. I did find it surprising here [in Westminster] I must admit. You would think that politicians would have some knowledge of what the world is like outside, but they all seemed to think that we're somehow exotic. I found that such an old-fashioned view of what the theatre was like, that it was very illuminating as to just how little many politicians know about the world outside this place. It can be very seductive, clearly, Parliament. I mean Parliament, I don't mean politics, I mean the actual place itself, which for many

politicians who happily no longer represent the people, was the be all and end all. For them it was not the result of the decisions that were made, nor how they affected people's lives outside, that mattered, but what was actually happening within these pseudo-Gothic corridors. I found that very surprising.

Glenda's greatest asset in the war to be taken seriously has always been self-deprecation. In all her interviews in her first years as an MP she dismissed any talk of promotion, and announced that she had not visited the theatre or a gallery for years. She openly and regularly laughed at herself for her incompetence. 'I am getting better,' she told the *Guardian*. 'Yesterday I only made three mistakes, including rising in a standing committee to say something, only to find that I was speaking on the wrong amendment.' Her so-called 'raunchy past' also came in for a few digs. She told one journalist, 'I was pulling my knickers up the other day and the door to my office was open, when my secretary shrieked in astonishment and rushed to protect my modesty. I reminded her that as two-thirds of the world has already seen me stark naked, I'm not really going to worry about my arse being exposed.'[5]

Certainly parliamentary colleagues found themselves caught off guard by Glenda. One Labour MP told me: 'I found it very difficult arguing with her over a Treasury bill early in 1993, because I kept on thinking of *Elizabeth R* and wondering whether she would require my immediate execution.' Another told me, 'Glenda seemed from the start to be resolutely interested in the least glamorous of issues, housing, public transport and dredgers, and it really disconcerted those of us who anticipated a constant run of theatrical anecdotes.' The left-winger Alan Simpson tells his own anecdote, however. Soon after the 1992 election he was stopped in the street in Nottingham by a constituent who wanted to shake his hand. Presuming he wanted to thank him for something or congratulate him on his recent election he was somewhat nonplussed to be told, 'I've always wanted to shake the hand of someone who sits next to Glenda Jackson.'

Glenda's past would not quite desert her. During the summer of 1992 Glenda's parliamentary office received a phone call from the airport. As the Commons switchboard had overridden the divert on the office phone, something that is normally done only for incoming calls from MPs, Sally Dobson presumed Glenda was on the line. In fact, it was Lauren Bacall, who had bullied her way through the operator. Miss Bacall had just landed at Heathrow and wondered whether Glenda was free for afternoon tea. Sally informed her that Glenda would be free in an hour's time. So Lauren Bacall came to tea at the House of Commons. Sadly, with Parliament in recess, the Commons tea-room was closed and tea had to be served in polystyrene cups in Glenda's tiny broom cupboard of an office. Nevertheless, several middle-aged MPs' heads were seen to turn as Glenda escorted her American guest around the Palace of Westminster.

Glenda also allowed herself a brief visit to Hollywood in 1992, although this was completely unnoticed by the UK Press, or even by her own office. The excuse was twofold. A new award for comedy had been initiated, in the name of the American comedian Jack Oakie, and the first recipient was to be Walter Matthau. When asked who he wanted to present the award to him Matthau had shown no hesitation in asking for Glenda. And at the same time the health of Glenda's friend Peter Bromilow was deteriorating dramatically, due to the ravages of HIV. In the summer recess Glenda took the opportunity of a brief holiday doing a tour of friends in Hollywood, catching up with John Schlesinger, Brenda Vaccaro and Charles Marowitz, and seeing Peter for the last time before his death. Apart from occasional visits by Matthau, Vaccaro and Segal to London, and her ongoing friendship with Dirk Bogarde, this was to be Glenda's last time spent hobnobbing with the stars.

Persistence has always been a Jackson strength, and in the five years of parliamentary Opposition that she had to endure she demonstrated that strength time and again. Like every other new MP she drafted vast arrays of parliamentary questions to ministers and to the prime minister. She spoke on everything from the Asylum and Immigration Appeals Bill to security in hospitals, homelessness and the civil rights of disabled people. Many of her speeches took a feminist turn: she was delighted to vote for the ordination of women; she complained that the House of Commons still had a shooting range but no crèche; and she supported Margaret Beckett for deputy leader of the Labour Party because it would be good 'to have a woman at the top'. Her gender is central to her politics.

> We are all standing on the shoulders of those women who went before us. Suffragettes died to give me the right to vote. One of the most heartbreaking experiences is when you meet a woman and she says, 'Oh, I never vote.' That really cuts me up. My feminism might well come from the fact that I was surrounded by women who were doing everything, but again, at the end of World War Two, they were told, as they were told at the end of the first, 'Thank you very much. Now you can go away. We can do it by ourselves.'

Surprisingly, she declared that:

> I do not believe that there is such a thing as a 'women's issue' and I would not be interested in arguing for it if I did. But undoubtedly there is a female dimension in all of us. For far too long the world has been governed and ruled by masculine perceptions, and has been presented as entirely their preserve. There is a whole other area of human experience, imagination and perception that could be dubbed female, although it does not always and exclusively reside in women. It is time for that balance to begin to percolate through, so that the world can indeed become a better and more equal place, not only for women, but for men too.[6]

The personal traits that had at times made her a difficult colleague as an actress have, instead, made her an excellent campaigning politician. Her candour lends her an aura of principle, while the sharpness of her tongue makes her adept at political invective. And her workaholism saw her through the countless late-night sittings. Some of her political positions have been unexpected. She argued for keeping Sunday special (on the grounds that people needed a rest from work). She voted *against* changing the age of consent for gay men from twenty-one to eighteen – on the grounds that she could not vote for continuing inequality, and that she preferred to emphasise her support for equality at sixteen.

Despite the myriad of bills and debates on which Glenda spoke, she soon devoted herself virtually exclusively to a single, unambiguously unglamorous issue – public transport. In part this was thanks to her constituency. Hampstead and Highgate lies within striking distance of Euston, King's Cross, St Pancras, Paddington and Marylebone stations, and British Rail is one of the biggest employers in her constituency. Moreover, the train drivers' union Aslef had not only provided Glenda with a campaign office, but had become official sponsors of her campaign. Glenda was also fired up with indignation about the Conservatives' apparent disregard for public transport. Even when she appeared on the *Michael Parkinson Show* in the seventies she confessed that she was racked with guilt every time she stepped into her own car rather than take the bus or train. As a long-time Londoner she was passionate about the London Underground and the plight of those condemned to commute on overcrowded, unreliable and often unsafe ancient rolling stock. When the Conservatives decided to privatise British Rail by selling off the stations and tracks to Railtrack, and selling separate franchises for different parts of the network, Glenda was prompted into action. She sat on all the privatisation bills' standing committees, and became an ardent opponent of privatisation, harrying ministers not only on the grounds of ideology but for their incompetence, their waste and the poverty of their ideas.

In the meantime the Labour Party had changed dramatically. Under Neil Kinnock Labour had started the process of ideological reform, abandoning unilateralism, recusing on opposition to the European Union and rejecting the rhetoric of class politics. The mantra of 'as resources allow' had become every Labour spokesperson's protection against rash financial commitments, but the 1992 manifesto still retained a belief in the redistribution of wealth at its economic core, and the trade unions were still considered an intrinsic and inalienable element of the Labour machinery. The electorate still mistrusted Labour's economic competence, and they believed every fiscal scare the Tories could dream up about life under Labour.

By the end of 1996 Labour was virtually unrecognisable. Even its name had changed, with the subtle interpolation of a single word, 'new', on the Labour Party conference set in Blackpool in autumn 1996. At first the changes were slow under John Smith, but when he died, suddenly, soon after the local elections in May 1994, the subsequent leadership election finally offered a chance to leave behind the disappointments of the 1992 election. Instead of clinging to security by electing one of their own, the party chose to risk a far more radical process of modernisation by overwhelmingly opting for a man with no roots in the party other than his own conscious choice – Tony Blair.

In both of these leadership races Glenda was on the winning side. She supported John Smith over Bryan Gould in 1992, and in 1994 she signed up early to the Blair campaign, this time, along with many others, renouncing her support for Margaret Beckett and backing John Prescott for deputy leader. At each of the staging posts on the route to New Labour Glenda sided with the modernisers. Against the advice of her local party's activists (but with her local members), she supported the introduction of Tony Blair's Clause IV to the Labour Party constitution, just as she had gone against her local party in supporting the leadership's position on the Gulf War.

Although she shares many perceptions with Blair, however, Glenda is not an instinctive moderniser. For instance, she has always argued for a right balance between rights and responsibilities, a political stance that, in the early 1990s, placed her firmly on the right of the Labour Party, and in the 1990s is an indispensable element of New Labour thinking. But her concern for radical causes such as homelessness and Third World aid and her class-consciousness, ally her more with Prescott than with Blair. Indeed she confesses that she is 'extremely doubtful that there is something called Blairism'. Many of her political views would not normally grace a Blairite conversation: 'If the Royal Family cannot change drastically and dramatically then I can see no place for them and it's ludicrous that we're expected to curtsy before minor royals,'[7] she declared in October 1992. Her hatred of Margaret Thatcher is intense and at odds with Blair's arms-length respect for the former premier: 'She acted as a poultice on the worst aspects of the English national character, and drew them like a boil to the surface.

Selfishness, greed, mean-spiritedness, wanting to see yourself one-up from your next-door neighbour.'[8] Even in 1992 Glenda was still complaining that 'we are reaping the whirlwind of that dreadful, dreadful woman'.[9] Glenda's list of political concerns looks and sounds very traditionally socialist: 'If Dickens were to return to London today he would find that much had changed. But not that much. There is quite a lot that he would recognise. He would recognise the poverty. He would recognise the homelessness. He would recognise the mentally ill wandering aimlessly about.' Her list of moral evils again gives the impression of a very traditional left-winger:

> If you leave people believing they can only survive in what is an increasingly hostile and dangerous world by their own efforts, in a sense you are giving a free pass to greed, selfishness, ruthlessness and exploitation of the weakest. Not everyone is capable of defending themselves: the very young, the old, the frail, the disabled. I think it behoves us as we claim to live in a civilised society to attempt to balance those inequities.[10]

Such rhetoric makes Glenda appear very old Labour, but, in her opinion, the 1992 election showed very clearly that an ideologically obsessed, or a disunited, party would not oust the Tories, and she believed that any serious politician had to be interested in more than just making fine speeches from the Opposition. In the cause of justice, power was every bit as important as ideological purity. After all, she had not renounced acting to spend all her time bemoaning the ills of the world, but to take action on behalf of those whose lives had been 'shot to hell' by politicians' decisions. She has always been far more practical than ideological. She was one of the initial signatories of Charter 88, calling for electoral reform and proportional representation. Thanks to pragmatism she changed her mind about the European Union, explaining that:

> I voted against joining the EEC all those years ago, but now I've had a complete turnaround really. It does seem to me to be the way forward for this country given that we have had to start punching our real weight, post-Empire, post the ascendancy of America. We can't

take on the rest of the world on our own, we simply aren't big enough. So economically it makes sense, but of course the reason the European Union came into being was to stop France and Germany going at each other and dragging the rest of the world after them and that seems to me to have worked.

Even on her pet subject, the privatisation of the railways, Glenda accepted the logic that Labour could not commit itself to buying back Railtrack or cancelling the rail franchises. Not only would this be immensely costly at a time when a Labour Chancellor would be hard-pressed to find money for equally urgent needs like schools and hospitals, but the dogmatic overtones of such a policy would frighten the electorate, both in Middle England, and in Labour's heartlands. Glenda rejoiced in the common-sense approach of new Labour, she saw the logic of Blair's position, and above all she believed in maintaining the united front of the party. She had been elected as a Labour MP, not as Glenda Jackson, and she would fight the party's corner come what may, even if it meant being derided by the left wing for her acquiescence. Neil Kinnock says that:

> She's not Blairite, she's Jacksonite. Her natural incli-
> nation is towards loyalty because she doesn't suffer fools
> gladly – and she hates loose ends. She understands that
> the victory of ideals has to be organised. And the great
> thing about her is that she could be the most loyal party
> machine woman and never lose the edge of her con-
> victions.

The new leadership of the Labour Party lost little time in recognising Glenda's campaigning élan and loyalty. It took a little longer, though, to comprehend that she was genuinely far more interested in public transport policy than in the arts. Even as a new backbench MP Glenda found it easy to get publicity, an ability that infuriated some of her colleagues, but was extremely useful to the Labour Party, whose long sojourn in the wilderness had made it hungry for publicity. John Prescott, who led the Labour Party's parliamentary campaign team, was keen in 1994 to enlist Glenda as a parliamentary campaigner on arts issues. Despite a close friendship with the MP for

Hull she adamantly refused even to consider such an arts portfolio, arguing that she was the last person the party should use to speak on arts issues. Her views, she felt, would simply be dismissed because, as a former actress 'she would say that, wouldn't she'. It would be far better, Glenda thought, for her to campaign on something nobody would expect a double Oscar-winner to have views on.

At first, this refusal of a minor campaigning role seemed a mistake – after all, it is unusual to say no to the offer of a job in politics – but thanks to Glenda's evident and passionate interest in public transport it soon paid off. In Tony Blair's reshuffle of August 1996, which saw Clare Short lose her post as shadow transport secretary to Andrew Smith, Glenda became shadow transport minister under Smith – she was the first of the 1992 intake of MPs to join the Labour front bench. In policy terms this was ideal. Glenda was interested in the subject, and knew something about it, which is more than many politicians can claim when they take on a new portfolio. On a personal level, though, this was not destined to be a perfect match. As shadow chief secretary to the Treasury Andrew Smith had gained a reputation as a clever and ardent Blairite, and he shares with Glenda the virtues of assiduity and sheer political determination, but he is not a natural showman. The fact that Glenda found it extremely easy to attract attention for everything she did made this political deficiency all the more evident. Week in, week out the new shadow minister, ably assisted by her astute son Dan, who churned out a steady stream of Glenda Jackson Press releases, made the news. There were weekly pictures of Glenda in all the national newspapers, there were full-spread interviews with her in the quality magazines, and she became a regular on BBC Radio 4's *Today*. All of this made it even more difficult for Smith to make his mark in his first full departmental job, and there were rumours of friction between them. At one point it was even maintained, in the *Sunday Telegraph*, that Smith had issued an edict that Glenda should desist from issuing Press releases.

The Labour Party, however, was keen to use Glenda whenever possible, and she was a regular 'key campaigner'. In the summer of 1996, just after the launch of the Tory 'demon eyes' posters, and not long after Glenda's promotion, she was sent to Benidorm, on the Costa Brava. The idea was simple. Labour was keen to maintain the momentum of its electioneering and deflect attention from the Tory posters, so it had decided to run a summertime 'beach offensive', with visits from key Labour figures to holiday resorts both at home and abroad. The campaign needed to be fronted by someone with chutzpah and flair, so Glenda was the party's inevitable first choice to launch it. Posters ('No wonder you need a break . . . same old Tories, same old lies') were printed, and she set off for the sizzling heat of Benidorm. Glenda explains: 'It was the very first time we put up posters outside the UK and we had selected Benidorm because something like 14 million British people go there for their holidays in a year.' The trip was, however, risky. There was a danger that Glenda would be told robustly to leave people alone on their holiday, and that the whole idea would come across as a silly-season gimmick. Even the flight out was complicated, as when Glenda and her Press-office minder arrived at Heathrow they found that there was a sizeable contingent of the Press travelling with them. Glenda explains the problem:

> They were all up in first class and we were in economy, so they kept demanding, 'Why are you keeping her away from us?' Of course, if we had been travelling first class that would have been a story, wouldn't it? It was perfectly clear to me that they were all hoping the story they could wire back was that Glenda Jackson was pursued from a Spanish beach by irate British tourists. But that isn't what happened at all, and people were genuinely pleased to see us and thought it was a very good idea. There were some great photos, too, especially that one of me with the guys with the tattoos. I loved that. 'I've seen her with her kit off,' one said, which was wonderful. 'You and all of several million other people around the world,' I thought.

The trip paid off. One topless sunbather declared, 'It's so mad, it's brilliant.' And every single British newspaper carried the photographs. When Glenda got back to London and heard that John Prescott was complaining that he had been sent off to Cleethorpes while Glenda did Benidorm, she delighted in teasing him, 'Well, virtue is its own reward.'

This was not the last of Glenda's high-profile outings. Later in the year the party sent her to New York with Gordon Brown to raise funds for the general election from the American branches of the Labour Party. Yet again Glenda caught the headlines and the front-page photographs with her appearance in the heart of Broadway. Glenda seems to have enjoyed this particular stunt: 'I must say, I have been there several times to appear on stages in New York, and it's the first time I'd stood in the middle of Time Square, arms akimbo saying New York, New York.'

But Glenda was not entirely happy as a 'key campaigner'. She felt that this trading on her celebrity status demeaned her seriousness as a politician, and saw her real value as an MP in rebutting Tory assaults on the welfare state, in preventing the break-up and privatisation of British Rail, and in representing her constituents. Despite a redrawing of the Camden constituencies' boundaries which gave her an extra-safe Labour ward, she was also nervous about her own electoral position in Hampstead and Highgate. When the national Labour Party drew up a general election campaign timetable which would take her out of Hampstead for nineteen days during the campaign itself, she rebelled and declared quite publicly that she thought it was a mistake, 'because I felt very strongly that I had to be there and be seen to be there'. As usual she won her way, eventually spending most of the general election in Hampstead. Unlike her shadow cabinet neighbour Frank Dobson, who spent all bar three days of the campaign outside his own constituency, Glenda only strayed beyond Camden's confines for half a dozen high-profile visits to marginal seats.

The 1992–7 Parliament was the longest since the Second World War, and when John Major finally summoned up the courage to face the electorate in April 1997 he had almost prolonged his stay to its legal limit. This time, everybody in the Labour Party refused to allow themselves to foresee victory, even though the opinion polls had shown the Conservatives trailing by nearly twenty points for nearly five years. There was a steely determination in the party, bred of the intense disappointment of 1992, to ensure a victory. In many ways this, the longest campaign this century, was dull, and

dominated by issues of sleaze, Tory divisions and Major's vacilla-
tions. There were local issues to fight, but the Labour national
campaign was tightly controlled, with the party determined to present a united front. Only the Tories, suffering from an apparent
death wish, provided any light entertainment. Tim Smith was
forced to withdraw as Conservative candidate for Beaconsfield following revelations about MPs receiving 'cash for questions'. A
similarly accused Neil Hamilton refused to stand aside as Conservative candidate in Tatton, and a BBC war correspondent, the white-
suited Martin Bell, stood against him as an independent, assisted
by both the Liberal Democrats and the Labour Party.

In Hampstead and Highgate the result seemed a foregone conclusion, but Glenda felt anxious throughout the campaign:

> I said, 'I'm not doing enough, I'm not doing enough.
> Why am I not doing enough?' Of course, this time people
> knew me so I didn't have that hill to climb, and my real
> worry was that everywhere I went people kept on telling
> me, 'You don't need my vote. You're a shoe-in.' So I
> thought, 'We are not going to get them out.' That was
> my real worry. So we were still knocking up at a quarter
> to ten on Thursday evening.

The campaign was very different in tone from that of 1992. The
Tories had no real expectations of winning the seat, and, having
lost her novelty value, Glenda had only a very reduced media pack to
contend with. One thing pleased her. The Hampstead and Highgate
electorate faced the largest number of women candidates ever seen
in any seat – five in total.

Glenda's electoral worries were grossly exaggerated. The first of
May – an inauspicious day for John Major to have chosen for the
election – proved to be Labour's day. The hundreds of loyal Labour
Party workers assembled at the Royal Festival Hall on the South
Bank were soon delighted beyond their wildest dreams. The scale
of the victory was phenomenal. The Conservative share of the vote
was lower than it had been at any time since 1832, and 127 Tory
MPs lost their seats. Throughout the night the heads of cabinet
ministers tumbled: Malcolm Rifkind, Ian Lang, Michael Forsyth,
Tony Newton, William Waldegrave and, most famously, Michael

Portillo. Not only did Glenda romp home with a majority of 13,284 votes, but Tony Blair's new Parliamentary Party numbered no fewer than 418. He had a larger majority than any Labour leader in history, and his supporters danced the night away to the strains of D:ream's 'Things Can Only Get Better'. The following day John Major visited the Queen shortly before noon, and publicly announced that he would be stepping down as Conservative leader. Minutes later Tony Blair was kissing hands at Buckingham Palace. In a final moment of electoral showmanship he abandoned his chauffeur-driven car and walked the final yards to 10 Downing Street, surrounded by flag-waving loyal troops (most of them Labour Party staff).

The atmosphere over the next few days was extraordinary. Lack of sleep made most Labour candidates and new MPs curiously tetchy, and while Tony Blair got on with the business of appointing a cabinet and moving house, the majority of his troops had to return to their mundane lives, conscious that they were part of a new era, but unsure quite what they should be doing about it.

For Glenda this meant returning to the suburban tranquillity of Blackheath and getting on with the housework and the gardening. As a shadow cabinet minister of nine months' standing she was clearly in the running for a job in Government, but there was no guarantee that Blair would necessarily summon everyone out of the shadows into Government. Glenda did not spend her time consumed with worry, though, and when Downing Street tried to get in touch with her on the Monday following the election, she had gone shopping at Tesco's:

> I had a call over the tannoy at Tesco's – would I go to the customer service desk? My son rang and said, 'You've had a call from No. 10, you'd better come back.' So I went back home and rang them, and the prime minister told me that he wanted me to be a minister and I said thank you and I put the phone down. The phone rang again and this voice said 'Minister?', and I said 'Yes' and the voice at the other end laughed and told me that a car would be there to take me to the Department of the Environment in twenty minutes, and there I was, in the middle of a big briefing session for new ministers.

The job of Parliamentary Under Secretary for Transport is not a glamorous one. Glenda's brief covers aviation, London transport and shipping, and her daily business is mundane to an extreme: dredgers, bus routes, London Underground rolling stock, franchises, health and safety and cycling. Glenda once admitted that 'I have a low boredom threshold which is one of the reasons I find acting interesting – it stays difficult. I'm sure being an MP would be equally difficult and therefore interesting.' It is fortunate that the workaholic in Glenda also relishes the mundane and the routine.

Like any other minister, Glenda's decisions have drawn fire from both political opponents and vested-interest groups. Her refusal to bring in a high-speed rail link to North Wales, or to ban early-morning flights to Gatwick have attracted criticism. The left has condemned her plans for the London Underground as semi-privatisation. The right has complained that she has not done enough to bring private investment into the transport system. The libertarians have argued that her insistence on integrated transport systems and her desire to get people out of their cars is an infringement of personal freedom.

Two decisions struck closer to Glenda's own history. In October 1997 the *Sapphire*, a Scottish trawler, went down with all hands off Peterhead. The families of the deceased argued passionately for the raising of the boat so that they could hold funerals on land, but after a period of prevarication the Government decided that it could not set the precedent and would not pay for the raising of the boat. Glenda had the unpleasant task of announcing the decision. She tried to explain that the sea was 'a noble grave', but both the decision and Glenda's manner of announcing it were immediately condemned by the *Sapphire* families, who soon collected the £500,000 they needed through Scottish newspapers. One Scottish MP told me, 'Glenda was so cold and arrogant in the way she told those families what they should feel it really came across very badly. For a while at least there certainly wasn't much love lost for Glenda in Scotland.' Shirley Stephen, the youngest of the widows, explained her feelings: 'Glenda Jackson's reaction only made us more determined. We wanted to prove her wrong. While our men were still at sea, our grieving had to be put on hold. For a long time, there was nothing tangible for us to cry over.'

Glenda's proposals for the replacement of four coastguard stations with digital equipment in August 1998 inspired similar personal lobbying and equally strong words from the trade unions, who claimed that 'health and safety is being sacrificed on the altar of accountancy'. Glenda snapped back on the *Today* programme, 'I am not prepared to tolerate this kind of misinformation and scaremongering that says this strategy would in any way put our lives at sea at risk. I repeat: this Government would not tolerate for ten seconds any such proposal in any manner or form.' For all her asseverations, the RNLI felt that Glenda was betraying her own family history, and they presented her with a photograph of 'Father' William Jackson and the Hoylake lifeboat as a reminder of the value of the personal touch in lifesaving – and in politics.

The brusque, even peremptory, tone that Glenda occasionally adopts as a minister has attracted its own fair share of criticism, especially at a time when the libertarian right in British politics has tried to attack Tony Blair's brand of socialism as 'nannyish'. It is an element of Glenda's ministerial style that has delighted the political sketch writers. In the *Guardian* Simon Hoggart chortled at Glenda's solemn parliamentary advocacy of the 'Walking Steering Group', which she chairs. In *The Times*, mindful of Glenda's experiences on a train in *The Music Lovers*, Matthew Parris delighted in one MP's request that the minister accompany him on a train journey through his constituency. In the *Daily Telegraph* Robert Hardman complained about Glenda's views on travel arrangements to the Millennium Dome in Greenwich:

> 'I am strongly against kiss and drop,' warned Miss Jackson. 'It is an anomaly and an anachronism and I would very strongly argue that the idea should be dropped.' There we have it. The parent doing the school run, the wife dropping the husband at the station, the neighbour giving a friend a lift to the shops – they are all guilty of an anachronistic anomaly. In New Britain, we should all be making our own way via wonderful public transport. Out, vile car. Uncharitable souls might conclude that Miss Jackson needs to be kissed more often.[11]

It is ironic that Glenda should come across as nannyish, for her instincts on nearly all matters of sexual and personal morality are liberal in the extreme. She has been a notable advocate of gay rights, tabling an amendment to the 1996 Housing Act, which would have given new tenancy rights to gay couples. She is a good and approachable employer. She is renowned in the Commons for spending time not just on her colleagues, but on the cleaners and the security staff. And among her friends she has none of the nanny about her at all – indeed, Sally Dobson believes that it is because Glenda is so even-handed with her attentions that some who feel that they should get more of her time get upset. One member of Blair's Policy Unit advances his own theory for Glenda's apparent dourness in Government: 'It's such a shame. Glenda brought a real sense of passion and excitement to all those films she did in the seventies, and she seems to have lost touch with that as an MP. It's as if she feels she can't really be herself, she has to be someone else. Maybe she's just frightened.'

Glenda's own explanations are quite different:

> When I became an MP some people expected me to fall flat on my face because I was a woman arriving from a profession thought to be occupied by idiots. Either that or they thought I would be a prima donna. Why anyone should have thought that, I'm in no position to know, as one of the things that was knocked out of me early on in acting was my ego. It was made clear to me that there was no place for ego whatsoever. I always eschewed media-related activities when I was involved in films. I don't have any natural affinity for it. All I did was the minimum I was contractually obliged to do when the film was released.[12]

In other words, Glenda is an extremely reluctant showhorse. When she chooses she can be immensely witty and affable, as in her recent appearance on the *Des O'Connor Show*, or her second outing on *Desert Island Discs*, and she comes across as candid and devoid of arrogance. But these appearances are rare, and far more common in recent years has been the deadly earnest Glenda who eschews such frivolity as theatrical anecdotes.

More substantial criticism of Glenda's ministerial career relates to her political originality – or lack of it. The *Guardian* reported one MP who had worked with Glenda as saying, 'People do express doubts about her capacity to originate ideas. About how brainy she is, at the end of the day,' and another has argued that 'Glenda doesn't have political ideas, she just has political concerns.' Nick Prior, a former chair of Hampstead and Highgate Labour Party, is more precise. 'Glenda's totally solid behind the Blair leadership – but she doesn't reek of modernisation because she's not prepared to take a chance. I've never known her take a chance since she was elected, and she is very dismissive of those who do take chances.' Others disagree. One special adviser says that

> Glenda has the amazing ability of getting to the nub of a problem in a matter of minutes. It's true that she doesn't come up with radical new ideas all the time, but I think what really matters to her is not flashy new ideas, but solutions that actually work. If anything she is rather suspicious of colleagues who are always parading their latest brainwave, and who never manage to get it implemented.

Few would gainsay Glenda's many strengths. Not only is she prepared to take a brief, but she also masters it well. Ron Bailey, the Friends of the Earth campaigner, who spent several months negotiating with Glenda over the Road Traffic Reduction Bill in 1998, was impressed:

> When I first met her in June [1998], all she did was repeat the mantra that Labour had an integrated transport policy. But she's been on a steep learning curve. When we started negotiations in December, she had really grasped the brief. At the moment she's just a minister, not a secretary of state. But I'm not saying she won't be in three or four years' time.[13]

It is something Kinnock, who has to deal with her regularly as the Transport Commissioner in the European Commission, has noted: 'She's very good on transport, because she's completely on top of it. She sticks to the line of the brief, but she's not afraid to add that little something.'

She also has a genuine passion for her work, and although she may think of herself as lazy, she works extraordinary hours, often remaining at the department late into the night, well after the time when the automatic energy-saving electrics switch off all the lights unless there is someone moving in the room. There have been achievements. Most notably Glenda points to success in getting an extra £365 million out of the Treasury for the London Underground. She has been central to the development of Labour's plans for an integrated transport policy, and although she confesses that the Government's successes have so far been minimal ('it will take years to redress the historic under-investment in the London Underground'), she believes that the slow but steady progress that has been made in convincing people 'that we cannot just go on as we are' is a political success in itself, 'because in London, as in the rest of the country, what is clearly essential is to start drawing all the strands of public transport together so that they are co-operating and not competing and so that we can reduce our over-dependence upon the private car'.

Overseas Glenda has also proved a significant asset. She is well-respected by her fellow European transport ministers. A 1998 trip to support Emily's List (which seeks to get more women elected) in the Australian elections found Glenda fêted everywhere, with fund-raising dinners full to capacity, and all the newspapers running full-page stories on Glenda and her feminist views. Glenda was not particularly impressed, however, when one gushing lady entranced her for minutes, waxing lyrical about her many great performances, before sighing that *The Avengers* was never as good after she left the series.

When she arrived in the House of Commons Glenda faced a tough challenge, to convince her colleagues that she was a serious politician, and although there are those who would like to see her adopt a lighter tone, she has for the most part managed the transition well. In large measure this is because of the similarities she sees between her two careers. When asked whether, in changing career, she had exchanged one form of theatre for another, she is prone to answer: 'If that's the case, the House of Commons is under-rehearsed and badly lit and the acoustic is terrible,' but her serious response is more instructive.

> The best theatre is about trying to find and tell the truth. It's not about covering up. It's not about playing games. It's not about hiding. It's not about pretending you're something you're not. It's trying to find out what it is to be a human being and why we behave towards each other the way we do. And the best politics is trying to find the truth as well.

It is the potency of this vocational understanding of politics that makes her both inspiring and unsettling as a politician.

So much so that ever since Tony Blair first declared that he intended to legislate for a directly elected Mayor of London, Glenda has been one of the front-runners. Chris Smith certainly feels that 'if we're looking for a good, attractive candidate from the centre-left then Glenda is a very good choice. She does after all have a major advantage – apart from her name – as I think the election will be won or lost on the issue of London transport and that's an issue she knows backwards.' Another cabinet member told me, 'The one thing that matters about the Mayor of London, especially the first one, is that it should be someone who, the moment they arrive in another city, the whole of that city knows that the Mayor of London is in town. There's only one candidate you'll get that from and that's Glenda.' At the time of writing Glenda is a keen and well-regarded candidate for Mayor. Every week there are rumours of a new Downing Street favourite. Tony Banks, Frank Dobson, Trevor Phillips and Glenda have all been touted as Blair's anointed. There have been rumours of a 'dream ticket' of Glenda and Phillips. The one constant has been the opinion polls. Ever since the idea of a London Mayor was first mooted Glenda has come third in all the opinion polls of Londoners, beaten only by Richard Branson, who has declared that he will not stand, and the former Leader of the GLC, Ken Livingstone, than whom the Blair leadership cannot imagine a more damaging Labour candidate. Whether Glenda eventually becomes the Labour candidate and Mayor of London is uncertain.

What is certain is that if she does stand she will do so as a politician and not as a former actress.

For it is now unlikely, although not impossible, that Glenda will act again. Before the 1997 election, while expressing the sincere hope that she would be re-elected, she confessed that if she were to lose her seat she would have to return to the theatre 'as the only thing I know how to do is act, and I would have to carry on working'. But the Conservatives are scarcely likely to overturn the Labour majority in Hampstead and Highgate at the next election, let alone in the country. Even if Glenda does not stand for Mayor of London in 2000 she will probably stand again as an MP whenever Tony Blair calls the next election, precluding any return to the stage.

As for her retirement and old age, Glenda has already stated her intentions: 'As long as I have got my health and my strength, I am going to be the most appalling old lady. I'm going to boss everyone about, make people stand up for me when I come into a room and generally capitalise on all the hypocrisy that society shows towards the old.'

Chronology
Select Bibliography
Notes
Index

Chronology

THEATRE

FIRST PERFORMANCE	TITLE	AUTHOR	THEATRE	DIRECTOR
1952				
	Mystery of Greenfingers	J. B. Priestley	YMCA Players, Hoylake	
1954				
20 March	*Nothing but the Truth*	James Montgomery	YMCA Players, Hoylake	
22 October	*To Kill a Cat*	Roland Pertwee and Harold Dearden	YMCA Players, Hoylake	
1956				
4 June	*The Caucasian Chalk Circle*	Bertolt Brecht	Vanbrugh	John Fernald
29 November	*Pygmalion*	George Bernard Shaw	St Pancras Town Hall	Ellen Pollack
1957				
28 January	*Doctor in the House*	Ted Willis	Connaught Theatre, Worthing	Melville Gillam
18 February	*Separate Tables*	Terence Rattigan	Queen's, Hornchurch	Nancy Poultney

FIRST PERFORMANCE	TITLE	AUTHOR	THEATRE	DIRECTOR
18 March	*Rum Punch*	A. P. Dearsley	Queen's, Hornchurch	Nancy Poultney
8 July	*Ring for Catty*	Patrick Cargill and Jack Beale	Queen's, Hornchurch	Nancy Poultney
5 August	*The White Sheep of the Family*	du Garde Peach and Ian Hay	Queen's, Hornchurch	Nancy Poultney
19 September	*All Kinds of Men*	Alex Samuels	Arts	Robert Mitchell
1958				
7 April	*An Inspector Calls*	J. B. Priestley	New Theatre, Crewe	Robert Mitchell
14 April	*My Three Angels*	B. & S. Spewak	New Theatre, Crewe	Robert Mitchell
28 April	*Macadam and Eve*	Roger Macdougal	New Theatre, Crewe	Robert Mitchell
5 May	*Trial and Error*	Kenneth Horne	New Theatre, Crewe	Robert Mitchell
12 May	*Book of the Month*	Basil Thomas	New Theatre, Crewe	Robert Mitchell
19 May	*Jane Eyre*		New Theatre, Crewe	Robert Mitchell
26 May	*The Glass Menagerie*	Tennessee Williams	New Theatre, Crewe	Robert Mitchell
2 June	*Burdalane*	Winifred Banister	New Theatre, Crewe	Robert Mitchell
16 June	Olde Tyme Music Hall		New Theatre, Crewe	Robert Mitchell
2 August	*A Girl Named Sadie*	Eugene Hamilton	National tour	David Kirk

FIRST PERFORMANCE	TITLE	AUTHOR	THEATRE	DIRECTOR
1961				
8 May	*Fools Rush In*	Kenneth Horne	Dundee Rep	Antony Page
22 May	*In Search of Happiness*	Victor Rozov	Dundee Rep	Antony Page
5 June	*The Durable Element*	Clifford Hanley	Dundee Rep	John Crockett
22 August	*The Kitchen*	Arnold Wesker	Royal Court	John Dexter
1962				
5 March	*The Idiot*	Jose Ruben (Dostoevsky)	Lyric, Hammersmith	John Crockett
21 May	*Come Back with Diamonds*	M. Lehmann	Lyric, Hammersmith	David Giles
24 September	*Guilty Party*		Palace Theatre, Watford	Ivan Butler
1 October	*Double Yolk*	Hugh and Margaret Williams	Palace Theatre, Watford	
1963				
19 June	*Alfie*	Bill Naughton	Mermaid, then Duchess	Donald McWhinnie
1964				
12 January	*Theatre of Cruelty*		LAMDA	Peter Brook and Charles Marowitz
April	*The Screens*	Jean Genet	Donmar Warehouse	Peter Brook
20 August	*Marat/Sade*	Peter Weiss	Aldwych	Peter Brook

FIRST PERFORMANCE	TITLE	AUTHOR	THEATRE	DIRECTOR
1 October	*The Jew of Malta*	Christopher Marlowe	Aldwych	Clifford Williams
1965				
7 April	*Love's Labour's Lost*	William Shakespeare	RST, Stratford-upon-Avon	John Barton
15 July	*Squire Puntila and His Servant Matti*	Bertolt Brecht	Aldwych	Michel Saint-Denis
19 August	*Hamlet*	William Shakespeare	RST, Stratford-upon-Avon	Peter Hall
21 October	*The Investigation*	Peter Weiss	Aldwych	Peter Brook
27 December	*Marat/Sade*	Peter Weiss	Martin Beck Theater, New York	Peter Brook
1966				
13 October	*US*		Aldwych	Peter Brook
1967				
18 April	*The Three Sisters*	Anton Chekhov	Royal Court	Bill Gaskill
16 November	*Fanghorn*	David Pinner	Fortune	Charles Marowitz
1973				
17 April	*Collaborators*	John Mortimer	Duchess	Eric Thompson
1974				
14 February	*The Maids*	Jean Genet	Greenwich	Milos Volonakis

Chronology

<table>
<tr><td>FIRST PERFORMANCE</td><td>TITLE</td><td>AUTHOR</td><td>THEATRE</td><td>DIRECTOR</td></tr>
<tr><td colspan="5">1975</td></tr>
<tr><td>27 February</td><td>Hedda Gabler</td><td>Henrik Ibsen</td><td>Richmond, world tour, Aldwych</td><td>Trevor Nunn</td></tr>
<tr><td colspan="5">1976</td></tr>
<tr><td>12 July</td><td>The White Devil</td><td>John Webster, adapted Edward Bond</td><td>Old Vic</td><td>Michael Lindsay-Hogg</td></tr>
<tr><td colspan="5">1977</td></tr>
<tr><td>23 March</td><td>Stevie</td><td>Hugh Whitemore</td><td>Vaudeville</td><td>Clifford Williams</td></tr>
<tr><td colspan="5">1978</td></tr>
<tr><td>4 October</td><td>Antony and Cleopatra</td><td>William Shakespeare</td><td>RST, Stratford-upon-Avon</td><td>Peter Brook</td></tr>
<tr><td colspan="5">1979</td></tr>
<tr><td>22 July</td><td>Antony and Cleopatra</td><td>William Shakespeare</td><td>Aldwych</td><td>Peter Brook</td></tr>
<tr><td colspan="5">1980</td></tr>
<tr><td>28 February</td><td>Rose</td><td>Andrew Davies</td><td>Duke of York's</td><td>Alan Dossor</td></tr>
<tr><td colspan="5">1981</td></tr>
<tr><td>26 March</td><td>Rose</td><td>Andrew Davies</td><td>Cort Theater, New York</td><td>Alan Dossor</td></tr>
<tr><td colspan="5">1982</td></tr>
<tr><td>28 April</td><td>Summit Conference</td><td>Robert David MacDonald</td><td>Lyric Theatre</td><td>Philip Prowse</td></tr>
<tr><td colspan="5">1983</td></tr>
<tr><td>25 August</td><td>Great and Small</td><td>Botho Strauss</td><td>provincial tour then Vaudeville</td><td>Keith Hack</td></tr>
</table>

FIRST PERFORMANCE	TITLE	AUTHOR	THEATRE	DIRECTOR
1984				
6 April	*Strange Interlude*	Eugene O'Neill	Duke of York's	Keith Hack
21 November	*Phedra*	Jean Racine trans. Robert David MacDonald	Old Vic	Philip Prowse
1985				
21 February	*Strange Interlude*	Eugene O'Neill	Nederlander Theater, New York	Keith Hack
15 October	*Phedra*	Jean Racine trans. Robert David MacDonald	Aldwych	Philip Prowse
1986				
27 February	*Across from the Garden of Allah*	Charles Wood	Comedy	Ron Daniels
8 September	*The House of Bernarda Alba*	Federico Garcia Lorca	Lyric Hammersmith	Nuria Espert
1987				
16 January	*The House of Bernarda Alba*	Federico Garcia Lorca	Globe	Nuria Espert
1988				
March	*Macbeth*	William Shakespeare	Canada and US tour	several directors
1989				
5 October	*Who's Afraid of Virginia Woolf?*	Edward Albee	Doolittle Theater, Los Angeles	Edward Albee

FIRST PERFORMANCE	TITLE	AUTHOR	THEATRE	DIRECTOR
1990				
9 January	*Scenes from an Execution*	Howard Barker	Almeida	Hugh MacDiarmid
May then 4 July	*Mother Courage*	Bertolt Brecht	Citizens, Glasgow then Mermaid	Philip Prowse
1991				
5–27 April	*Mourning Becomes Electra*	Eugene O'Neill	Citizens, Glasgow	Philip Prowse

RADIO AND TELEVISION

BROADCAST	TITLE	DETAILS
18 December 1957	*A Voice in Vision*	ITV, produced Peter Graham Scott
1962	*Dr Everyman's Hour*	ITV, produced Peter Graham Scott
12 December 1964	*Ars Longa Vita Brevis* by John Arden and Margaretta D'Arcy	BBC Third Programme, produced Charles Lefeaux
10 March 1965	*Horror of Darkness* by John Hopkins	BBC TV, The Wednesday Play, directed Alan Bridges
23 November 1965	*The Investigation* by Peter Weiss	BBC Third Programme, directed Peter Brook and David Jones
1967	*Home Movies*	Thames TV, Armchair Theatre
12 July 1967	*Which of These Two Ladies is He Married to?* by Edna O'Brien	ITV, directed Alan Clarke
18 December 1967	*The Representative of the Poem* (poetry of Emily Dickinson)	BBC Third Programme, produced Hallam Tennyson
10 April 1968	*Let's Murder Vivaldi* by David Mercer	BBC TV, The Wednesday Play, directed by Alan Bridges
27 February 1969	*Danton's Death* by Georg Buchner	BBC Third Programme, produced Martin Esslin
19 April 1970	*Howards End*	BBC1, directed Donald McWhinnie
17 February to 24 March 1971	*Elizabeth R*	BBC2, produced Roderick Graham
3 June 1971	*The Morecambe and Wise Show*	BBC1, produced John Ammonds

BROADCAST	TITLE	DETAILS
19 September 1971	*Omnibus: A Private Face in a Public Place – with Kenneth Tynan*	BBC1
25 December 1971	*The Morecambe and Wise Christmas Show*	BBC1, produced John Ammonds
25 December 1972	*The Morecambe and Wise Christmas Show*	BBC1, produced John Ammonds
25 December 1979	*The Morecambe and Wise Christmas Show*	Thames TV
25 May 1980	*The Yellow Wallpaper* by Charlotte Perkins Gilman	BBC Radio 3, produced Liane Aukin
1980	*The Muppet Show*	ATV, produced Jim Henson and Jon Stone
28 August 1981	*You Will Hear Thunder*	BBC Radio poetry reading
8 December 1981	*The Patricia Neal Story*	Thames TV, directed Anthony Harvey and Anthony Page
27 December 1982	*The Morecambe and Wise Christmas Show*	Thames TV
14 October 1984	*Scenes from an Execution* by Howard Barker	BBC Radio 4, produced Richard Wortley
24 April 1990	*Women Mean Business*	BBC Educational series
1989	*Doombeach*	Channel 4
26 December 1990	*T-Bag's Christmas Ding-Dong*	Thames TV
10 April 1991	*A Murder of Quality* by John Le Carré	Thames TV, directed Gavin Millar
20 December 1991	*The House of Bernarda Alba*	BBC2, directed Nuria Espert
22 November 1992	*The Secret Live of Arnoldo Bax*	LWT, directed Ken Russell

CHARITABLE FILMS

YEAR OF RELEASE	TITLE
1979	*Build Me a World, International Year of the Child*
1981	*Stop Polio*
1982	*Save the Children in the Sudan*
1982	*Let Poland be Poland*
1986	*Man-Made Famine*
1986	*Labour Party Election Broadcast*
1987	*Facing South, VSO in Thailand*
1988	*One Child Family and Yunnan, China in Change, Oxfam*
1990	*Death on Delivery, Campaign Against the Arms Trade*
1992	*Rise Up, Women! The Suffragette Campaign in London*

FILMS

YEAR OF RELEASE	TITLE	DIRECTOR
1963	*This Sporting Life*	Lindsay Anderson
1966	*Marat/Sade*	Peter Brook
1967	*Tell Me Lies*	Peter Brook
1968	*Negatives*	Peter Medak
1969	*Women in Love*	Ken Russell
1970	*The Music Lovers*	Ken Russell
1971	*Sunday, Bloody Sunday*	John Schlesinger
1971	*The Boyfriend*	Ken Russell
1971	*Mary, Queen of Scots*	Charles Jarrott
1972	*The Triple Echo (Soldier in Skirts)*	Michael Apted
1972	*A Touch of Class*	Melvin Frank
1973	*Bequest to the Nation (The Nelson Affair)*	James Cellan Jones
1973	*The Tempter (Il Sorriso del Grande Tentatore)*	Damiano Damiani

YEAR OF RELEASE	TITLE	DIRECTOR
1974	*The Maids*	Christopher Miles
1975	*The Romantic Englishwoman*	Joseph Losey
1975	*Hedda*	Trevor Nunn
1976	*The Incredible Sarah*	Richard Fleischer
1976	*Nasty Habits*	Michael Lindsay-Hogg
1978	*House Calls*	Howard Zieff
1978	*Stevie*	Robert Enders
1978	*The Class of Miss McMichael*	Silvio Narizzano
1979	*Lost and Found*	Melvin Frank
1979	*Health*	Robert Altman
1980	*Hopscotch*	Ronald Neame
1982	*Giro City (And Nothing but the Truth)*	Karl Francis
1982	*The Return of the Soldier*	Alan Bridges
1983	*Sakharov*	Jack Gold
1985	*Turtle Diary*	John Irvin
1986	*Beyond Therapy*	Robert Altman
1988	*Business As Usual*	Lezli-An Barret
1988	*The Strange Interlude*	Keith Hack
1988	*Salome's Last Dance*	Ken Russell
1988	*The Rainbow*	Ken Russell
1989	*King of the Wind*	Peter Duffell

AWARDS AND HONOURS

YEAR	PERFORMANCE	AWARD
1966	*Marat/Sade*	Variety Award (US), Most Promising Actress
1966	*Marat/Sade*	New York Drama Critics Circle, Best Actress

YEAR	PERFORMANCE	AWARD
1966	*Marat/Sade*	Tony Nomination, Outstanding Dramatic Actress
1970	*Women in Love*	Variety Club of Great Britain, Best Actress
1970	*Women in Love*	New York Film Critics, Best Actress
1971	*Women in Love*	Academy Award, Best Actress
1971	*Sunday, Bloody Sunday*	Variety Club of Great Britain, Best Actress
1971	*Sunday, Bloody Sunday*	New York Film Critics, Best Actress
1971	*Women in Love*	National Society of Film Critics, Best Actress
1972	*Sunday, Bloody Sunday*	Society of Film and Television Arts (UK), Best Actress
1972	*Sunday, Bloody Sunday*	Academy Award nomination, Best Actress
1972		French Film Academy, Best Actress
1972	*Elizabeth R*	Emmies for Best Actress in a series and Best Actress in a single episode (Shadow in the Sun)
1973	*A Touch of Class*	London Evening News, Best Actress
1973	*A Touch of Class*	Golden Globe nomination, Best Actress
1974	*A Touch of Class*	Academy Award, Best Actress
1975	*Hedda*	Variety Club of Great Britain, Best Actress
1976	*Hedda*	Academy Award nomination, Best Actress
1978		Commander of the British Empire (CBE)
1979	*House Calls, Stevie* and *The Class of Miss McMichael*	Variety Club of Great Britain, Best Actress
1981	*Stevie*	New York Film Critics, Best Actress
1981	*Rose*	Tony nomination for Best Actress

YEAR	PERFORMANCE	AWARD
1981	*Stevie*	National Board of Review of Motion Pictures, Best Actress
1981	*The Patricia Neal Story*	Emmy nomination, Best Actress
1981		Montreal Film Festival Award
1983		Distinguished Service to the Cinema Award, Cannes Film Festival
1984	*Strange Interlude/Phedra*	Plays and Players Best Actress Award
1984	*Strange Interlude*	Critics' Circle Best Actress Award (UK)
1985	*Strange Interlude*	Tony nomination for Best Actress
1986	*Turtle Diary*	Rio de Janeiro Film Festival, Best Actress
1988	*Macbeth*	Tony nomination for Best Actress
1988		Honorary Doctor of Letters, Exeter University

Select Bibliography

Ackland, Joss, *I Must be in There Somewhere, the Autobiography of Joss Ackland*, Hodder & Stoughton, London, 1989

Artaud, Antonin, *The Theatre and Its Double*, Calder, London, 1993

Ayers, Pat, *Women at War*, Liver Press, Birkenhead, 1988

Barnes, Julian, *Letters from London*, Picador, London, 1995

Billington, Michael, *One Night Stands*, Penguin, London, 1994

Black, Kitty, *A Theatrical Chronicle*, Methuen, London, 1984

Bogarde, Dirk, *Backcloth*, Penguin, London, 1987

Brook, Peter, *The Shifting Point*, Methuen, London, 1988

Brook, Peter, *Threads of Time*, Methuen, London, 1998

Caute, David, *Joseph Losey, a Revenge on Life*, Faber, London, 1994

Coveney, Michael, *The Citz*, Nick Hern, London, 1990

Dundy, Elaine, *Finch, Bloody Finch*, Michael Joseph, London, 1980

Falk, Quentin, *Albert Finney in Character*, Robson, London, 1992

Faulkner, Trader, *Peter Finch, a Biography*, Angus & Robertson, London, 1979

Fay, Stephen, *Power Play, the Life and Times of Peter Hall*, Hodder & Stoughton, London, 1995

Fleischer, Richard, *Just Tell Me When to Cry*, Carol and Graf, New York, 1993

Freedland, Michael, *Peter O'Toole, a Biography*, W. H. Allen, London, 1983

Goodwin, John (ed.), *Peter Hall's Diaries*, Hamish Hamilton, London, 1983

Grotowski, Jerzy, *Towards a Poor Theatre*, Methuen, London, 1969

Hunt, Albert and Reeves, Geoffrey, *Peter Brook*, CUP, Cambridge, 1995

Hunter, Allan, *Walter Matthau*, St Martin's Press, New York, 1984

McCall, Margaret, *My Drama School*, Robson, London, 1978

McCann, Graham, *Morecambe and Wise*, Fourth Estate, London, 1998

McCulloch, Agnes, *The Headland with the Birches*, Countrywise, Birkenhead, 1991

McFarlane, Brian, *An Autobiography of British Cinema*, Methuen, London, 1997

Marowitz, Charles, *Burnt Bridges*, Hodder & Stoughton, London, 1990

Marowitz, Charles, *Prospero's Staff – Acting and Directing*, Indiana University Press, Bloomington, 1986

Munn, Michael, *Trevor Howard, the Man and His Films*, Robson Books, London, 1989

Nathan, David, *Glenda Jackson*, Spellmount, Tunbridge Wells, 1984

O'Brien, Daniel, *Robert Altman, Hollywood Survivor*, Batsford, London, 1995

Palmer, James and Riley, Michael, *The Films of Joseph Losey*, CUP, Cambridge, 1993

Petrie, Duncan, *The British Cinematographer*, British Film Institute, London, 1996

Quinlan, David, *Quinlan's Illustrated Guide to Film Directors*, Batsford, London, 1983

Reed, Oliver, *Reed All About Me*, W. H. Allen, London, 1979

Roberts, Stephen, *Hoylake and Meols Past*, Phillimore, Chichester, 1992

Russell, Ken, *A British Picture*, Heinemann, London, 1989

Russell, Ken, *Fire Over England*, Hutchinson, London, 1993

Sherwin, David, *Going Mad in Hollywood*, Penguin, London, 1993

Street, Sarah, *British National Cinema*, Routledge, London, 1997

Swift, Clive, *The Performing World of the Actor*, Hamish Hamilton, London, 1991

Trewin, J. C., *Peter Brook*, Macdonald, London, 1971

Walker, Alexander, *English Heroes, British Cinema in the 70s and 80s*, Harrap, London, 1985

West, Timothy, *I'm Here, I Think. Where are You?*, Coronet, London, 1995

Wiley, Mason and Bona, Damien, *Inside Oscar*, Ballantine, New York, 1986

Williams, David (ed.), *Peter Brook, A Theatrical Casebook*, Methuen, London, 1992

Wilson, Harold, *The Labour Government 1964–70*, Weidenfeld & Nicolson, London, 1971

Woodward, Ian, *Glenda Jackson, a Study in Fire and Ice*, Weidenfeld & Nicolson, London, 1985

Notes

Chapter One

1. *Moss's Illustrated Guide to Hoylake and West Kirby*, Birkenhead, 1899, p. 44
2. Norman Ellison, *The Wirral Peninsula*, Robert Hale, London, 1955
3. *Cheshire Life*, August 1996, p. 28
4. Ibid., p. 29
5. *Independent on Sunday Magazine*, 16 February 1997
6. *Cheshire Life*, August 1996, p. 29
7. *Evening Standard*, 6 October 1995
8. Ibid.
9. *Daily Express*, 16 March 1978
10. *Sunday Telegraph*, 25 April 1982
11. *Daily Post*, 19 July 1990
12. Jean Rafferty, *Plus*, 27 September 1989
13. Ian Woodward, *Glenda Jackson, A Study in Fire and Ice*, Weidenfeld & Nicolson, London, 1971, p. 15
14. P. A. Carson and C. R. Garner, *The Silver Screens of the Wirral*, Countrywise, Birkenhead, 1989, p. 96
15. Nor was it, as Glenda herself states, *Murder at the Vicarage*, a production she was cast in but did not end up playing.
16. Ian Woodward, op. cit., p. 21

Chapter Two

1. Hugh Whitemore in Margaret McCall (ed.), *My Drama School*, Robson Books, London, 1978, p. 176
2. Memories of this production are extremely hazy. Pauline Devaney recalls quite clearly that Peter O'Toole played the narrator, and that she was desperately over-awed: 'he was so chatty and so drunk'. In fact Neville Jacobson played the part. Charles Kay has a similarly clear memory that on the first night, when Glenda was meant to follow him on stage for the very opening scene, he tripped, she fell on top of him and they brought the whole of the set down around them. As all three members of the chorus, Pauline, Josie and Glenda, maintain that they never once left the balcony, it seems it must have been another actress or another play.
3. *People*, 12 April 1970
4. Ian Woodward, op. cit., p. 26
5. Hugh Whitemore in Margaret McCall (ed.), op. cit., pp. 180–1
6. *Watford Observer*, 5 October 1962
7. *The Sunday Times*, 4 August 1963

Chapter Three

1. His attempts to transform the world had also included an impressive French Resistance record in the war that had earned him a British pension.
2. Peter Brook, 'From Zero to the Infinite', *Encore*, Nov–Dec 1960, p. 7
3. Charles Marowitz, *Encore*, Jan–Feb 1959, p. 25
4. Ibid., p. 29
5. Peter Brook, ibid., p. 11
6. Peter Brook, ibid., p. 15
7. Indeed memories are now so confused that it is even uncertain whether she auditioned just once – in front of both Marowitz and Brook – or twice – for Marowitz alone and then for them both together. Glenda's memory is of two auditions with both directors.
8. Charles Marowitz, *Burnt Bridges*, Hodder & Stoughton, London, 1990, p. 88
9. Peter Brook, letter to Charles Marowitz, ibid., p. 88
10. Peter Brook, *Threads of Time*, Methuen, London, 1998, p. 136

11. Charles Marowitz, *Burnt Bridges*, pp. 88–9
12. *Independent Magazine*, 21 January 1995
13. Albert Hunt and Geoffrey Reeves, *Peter Brook*, CUP, Cambridge, 1995, p. 71
14. Cited in Albert Hunt and Geoffrey Reeves, op. cit., 1995, p. 71
15. Peter Brook, *The Empty Space*, Penguin, London, 1972, pp. 54–5
16. Peter Brook, programme notes, reprinted in *The Shifting Point*, Methuen, London, 1987, p. 56
17. Antonin Artaud, *The Theatre and Its Double*, Calder, London, 1993, p. 79
18. Peter Brook, programme notes, op. cit., p. 60
19. Glenda Jackson in RSC profile in 1965.
20. *Observer*, 13 July 1975
21. Cited in Albert Hunt and Geoffrey Reeves, op. cit., p. 83
22. Ibid.
23. Ibid., p. 85
24. Ibid., p. 86
25. Cited in ibid., p. 94
26. Ibid., p. 89
27. Ivor Brown to Fordham Flower, 9 November 1964, Fordham Flower Papers, Shakespeare Centre Library, Stratford-upon-Avon
28. Letter to Peter Hall, 24 August 1964
29. Cited in Stephen Fay, *Power Play, The Life and Times of Peter Hall*, Hodder & Stoughton, London, 1995
30. Glenda was also shaken by a rather snide first-night comment from Elizabeth Spriggs, who was playing the Queen, and turned to Glenda just as she was about to go on stage. 'Who would have ever thought *you* would end up here?' she said.
31. *Nova*, August 1967
32. David Nathan, *Glenda Jackson*, Spellmount, Tunbridge Wells, 1984, p. 36
33. Cited in Albert Hunt and Geoffrey Reeves, op. cit., p. 91
34. Ian Woodward, op. cit., p. 91

Chapter Four

1. Harold Wilson, *The Labour Government 1964–70*, Weidenfeld & Nicolson, London, 1971, p. 23
2. Albert Hunt and Geoffrey Reeves, op. cit., p. 97
3. Cited in ibid., p. 103
4. Ibid., pp. 114–15
5. Cited in ibid., p. 110
6. *Theatre Quarterly*, no. 25, spring 1967
7. Peter Brook, *The Shifting Point*, Methuen, London, 1988, p. 63
8. Cited in David Nathan, op. cit., p. 44
9. Peter Brook, *Threads of Time*, op. cit., p. 136

Chapter Five

1. *Evening Standard*, 13 March 1967
2. Ian Woodward, op. cit., p. 62
3. Ibid.
4. *Daily Mirror*, 13 August 1970
5. Ian Woodward, op. cit., p. 67
6. In fact there are plenty of photos of Daniel in a pram at Coleraine Road, so this is another example of the Glenda Jackson apocrypha.
7. *Daily Express*, 6 December 1971
8. Ken Russell, *Fire Over England*, Hutchinson, London, 1993, p. 75
9. Barry Norman, *Daily Mail*, 2 April 1970
10. *Sunday Times*, 17 March 1971
11. *Daily Mail*, 19 September 1981
12. *Daily Express*, 4 December 1969
13. Peter Evans, *People*, 12 April 1970
14. *Guardian*, 28 November 1969
15. *Vogue*, 15 March 1972
16. *Daily Express*, 4 December 1969
17. *Time*, 26 April 1971
18. Cited in Brian McFarlane, *An Autobiography of British Cinema*, Methuen, London, 1997, p. 513
19. Trader Faulkner, *Peter Finch, a Biography*, Angus & Robertson, 1979, London, p. 250
20. David Sherwin, *Going Mad in Hollywood*, Penguin, London, 1997, p. 39
21. Trader Faulkner, op. cit., p. 251

22. Cited in Brian McFarlane, op. cit., p. 316
23. Ken Russell, op. cit., p. 93
24. Cited in Brian McFarlane, op. cit., p. 316
25. Ian Woodward, op. cit., p. 80
26. Cited in Michael Munn, *Trevor Howard, the Man and His Films*, Robson, 1989, p. 148
27. Ian Woodward, op. cit., p. 82

Chapter Six

1. Ian Woodward, op. cit., p. 83
2. Oliver Reed, *Reed All About Me*, W. H. Allen, London, 1979, p. 209
3. *Daily Mail*, 6 June 1978
4. Ian Woodward, op. cit., p. 88
5. Ibid.
6. *Time Out*, no. 335, 1976
7. *Guardian*, 22 March 1973; *The Sunday Times*, 25 March 1973
8. Cited in David Nathan, op. cit., p. 65
9. Cited in Brian McFarlane, op. cit., p. 317
10. Joss Ackland, *I Must Be in There Somewhere, the Autobiography of Joss Ackland*, Hodder & Stoughton, London, 1989, p. 179
11. Cited in David Nathan, op. cit., pp. 75–6
12. Cited in David Caute, *Joseph Losey, A Revenge on Life*, Faber & Faber, London, 1996, p. 375
13. Cited in David Caute, op. cit., pp. 232–3
14. Cited in Ian Woodward, op. cit., p. 111
15. David Caute, op. cit., p. 336
16. Cited in ibid., p. 378

Chapter Seven

1. *The Sunday Times*, 17 March 1971
2. *Daily Mail*, 17 May 1972
3. *Evening Standard*, 15 January 1972
4. Ibid.
5. Glenda's tax advisers also recommended that she buy a smart Mercedes sports car, although Pauline Devaney thinks that Glenda felt so guilty about its ostentation that she refused to care for it properly, so it was always a tip inside.
6. *Sunday Express*, 29 June 1980
7. Ian Woodward, op. cit., p. 113
8. Ibid., p. 115
9. *Films and Filming*, January 1977
10. *Observer*, 13 July 1975
11. Timothy West, *I'm Still Here I Think, Where Are You?*, Nick Hern Books, London, 1994, pp. 55–6
12. *Sunday Express*, 22 April 1979
13. Ian Woodward, op. cit., p. 124
14. *Time*, 10 April 1975
15. *Los Angeles Times*, 8 April 1975
16. *Daily Express*, 4 August 1975
17. *Daily Telegraph*, 4 August 1975
18. *Guardian*, 11 November 1976
19. Patrick Gibbs, *Daily Telegraph*, 12 November 1976
20. One rumour current after the divorce maintained that Roy had taken to wearing Glenda's clothes. 'Completely untrue', Roy told me.

Chapter Eight

1. Cited in Michael Munn, op. cit. p. 148
2. Cited in Albert Hunt and Geoffrey Reeves, op. cit., p. 224
3. Ibid., p. 233
4. Albert Hunt, *Peter Brook*, p. 230

Chapter Nine

1. Alexander Walker, *English Heroes, British Cinema in the 70s and 80s*, Harrap, London, 1985, p. 19
2. *Time Out*, 20 August 1976
3. *Evening News*, 19 January 1971
4. *Radio Times*, 1 June 1972
5. *Daily Mirror*, 17 February 1979
6. *New Standard*, 5 December 1980
7. Ian Woodward, op. cit., p. 163
8. *Evening Standard*, 2 November 1979
9. *Independent*, 2 November 1992
10. Ed. Otis L. Guernsey Jr, *Best Plays of 1980–81*, Dodd Mead and Co., New York, 1981, p. 16

11. *News of the World*, 12 December
    1976
12. Dirk Bogarde, *Backcloth*, Penguin,
    London, 1987, p. 199
13. Ibid., p. 202
14. *What's On in London*, 2 December
    1977
15. *Daily Mail*, 9 April 1984
16. *Punch*, 6 June 1984
17. Michael Coveney, *The Citz*, Nick
    Hern Books, London, 1990,
    pp. 211–12
18. *Daily Telegraph*, 22 November 1985
19. *Observer*, 14 September 1987
20. *Guardian*, 14 January 1987
21. *Evening Standard*, 16 March 1988
22. *Guardian*, 23 April 1988
23. *Guardian*, 17 March 1988
24. Charles Marowitz, *Herald Examiner*, 12
    October 1989
25. Bruce Feld, *Drama Logue*,
    12–18 October 1989
26. Dan Sullivan, *Los Angeles Times*,
    6 October 1989, pt. vi, p. 1

Chapter Ten

1. Clive Swift, *The Performing World of
   the Actor*, Hamish Hamilton, London,
   1991, p. 40
2. *Observer*, 12 December 1965
3. Peter Brook, *Threads of Time*, op. cit.,
   p. 137
4. Clive Swift, op. cit., pp. 50–1
5. *Guardian*, 2 February 1998
6. *Independent*, 8 February 1989
7. *Plus*, 27 September 1989
8. *The Times*, 8 December 1989
9. Julian Barnes, Richard Wilson, Melvyn
   Bragg, Michael Foot, Gary Kemp
   (Spandau Ballet), Gordon Sumner
   (Sting), Dominic Lawson (then editor
   of the *Spectator*), Hunter Davies, Jenny
   Abramsky, Jeanette Winterson, Sue
   Cook, Emma Thompson, Terry
   Gilliam, Lynsey de Paul, Conrad
   Black, Peggy Ashcroft, Hugh
   Manning, Juliet Stevenson, all lived
   there in 1990, and the redrawn
   boundary now gives Glenda Michael
   Palin and the prime minister's press
   secretary, Alistair Campbell, as
   constituents as well.
10. *Hampstead and Highgate Express*,
    30 March 1990
11. *Observer*, 14 January 1990
12. *Guardian*, 11 January 1990
13. *Financial Times*, 10 January 1990
14. *Daily Mail*, 10 January 1990
15. *Daily Express*, 10 January 1990
16. *Daily Mail*, 5 July 1990
17. Jean Rafferty, *Plus*, 27 September 1989
18. *Independent*, 18 September 1993
19. *Sunday Express*, 8 July 1990
20. *The Times*, 6 July 1990
21. *Guardian*, 6 July 1990
22. *Independent*, 6 July 1990
23. My own memory of the London
    production is of watching a procession
    of soldiers frog-marching across the
    back of the stage, with one of them
    constantly missing the beat. It would
    have been a supernatural feat to have
    concentrated on Glenda's downstage
    performance.
24. *The Sunday Times*, 14 April 1991
25. *The Times*, 8 April 1991
26. *Guardian*, 8 April 1991
27. *Observer*, 14 April 1991

Chapter Eleven

1. *Sun*, Tuesday 25 February 1992
2. *Daily Telegraph*, 21 May 1992
3. *Sunday Express*, 22 March 1992
4. *Hampstead and Highgate Express*,
   30 March 1990
5. Julian Barnes, *Letters from London*,
   Picador, London, 1995, p. 110
6. *Sunday Telegraph Magazine*,
   9 November 1997
7. *Evening Standard*, 19 March 1992

Chapter Twelve

1. *The Times*, 11 April 1992
2. *Independent*, 3 May 1992
3. Ibid.
4. *Independent Magazine*, 21 January 1995
5. *Guardian*, 20 June 1992
6. *Hansard*, 7 March 1996

Notes

7. *Reuters News Service*, 29 October 1992
8. *City Limits*, 13 June 1991
9. *Reuters News Service*, 14 October 1992
10. *Guardian*, 20 June 1992
11. *Daily Telegraph*, 10 December 1998
12. *New Statesman*, 22 May 1998
13. *Guardian*, 2 February 1998

Index

Abbess of Crewe, The 146
Abell, Ray 49
Abelman, Paul 56
Abrahams, Penny 195, 201
Academy Awards (Oscars) 99–100, 103, 115–16, 137–8, 142, 171, 199
Ackland, Joss 121
Across From the Garden of Allah 183
Actors' Equity *see* Equity
Afore Night Come 49, 64
Albee, Edward 186
Aldridge, Joan 13, 17–18, 20, 21, 36, 94, 95
Aldwych Theatre, London 47, 62, 64, 65, 67, 82, 85, 121, 182
Alexander, Jane 99
Alfie 43–4, 50, 54, 55, 128
Alice in Wonderland 26
All Gas and Gaiters 25, 74
All Kinds of Men 31–3, 104
All Saints Pastoral Centre, London Colney 146
Allcock, Dawn 104
Allen, Kate 196–7, 199
Allen, Mary 51, 76, 80
Almeida Theatre, Islington 187, 196, 198
Altman, Robert 167, 183
Amadeus 170
American Equity 180
American Film Theatre 123
Ammonds, John 107
Anastasia 21
ANC 193
Andrew, Prince 221
Andrews, Julie 105
Ann-Margret 173–4
Annie Get Your Gun 203
Antony and Cleopatra 108, 130, 151, 157–62, 186, 189

Any Questions 166
Apps, Barnaby 94, 130
Apps, Edwin 25, 94, 130
Apted, Michael 110–12
Arden, John 47, 66
Aristophanes 28
Armchair Theatre 29
Armstrong, Bridget 96, 104, 138
Artaud, Antonin 49, 55–6, 61, 62, 65
Arts Council 29, 46, 49, 81
Arts for Labour 166
Arts Theatre Club, Soho 31–2, 47, 49
Ashcroft, Peggy 47, 58, 81, 160, 166
Ashdown, Paddy 219
Ashton, Marcia 39, 44
Ashton, Terry 197
Aslef 199, 213, 236
Astaire, Fred 108
Asylum and Immigration Appeals Bill 234
Atkins, Coral 164
Atkins, Eileen 52
Attlee, Clement 7
Avengers, The 61, 249

Bacall, Lauren 73, 167, 234
Bailey, Ron 248
Ball, Lucille 109
Banks, Joan and Tom 20, 21, 22
Banks, Tony 250
Bannen, Ian 101
Barber, John 181
Barker, Howard 175, 187, 199
Barker, Katie 68
Barnes, Julian 219–20
Barnes, Sir Kenneth 24–5
Barrault, Jean-Louis 84–5
Barrie, George 136, 141–2
Barton, John 48, 68
Bassett, Tarn 37

277

Bassey, Shirley 108
Bates, Alan 25, 89, 124, 173, 174
Bates, H.E. 110
Bax, Arnoldo 212
BBC
  election coverage ix, 96, 214, 223,
    224
  radio 20, 166, 240
  television 29, 100, 103–4, 107, 111,
    212
Beaumont, Hugh 'Binkie' 46, 48
Beckett, Margaret 235, 237
Beckett, Samuel 47, 49, 121, 179
Beecham, Sir Thomas 213
Behan, Brendan 47
Bell, Martin 243
Bell, Tom 37
Beloved Friend 96
Benefit of the Doubt 83
Benn, Tony 166
Bennett, Arnold 191
Bennett, Jennifer 218
Bennett, Tony 113
Bequest to the Nation 116–20
Berger, Helmut 124, 125
Bergman, Ingrid 116, 138
Berliner Ensemble 48
Bernhardt, Sarah 143–4, 149, 182
Berry, Anne 144
Beyond Therapy 183
Billington, Michael 176, 182, 199–200,
  211
Billion Dollar Brain 89
Billy Liar 100
Birkenhead 1–2, 3, 7, 8, 9
Birmingham Repertory Theatre 67
Birthday Party, The 66
Black, Cilla 43
Blackboard Jungle 24
Blair, Tony x, 237, 239, 240, 244, 246,
  247, 248, 250, 251
Blalock, Julia 176
Blue Anchor pub, Hoylake 5
Blunkett, David 208, 209
Boalth, Amy 27
Bogarde, Dirk 123, 171–3, 191, 234
Bond, Edward 191
Boots the Chemist 16–17, 19, 22, 26,
  41, 198
Boston Strangler, The 143
Bowden Productions 141, 148, 184
Bowe, John 159, 160

Bowen, Catherine Drinker 96
Box Office 121
Boy Friend, The 178
Boy George 222
Bradbury, Ray 56
Bradford Civic Theatre 37
Bradford Drama School 34
Bragg, Melvyn 96
Braithwhaite, Beryl 26, 73
Brando, Marlon 24
Brandreth, Gyles 231
Branson, Richard 250
Brecht, Bertolt 48, 175, 178, 203–4
Brickman, Miriam 42
Bridges, Alan 173
Brigadoon 46
British Home Stores 38
British Rail 236, 242
Britton, Tony 119
Bromilow, Peter 37, 59, 73, 140, 155,
  178, 186, 234
Bronston, Samuel 107
Brontës, The 107
Brook, Peter 48–66, 68–71, 75–88, 89,
  92–3, 97, 121, 151, 152, 157–62,
  186, 189
Brown, Gordon 242
Brown, Ivor 65
Brown, William Cullerne 201, 215,
  217–18, 224
Brueghel, Pieter 62
Brut Productions 136, 141
Bryden, Ronald 68
Bull, Mac 199
Bullfinch 148–9, 150, 184
Buried Alive 191
Burn, Jonathan 50, 53–4, 61, 64, 72
Burnett, Carol 167, 173
Burnham, Edward 27
Burstyn, Ellen 138
Burton, Donald 67
Burton, Richard 112
Butlins 39–40
Byrne, Colin 209
Byrne, Patsy 67

Cactus Flower 73
Café Royal, London 147
Caine, Michael 43, 89, 124, 125
Caldwell, Zoe 72, 184
Cambridge Theatre, London 65, 164,
  166

Index

Camden Council x, 195, 196, 205, 217, 223, 224
Camden Education Institute 205
Camden New Journal 218
Camden Palais 223, 224
Cammel Laird 1
Canby, Vincent 149
Cannan, Denis 79
Capote, Truman 48
Carney, Art 138, 156
Carousel 46
Carter, Nell 28
Casey's Shadow 156
Castle, Barbara 208
Cathcart Street Primary School, Birkenhead 9
Caucasian Chalk Circle, The 28
Caute, David 125
Cellan Jones, James 116–18, 132
Cello, Paul 185
Chaikin, Joe 76
Chaing Lui 77
Chamberlain, Neville 7
Champions 184
Chaplin, Charlie 184
Charades 200
Charter 88 238
Cheshire County Council Education Committee 22, 25, 26
Christie, Agatha 20
Christie, Julie 123–4, 173–4
Church, Esmee 34
Churchill, Winston 7, 9, 24, 25, 226
Cieslak, Ryszard 77
Cilento, Diane 83
Cinderella 17–18
Citizens Theatre, Glasgow 175–6, 181, 187, 203–4, 210–11
Clarke, Oz 132
Class of Miss McMichael, The 156
Clift, Montgomery 24
Clinton-Davies, Lord Stanley 215
Clunes, Alec 31
Clunes, Martin 31
CNN 224
Cobbold, Lord 60, 80
Coe, Sebastian 231
Colbourne, Maurice 65
Collaborators 121–2
Colley, Ken 95, 111
Collins, Joan 30
Comédie de l'Est, Paris 48

Comedy of Errors, The 61, 66
Commonweal 71
Communism 155
Communist Youth League 155
Connaught Theatre, Worthing 30
Connolly, Cyril 56
Connor, Patrick 43, 44
Conservative Party ix–x, 7, 8, 57
    leadership 205, 221
    representation in Hampstead and Highgate 195, 199, 200, 217, 224, 229, 230
    see also general elections
Conti, Tom 183
Coppola, Francis Ford 137
Corn is Green, The 34
Coronation Street 110
Cort Theater, New York 169
Cortese, Valentina 137, 138
Cottle, Graham 110
Court Jester, The 109
Coveney, Michael 176, 181, 199, 211–12
Coward, Noël 27, 142, 175
Cox, Brian 42, 180, 181
Crawford, Joan 1, 18, 180
Crewe Chronicle 33
Crockett, John 43
Croft, Michael 166
Crosbie, Annette 103
Crouch, Peter 28–9, 30, 38, 40, 42, 89, 90, 100, 105, 119, 140, 151
Cunningham, Jack 215
Cunningham, Sir Knox 81
Curtis, Alan 33
Cushman, Robert 176, 185
Cymbeline 47

Dad's Army 43
Dahl, Roald 171–3
Dahl, Tessa 172, 173
Daily Express 12, 99, 142, 196, 200
Daily Mail 65, 96, 112, 200, 202, 209
Daily Mirror 165, 221
Daily Telegraph 69, 142, 181, 214, 246
Dalton, Timothy 143
Damiani, Damiano 122
Damned, The 124
Dance, Brian 209
Dance with a Stranger 218
D'Arcy, Margaretta 66
Dare, Richard 50–1

Index

Darlington, W.A. 69
Dave Morris' Club Night 20
Davenport, Nigel 166
Davies, Andrew 168–70
Davis, Bette 1, 18, 52, 71–2, 100, 116, 137
Davis Junior, Sammy 138
Davis, Victor 99
Days in the Trees 81
de Havilland, Olivia 116
De Jongh, Nicholas 204, 221
de la Tour, Frances 148, 149
de Manio, Jack 98
Deacon, Brian 111–12, 179
Dean, James 146
Dearden, Harold 21
Delaney, Shelagh 47
Delon, Alain 123
Dennis, Sandy 146
Des O'Connor Show 247
Desert Island Discs 247
Devaney, Pauline 25, 26, 27, 28, 29, 37, 39–40, 53, 73, 74, 94, 95, 98, 127, 130, 131, 138, 139, 152
Devils, The 100, 103
Devine, George 47, 48
Diary of a Mad Housewife 99
Dickens, Charles 238
Dickens' Women 205
Dickinson, Angie 173
Dionisotti, Paola 158, 160–1, 203
Disney, Anthea 112, 156
Dixon of Dock Green 29
Dobson, Frank 197, 199, 201, 206, 207, 209, 213, 215–16, 223, 224, 242, 250
Dobson, Sally 201, 207–10, 213, 224, 227, 234, 247
Doctor Doolittle 143
Doctor In the House 30
Doll, Aunt 6, 9
Donmar Warehouse, London 60, 66, 80
Dotrice, Roy 70
Douglas, Michael 73, 128
Douglas-Home, Sir Alec 57
Dowie, Freda 51
Downing Street Policy Unit 200
Drabinsky, Garth 184
Duchess of Malfi, The 148
Duchess Theatre, London 44, 121
Duke of York's Theatre, London 168

Dundee Repertory Theatre 42
Durable Element, The 42
Duras, Marguerite 81
Duthy Theatre, Southwark 130
Dvorak, Anne 1
Dynasty 180, 210

East of Eden 24
Eden, Sir Anthony 25
El Cid 107
Electrolux 6
Elizabeth R 97, 103–5, 107, 233
Elizabethan Theatre, Sydney 135
Elliott, Denholm 212
Ellison, Jane 14
Elwyn, Michael 113, 115
Embassy Communications 184
Emily's List 249
Emmy Awards 106, 173
Encore 48, 49
Enders, Robert 123, 141–2, 148, 149, 150, 151
Enfants du Paradis, Les 84
Enfield, Harry 216
English Stage Company 47
Entertainer, The 89
Epstein Brothers 157
Equity 166
Espert, Nuria 182
Esslin, Martin 60–1, 81
Etoile de Cristal Award 122
European Union 236, 238, 239
Evans, Edith 146, 160, 222
Evans, Peter 98
Evening News 65, 122, 169
Evening Standard 88, 115, 129, 151, 169, 179, 221
Execution of Stepan Razin, The 97
Eyre, Peter 104, 132, 135, 136, 137, 139, 141, 150, 151

Fabergé 136, 141
Fairbanks, Douglas 184
Faithfull, Marianne 83, 148
Fanghorn 83, 176
Far From the Madding Crowd 89, 101
Farmer, George 80
Farrell, Barry 171
Farrell, Glenda 1
Feld, Bruce 186–7
Fernald, John 25, 28, 30, 31, 147
Ferris, Fred 20

Index

Feuillère, Edwige 182
Field, Sally 116
Fields, Gracie 1
Financial Times 69, 176, 200, 218
Finch, Peter 101, 102, 116–18
Findlay, Deborah 182
Finlay, Frank 173
Finney, Albert 25, 89, 184
Finsberg, Sir Geoffrey 195, 200, 230
Fisher, Gerry 125
Fitzgerald, Julie 206
Flanagan, Desmond 33
Fleischer, Richard 107, 143–4
Flower, Fordham 48, 65
Folk Theatre Limited 33
Fonda, Jane 103, 116, 163
Fools Rush In 42
Formby, George 5
Forsyth, Michael 243
Fortune Theatre 83
Foster, Charlie 20, 21, 22
Foster, Jodi 116, 173
Four Weddings and a Funeral 218
Fox, Bobby 178
Fox, Edward 42
Fraenkel, Kenneth 184–5
Frank, Melvin 109, 112–14, 151, 156
Fraser, Lady Antonia 105
Fraulein Elsa 58
French Dressing 89
Friends of the Earth 248
Frigerio, Ezio 182
Frogs, The 28

Gaitskell, Hugh 56
Garland, Judy 24
Garner, James 167
Garrick Theatre, London 184
Garside, Esther and George (aunt and uncle) 3, 4, 5, 6, 9, 11, 13, 17, 36, 171
Garson, Greer 137
Gascoine, Jill 130
Gaskill, Bill 83, 148
Gasthalter, Dr ('Miss Guest') 11
general election
  (1964) 75
  (1979) 163
  (1987) 183
  (1992) ix–x, 96, 207–8, 213–26, 238
  (1997) 242–4

Genet, Jean 49–50, 60
Gibson, Carl 229
Gielgud, John 48, 84
Gillam, Melville 30
Gilliatt, Penelope 69, 101
Girl Named Sadie, A 37, 52
Givenchy 14
Glass, Peter 28
Glass Menagerie, The 33
Globe Theatre, London 182
Go-Between, The 123
Go Into Your Dance 1
Gold, Jack 183
Gold Diggers of 1935 1
Goldblum, Jeff 183
Gonner, Sir Edward 11
Good Morning America 71–2
Good Morning, Goodnight 122
Goring, Marius 166
Gorky, Maxim 49
Gould, Bryan 183, 237
Goya y Lucientes, Francisco 63
Grade, Lord 184
Graham, Roderick 104
Grainger, Gawn 42
Granada Television 20
Great and Small 178–9
Great White Hope, The 99
Greater London Authority 205
Green Party 215
Greenwich Borough Council 194
Greenwich General Hospital 214
Greenwich Theatre 122–3
Griffiths, Miss 10
Griffiths, Richard 159, 161
Grotowski, Jerzy 77–9
Grove Family, The 29
Guardian 82, 118, 176, 179, 182, 185, 211, 221, 233, 246, 248
Gulbenkian Foundation 50
Gulf War (1992) 205, 237
Gurdjieff 84
Guthrie, Janet 195, 201
Guthrie, Tyrone 34

Hack, Keith 179
Hailey, Bill 24
Hale, Georgina 176–8, 181, 210–11
Hall, Sir Peter 47, 48, 49, 50, 65, 66, 68–70, 80, 83, 132
Hamilton, Lady Emma 116–18
Hamilton, Eugene 37

Index

Hamilton, Neil 243
Hamlet 18, 56, 68–9, 70, 149
Hammer Horror 89
Hampshire, Susan 32
Hampstead and Highgate constituency ix–x, 195–203, 213–24, 226, 228–31, 236, 242–3, 251
Hampstead and Highgate Express 218
Hampstead Theatre 205
Hancock, Sheila 19
Hanley, Clifford 42
Hanna, Gillian 182
Hannibal Brooks 90
Hanson, Lord 198
Hanson Trust 209
Harding, Olive 101
Hardman, Robert 246
Hardy, Robert 104
Hare, David 148
Harrison, Sir Rex 104
Harry and the Hendersons 186
Hart to Hart 173
Harvey, Anthony 172
Harwood, John 63
Haverstock School, Camden 216
Hawthorne, Nigel 183
Hayes, Patricia 182
Hayter, Dianne 197
Hazeldine, James 169, 177, 180, 181
Head, Murray 102
Healey, Denis 194
Health 167–8
Hedda 141–2, 143
Hedda Gabler 127, 131–42, 189, 191
Hepburn, Audrey 14
Hepburn, Katharine 1, 18, 116
Hepton, Bernard 104
Herald Examiner 186
Hervey Road, Blackheath 94, 140, 144, 145, 152, 155, 170
Heyer, Georgette 123
Hibbert, Jean 15, 17, 19, 20, 73
Hill, Mrs 26
Hines, Ronald 104
Hirschhorn, Clive 203–4
Hitchcock, Laura 192
H. M. Tennent Productions Ltd 46
Hobson, Harold 43–4
Hodge, Douglas 183
Hodges, Mervyn 34, 37
Hodges, Daniel (son)
  birth and early years 94–5, 120, 121, 122, 125, 130
  closeness to Glenda 120, 130–1, 134, 156
  joins Glenda in Toronto 139–41
  parents granted joint custody 145
  father continues to look after 152, 156
  holidays with father and Glenda 154–5
  attends grandmother's funeral 171
  school and exams 181, 209
  godparents 186
  college 201, 209, 213
  becomes part of Glenda's election team 208, 213
  loses eye after attack in pub 214
  appointed researcher for Glenda 227, 240
Hodges, Roy (former husband)
  family background 34, 59
  meets Glenda 34–6
  theatrical career 34–5, 37–8, 41, 43, 93, 94, 128, 129–30
  marriage 36–7, 42, 52–3, 59, 88
  poverty 38–9, 45, 54, 93, 94
  works at Butlins 39–40, 128
  rows with Glenda 52–3, 127–9, 153
  views on Glenda's career 42, 58, 104
  in Stratford with Glenda 67
  joins Glenda in New York 71–3
  meets Bette Davis 71–2, 100
  organises Glenda's social life 74, 128
  holidays 84
  Glenda's pregnancy and birth of Dan 89, 91, 94–5
  move to Blackheath 94
  role of house-husband 95, 96, 122, 128–30
  marriage under stress 127–31, 132, 134, 139–41
  opens art gallery 130
  attends Oscar ceremony (1975) 138
  learns of Glenda's affair 139–41
  divorce 144–6
  sexuality 144–5
  studies at Warwick University 145
  accompanies Glenda on tours 145
  continues to look after Dan 152, 154–5, 156
  controversy over Dan's school 209
Hoey, Kate 209

Hoffman, Dustin 112
Hogarth, William 63
Hoggart, Simon 246
Holborn and St Pancras constituency
    197, 206, 213, 218, 223
Holborn Centre 205
Holly Lodge Community Centre,
    Camden 221
Holm, Ian 173
Holy Trinity Church of England
    Primary School, Hoylake 8, 17
Home Office 229
Hope, Bob 109, 138
Hopkins, Anthony 173
Hopscotch 168
Horne, Kenneth 42
Hostage, The 47
House Calls 154–6, 168, 214
House of Bernarda Alba, The 182, 191,
    212
House of Flowers 48
Housing Act (1996) 247
Howard, Alan 158
Howard, Melinda 184
Howard, Trevor 105, 150, 151
Howerd, Frankie 204
Hoxton Music Hall 130
Hoylake 2–9, 17, 26, 29, 45, 94, 131,
    141, 171, 201
    lifeboat 3–4, 246
Hoylake Amateur Operatic and
    Dramatic Society 20
Hoylake and West Kirby Advertiser 21
Hud 171
Hudson, Norah 10, 11
Hughes, Ted 84
Humperdinck, Engelbert 5
Hunt, Albert 64, 77–9, 161
Huntingdon Theater, Los Angeles 137
Hurd, Douglas 226
Hurt, John 184

Ibsen, Henrik 127
Idiot, The 43
Ikon Theatre Company 43
Importance of Being Ernest, The 24
Imrie, Celia 132, 136
In Caliente 1
In Search of Happiness 42
In-Stage 49
Incredible Sarah, The 96, 143–4
Independent 227

Independent Broadcasting Authority 29
Inglis, Rob 51
Inland Revenue 165
Inspector Calls, An 33, 35
Investigation, The 70
Irma La Douce 53
Isabella of Spain 107, 110
Irving, Henry 25
ITN 224
ITV 212

Jackson, Arthur 4
Jackson, Edgar 4
Jackson, Edith ('Queenie') 4
Jackson, Elizabeth ('Liz', sister) 5, 12,
    14
Jackson, Eric 4
Jackson, Gill (sister) 9, 12, 14, 22, 37,
    95, 214
Jackson, Glenda (*see also names of
    productions*)
    birth 1–2, 5
    family background 1–9, 38, 59, 73,
        95, 131
    childhood 2–8
    character xi, 6, 14–15, 19–20, 41,
        51–3, 102, 120, 122–3, 125–6,
        133–4, 152–3, 154, 155, 170, 177,
        235
    feminism 6–7, 95–6, 113–14, 163,
        174–5, 198, 235, 249
    school 8–16
    teenage years 11–15
    appearance 11, 13–14, 30–1, 40, 51,
        97–8, 152, 202, 210
    work ethic 14, 39, 45, 128–9, 143,
        147, 235
    works at Boots the Chemist 16–17,
        19, 22, 26, 41
    amateur dramatics 17–22
    awards ix, 27, 72, 99–100, 105,
        115–16, 122, 142, 169, 199, 201
    RADA ix, 21, 22–3, 24–8, 30, 41, 73,
        107, 189, 208
    taken on by agent 28–9
    begins career as professional actress
        29–33
    meets Roy Hodges 34–6
    marriage 36–7, 42, 52–3, 59, 88
    touring 37–8
    poverty 38–9, 41, 45, 54, 93, 94
    unemployment 38–41, 42

Index

Jackson, Glenda – *cont.*
in repertory theatre 30–7, 42–4
works at Butlins 39–40
illness 39–40
notices 43, 69, 82, 121, 142, 144, 150,
160, 169, 170, 174, 176, 179–80,
181, 182, 185, 186–7, 199, 204, 211
works in West End 44–5, 175
RSC experimental theatre group
48–66
rows with Roy 52–3, 127–9, 153
left-wing sympathies 57, 163–7
nudity 58, 93, 96, 153, 165
continues work with RSC 67–85, 128,
157–62
friendships 73–4, 152, 154, 177–8
pregnancy and birth of Dan 88–9, 91,
93, 94–5
desire to act in films 88
move to Blackheath 94
buys house for parents 94–5
family holidays 95
wins Oscar for *Women in Love* 99–10,
107, 138
Oscar nomination for *Sunday, Bloody
Sunday* 103
Emmy Award for *Elizabeth R* 105
artistic principles 105–6, 119–20
ability as comic actress 107–9, 156, 189
views on fame 114–15
awarded second Oscar 115–16, 126,
131
behaviour with other actors 119–20,
122–3, 124–5, 132–4, 137, 178,
188
closeness to Dan 120, 130–1, 134,
156
marriage under stress 127–31, 132,
134, 139
affair with Andy Phillips 134, 136,
138–41, 144–5
attends Oscar ceremony (1975) 137–8
nominated for third Oscar 142
divorce from Roy 144–6
celebrates 40th birthday 147
considers changing profession 147–8
sets up Bullfinch co-operative theatre
company 148–9
difficulties with Andy Phillips 152,
153–4
control of public image 152–3
views on men 154, 170–1

political views 163–82, 192–4
charity work 164, 192
views on personal morality 165, 170,
247
separates from Andy Phillips 170, 177
death of father 171, 175
views on parts for women 174–5
forms United British Artists 184
views on her greatness as actress
188–91
desire to do socially valuable work
191–2
studies for degree 192
abhorrence of Thatcherism 192–4,
237–8
approached to stand in by-elections
192, 194–5
selection as candidate for Hampstead
and Highgate constituency ix–x,
195–203
press coverage of political life 200,
209, 216–17, 218, 220, 221–2, 227,
231, 246–7
mother dies 201
attends Labour Party conference
(1990) 204
campaigns as Prospective
Parliamentary Candidate 205–10
speech at Labour Party conference
(1991) 206–9
speech to Parliamentary Lobby
Correspondents 209–10
Daniel becomes part of election team
208, 213
general election campaign (1992) ix–x,
96, 213–24
Daniel injured in attack 214
nervousness about speaking in public
220–1, 231
wins seat 224–6
constituency casework 228–9
life as new MP 226–35
vote-rigging row 229
maiden speech in Commons 229–31
views on actors-turned-politicians
231–3, 249–50
public transport issues 236, 239–40,
245–9
appointment as shadow transport
minister x, 240
seen as 'key campaigner' for Labour
240–2

campaigns in Benidorm 241–2
general election campaign (1997)
    242–4
appointment as minister x, 244–6
views on Glenda as an MP and
    minister 245–50
possible candidacy as Mayor of
    London x, 250–1
views on retirement and old age 251
Jackson, Harry 4
Jackson, Jack 4
Jackson, Jane ('Aunt Pop', step-
    grandmother) 3, 6
Jackson, Joan (mother) 1, 3, 5, 6–7, 9,
    11, 12–13, 22–3, 36, 65, 94–5, 114,
    131, 139–40, 141, 201
Jackson, Lynne (sister) 5, 6, 9, 12, 13,
    131, 139, 156, 201
Jackson, Micky (father) 1, 3, 4, 5, 6, 7,
    9, 14, 22–3, 36, 65, 94–5, 114
    death 171, 175, 201
Jackson, Tom (uncle) 4
Jackson, William ('Father', grandfather)
    3–4, 246
Jackson, William (uncle) 3–4, 6
Jacobs, Sally 62
Jagger, Mick 83
James, Viv 11, 12
Jane Eyre 35
Janni, Joe 101, 102
Jarrott, Charles 105, 132
Jenkins, Roy 209
Jennings, Miss 11
Jew of Malta, The 66
Johnson, Lyndon B. 75
Johnson, Richard 184
Jones, Freddie 61, 66
Jones, Gemma 44
Jones, Mark 79

Kallinan, Richard 72
Kanner, Alexis 51, 56
Karlin, Miriam 32, 166
Kaye, Danny 109
Keach, Stacy 157–8
Keats, John 231
Keeler, Christine 57–8
Keith, Penelope 70
Kelly, Clare 33
Kempson, Rachel 104
Kendrick, Myra 15, 18
Kennedy, Bobby 71

Kennedy, Jackie 57, 58, 72
Kennedy, John Fitzgerald 57
Kenright, Bill 204
Khrushchev, Nikita 75
Kidbrooke Comprehensive School,
    Greenwich 209
Kidd, Josie 25, 28, 30, 41
King Henry's Road, Swiss Cottage 40,
    45, 94
King Lear 61, 66
Kings Cross fire (1987) 216
Kingsley, Ben 183
Kingsway Cinema, Hoylake 18
Kinnear, Roy 25, 81
Kinnock, Glenys 197–8, 205
Kinnock, Neil ix, 183, 196, 197–8, 205,
    207, 218–19, 225, 236, 239, 248
Kirk, David 37, 38
Kissinger, Henry 146
Kitchen, The 42, 90
Klute 103
Koch, Howard W. 138
Kozintsev, Grigori 60
Kramer, Larry 89, 90, 91
Kretzmer, Herbert 142
Kroll, Dr Una 165

Labour Party 57, 164, 166
    by-elections 192, 194–5, 196
    Clause IV 205, 237
    conferences 204, 206–9, 237
    infiltration by Militant Labour 193–4
    'key campaigners' 240–2
    leadership 166, 237, 239
    public transport policy 236, 239–40,
        245–9
    reform of 236–7, 238
    selection of Glenda as prospective
        parliamentary candidate 195–203
    see also general elections
Lake Place, Hoylake 3, 4, 5, 8–9, 94
Lake Pub, Hoylake 5
Lancaster University 209, 213
Landau, Ely 123
Lane, Graham 208
Lang, Ian 243
Lapotaire, Jane 169
Lawrence, D.H. 89, 92, 93, 183
Lawson, Wilfred 32
Le Carré, John 103, 212
Lear, King 49
Lee, Jenny 65, 81

Lee Repertory Theatre 34
Legrand, Julie 182
Leigh, Vivien 30, 116
Leighton, Margaret 118, 160
L'Escargot 98
Letwin, Oliver 200, 217, 224
Levin, Bernard 65
Liberal Democrat Party 219
  see also general elections
Lighthouse Pavilion Cinema, Hoylake
  19
Linden, Jenny 90, 91, 120, 132, 136,
  147, 154
Lindsay-Hogg, Michael 146, 148–9
Lissek, Leon 51, 61, 76
Lister, Alison 208
Lithgow, John 169, 186
Little Something for the Maid, A 49
Littler, Emile 65
Littler, Prince 29, 46, 47–8, 65
Littlewood, Joan 47
Liverpool College for Girls 10
Liverpool Empire 18
Liverpool Playhouse 25
Livingstone, Ken x, 196, 210, 250
Lloyd, Robert 51, 61, 63, 76, 79, 81
Lloyd, Selwyn 7
Locke, Joseph 19
London Academy of Music and
  Dramatic Art (LAMDA) 48, 55, 56,
  57, 58
London, Mayor of x, 250–1
London School of Economics 194
London Theatre Studio 48
London Underground 236, 245, 249
Look Back in Anger 33, 47, 48
Lorca, Federico Garcia 175, 182
Lord Chamberlain *see* theatre, British:
  censorship
Los Angeles Times 142
Losey, Joseph 122–5, 132
Losey, Patricia 124
Lost and Found 151, 156–7
Love Story 99
Love's Labour's Lost 47, 48, 68
Lower Depths 49
Lucan, Lord 226
Luscombe, Jill 21
Lyric Theatre, Hammersmith 43, 176,
  182

Macbeth 184–6

McCarthyism 123, 155
McColl, Ewan 47
McCowen, Alex 151
MacDiarmid, Hugh 186, 187
MacDonald, Robert David 175–7, 181,
  182
MacDonald, Simon 222
McDowall, Roddy 138
McEnery, Peter 83
MacGraw, Ali 99
McKellen, Ian 169
McKenna, Siobhan 30
Macmillan, Harold 57
MacWhinnie, Donald 43–4
Madoc, Philip 130
Magee, Patrick 61, 72, 148
Maids, The 122–3, 141
Major, John ix, 205, 208, 210, 213, 214,
  223, 230, 242–4
Malcolm, Derek 118
Mandela Theatre, Camden 205
Mandelson, Peter 183
Manning, Hugh 166, 199
Man's Fate 101
Marat/Sade 60–6, 70–2, 75, 83, 90,
  104, 128, 134, 212
Margolyes, Miriam 148, 205
Marlow, Joyce 43, 69, 128, 134, 188,
  195
Marlowe, Christopher 18, 66
Marlowe Society 48
Marowitz, Charles 48–58, 61, 62, 83,
  85–6, 98, 116, 119, 153, 186, 191,
  234
Martin Beck Theater, New York 70
Mary, Queen of Scots 105, 150
M*A*S*H 167
Matthau, Walter 99, 138, 151, 154–6,
  168, 172, 191, 234
Measure for Measure 48
Medak, Peter 83
Merchant of Venice, The 24
Merchant, Vivian 30, 122, 124
Mercouri, Melina 146
Mermaid Theatre, London 44, 204
Merman, Ethel 203
MGM 101
Michael Parkinson Show, The 236
Michell, Keith 103
Middleton, Robert 109
Middleton, Thomas 49
Midnight Cowboy 73, 100–1

Midsummer Night's Dream, A 18, 121
Miles, Bernard 44
Miles, Christopher 123
Miles, Sarah 99
Militant Labour 193–4
Millbank 225
Millennium Dome, Greenwich 246
Mills, Barbara 215
Mills, John 99, 215
Milukova, Nina 96
Minnelli, Liza 138
Mishkin, Alan 33
Mitchell, Ann 176
Mitchell, Joni 135
Mitchell, Robert 33, 34, 36
Molyneaux, John 8
Monitor 89, 90
Montez, Maria 19
Montgomery, James 21
Moreau, Jeanne 40, 86, 151
Morecambe, Eric 107–9, 116
Morecambe and Wise Show, The ix,
     107–9, 189
Morell, André 166
Morgan, Fidelis 132, 136, 144–5
Morley, Sheridan 180
Morrison, Norman 79
Mortimer, John 121
Mother Courage 178, 187, 203–4,
     210–11
Mourning Becomes Electra 210–12
Mower, Patrick 44
Muir, Jean 14, 114, 202
Muppets, The 189
Murder at Gleneagles 20
Murder of Quality, A 212
Murphy, Gerald 203
Music Lovers, The 94, 96–9, 102, 111,
     128, 246
My Three Angels 36
Mystery of Greenfingers 20
Mystery of the Wax Museum, The 1

Nabokov, Vladimir 101
Narizzano, Silvio 156
Nasty Habits 146
National Abortion Campaign (NAC)
     164, 166
National Association of Voluntary
     Hostels 164
National Health Service (NHS) 163,
     164, 203

National Theatre 61, 175
National Youth Theatre 205
Naughton, Bill 43–4
Neagle, Anna 1, 193
Neal Patricia 171–3, 188–9
Nederlander Theater, New York 180
Negatives 83, 84
Nelson, Admiral Horatio 116–17
Nettleton, John 32, 33, 66, 70, 104
Neville, John 43–4
New Labour *see* Labour Party
New Scientist 201
New Statesman 68, 176, 179
New Theatre, Crewe 33–6
New York Daily News 99
New York Film Critics' Award 143
New York Times, The 81, 149
New Yorker 220
Newell, Mike 218
Newman, Paul 171
News of the World 170
Newsweek 169
Newton, Tony 243
Nicholson, Pat 6
Nightingale, Benedict 176, 204, 211
Nineteen Eighty-Four 227
Norman, Barry 96
Norris, Jason 214
Not I 121
Nothing but the Truth 21
Nova 70
Novak, Kim 30
Now Voyager 52
Nunn, Trevor 85, 132–6, 141–2, 162
Nureyev, Rudolf 149

Oakie, Jack 234
Observer 69, 101, 176, 182, 211
O'Connor, Des 108, 247
Odéon, l', Paris 85
Oedipus 84
Oh, What a Lovely War! 47
Old Vic Theatre, London 43, 48, 61,
     84, 148–9, 181, 182
Oldman, Gary 176, 178
Olivier, Laurence, Lord 27, 48, 67, 89
On Stage 130
O'Neill, Eugene 175, 179, 188, 210–12
Open Space, The 55
Open University 192
Open Theater 84
Oresteia, The 210

Osborne, John 47, 101
Oscars *see* Academy Awards
Othello 67
O'Toole, Peter 25
Owen, Armitage 33
Owen, Warren 20, 21
Owl and the Pussycat, The 112
Oxfam 164, 192

Page, Anthony 42, 172
Palace Theatre, Manchester 179
Palace Theatre, Watford 43, 44, 51
Palestine Liberation Organisation
    (PLO) 163
Palmer, Sarah 198, 199
Panama, Norman 109
Papp, Joseph 149
Parish, Jim 207
Parker, Dorothy 51
Parkinson, Michael 14
Parris, Matthew 246
Pat and Roald 171–2
Patricia Neal Story, The 171–3
Patten, Chris 223
Pearce, May (Mabel) and James
    (grandparents) 1, 2, 6
Pennington, Michael 67
Penny, Barbara 132, 136
People 98
Perry, Jimmy and Gilda 43
*Persecution and Assassination of Marat as
    performed by the Inmates of the
    Asylum of Charenton under the
    Direction of the Marquis de Sade see
    Marat/Sade, The*
Pertwee, Roland 21
Peter, John 211
Petherbridge, Edward 180, 181
Phedra 177, 181–2, 191, 200
Phillips, Andy 134, 136, 138–41, 144–5,
    148, 150, 152, 154–5, 156, 170, 177
Phillips, Robin 184
Phillips, Trevor 250
Phoenix, Pat 110
Piaf 169
Pickford, Mary 184
Pinner, David 83
Pinter, Harold 65, 66, 124
Platonov or Wild Honey 104
Plowright, Joan 182
Plummer, Christopher 184–5
Polanski, Roman 100

Pope, Miss 11
Portillo, Michael 243
Potter, Diana 27
Pound, Ezra 62
Powell, Miss 11
Prescott, John 237, 239–40, 241–2
Previn, André 108
Priestley, J.B. 20
Prior, Nick 201, 248
Prix Italia Award 199
Profumo, John 57–8
Prowse, Philip 176, 178, 181, 182, 186,
    203, 210
Pryce, Jonathan 148, 157, 158
'Public Bath, The' 57–8
Punch 180
Pygmalion ix, 28, 32

Quare Fellow, The 47
Quayle, Anthony 117
Queen's Theatre, Hornchurch 31
Quirke, Pauline 174

Racine, Jean 175, 177, 181–2
Rafferty, Jean 202
Rag Trade, The 32
Railtrack 236, 237
Rainbow, The 183
Rainer, Luise 116
Rainmaker, The 32
Ralph, Simon 111
Rankin, Jean 15, 73
Ratcliffe, Michael 182
Rattigan, Terence 31, 116–18
Readers' Digest 143, 144
Rebel Without a Cause 24
Redgrave, Vanessa 100, 103, 105, 160,
    163, 166
Reed, Oliver 89–93, 110–12, 156
Relph, Simon 174
Representation of the People Act 229
Requiem for a Heavyweight 169
Return of the Soldier, The 173–4, 191
Revenger's Tragedy 132
Revill, Clive 61, 66
Rhys, Jean 122
Rich, Frank 169
Richardson, Ian 61, 70
Richardson, Sir Ralph 31, 89
Richardson, Tony 47
Rickman, Alan 159
Rifkind, Malcolm 243

Index

Rigg, Diana 61, 181, 184
Rippon, Angela 108
Riverside Theatre 150
Road Traffic Reduction Bill (1998) 248
Robbe-Grillet, Alain 56
Robinson, Ann 210
Robinson, Bill 151
Robinson, John, Bishop of Woolwich 82
Robinson, Maureen 197, 199
Rocky Horror Show, The 104
Rogers, Ginger 108, 109
Romantic Englishwoman, The 122–5
Romeo and Juliet 54, 78, 130
Root, Amanda 182
Rose 168–71, 172, 173, 184
Rose, Clifford 61, 63, 67, 71, 76, 77, 79, 104
Rosen, Marty 90, 91
Roundhouse, London 85, 88
Royal Academy of Dramatic Art (RADA) ix, 21, 22–3, 24–8, 30, 41, 73, 107, 189, 208
Royal Alexandra Theatre, Toronto 139
Royal Court Theatre, London 42, 47, 83, 121, 134, 148
Royal Festival Hall 243
Royal Free Hospital 203, 207
Royal Liverpool Golf Course 2, 5
Royal National Lifeboat Institution (RNLI) 3–4, 246
Royal Shakespeare Company (RSC) 32, 38, 65–74, 80, 81, 83, 97, 101, 121, 128, 132, 141, 157–62, 175, 178, 203
  experimental theatre group 48–65, 75–85, 119
Royal Shakespeare Theatre, Stratford-upon-Avon 159 *see also* Royal Shakespeare Company
Rozov, Victor 42
Rudkin, David 49
Russell, Ken 89–94, 96–7, 99–100, 102, 103, 112, 173, 183, 186, 212
Ryan's Daughter 99

Sachs, Leonard 104
Sade, Marquis de 60–6
St Clement, Pam 132, 136
St Dunstan's College, Catford 209
Saint Joan 30, 130
St Martin's Theatre, London 32
St Pancras Town Hall ix, 223–4

St Thomas' Hospital, Lewisham 94
Saint-Denis, Michel 48, 55
Sakharov 183
Salad Days 42
Salome 183
Salome's Last Dance 183
Salzmann, Madame de 84
Samuels, Alex 31
Sapphire, sinking of 245–6
Scales, Prunella 42
Scargill, Arthur 193
Scenes from an Execution 198, 199
Schlesinger, John 73, 89, 100–3, 130, 234
Schneider, Bert 138
Schubert Theater, New York 151
Scofield, Paul 49, 81, 101, 113
Scottish National Party (SNP) 163
Scottish Television 42
Screens, The (Paravents, Les) 49, 56, 60, 62
Seeley, Tim 27
Segal, George 71, 108, 109, 112–15, 137, 151, 156–7, 166, 169, 178, 198, 234
Semi-Monde 175
Seneca 84
Separate Tables 31
Serjeant Musgrave's Dance 47
Servant, The 123
Seynor, John 201
Shakespeare Festival, Stratford, Ontario 184
Shakespeare Memorial Theatre, Stratford-upon-Avon 27, 47, 48 *see also* Royal Shakespeare Theatre
Sharples, Ena 110
Shaw, George Bernard ix, 28, 130
Shaw, Sandie 130
Sheed, Wilfred 71
Shelter 164
Shepherd, Jack 65, 83, 148, 190
Sherwin, David 101, 102
Sheybal, Vladek 92
Short, Clare 221, 240
Shorter, Eric 142
Shostakovich, Dmitry 97
Shulman, Milton 179
Silvers, Phil 109
Simpson, Alan 233
Sims, Joan 27
Sinatra, Frank 138

Sinden, Donald 68
Sister Act 146
Six Wives of Henry VIII, The 103
Slater, Daphne 104
Slocombe, Dougie 97, 98, 141
Smith, Andrew 240
Smith, Chris 232, 250
Smith, John 207, 217, 219, 225, 237
Smith, Maggie 184
Smith, Nick 197
Smith, Shirley 15, 73
Smith, Stevie 150–1
Smith, Tim 243
Snodgrass, Carrie 99
Society for the Protection of the
    Unborn Child 164
Society of Authors' Sony Award 199
Spark, Muriel 146
Sparks, Betty 15, 73
Spectator 81
Spriggs, Elizabeth 30–1, 40, 41, 61, 69,
    188
Spurling, Hilary 81
Spurt of Blood 56
Staircase, The 81
Stanton, Barry 76, 77, 79, 84, 85, 87,
    179, 188, 190
Stanwyck, Barbara 1
Steinem, Gloria 96
Stephen, Shirley 245
Stephens, Robert 37
Stevenson, Juliet 147, 157–61
Stevie 105, 142–3, 150–1
Stewart, James 137
Stewart, Patrick 131–2, 133, 135–6,
    141, 142, 157, 158, 161, 162
Stone, Margery 9, 10, 15, 16, 73
Stoppard, Tom 123, 124
Strange Interlude 177–8, 179–81, 182,
    189, 191, 200
Strauss, Botho 175, 178
Strauss, Helen 143
Streetcar Named Desire, A 42
Strehler 182
Streisand, Barbra 112
Subject Was Roses, The 171
Suchet, David 157
Sullivan, Dan 187
Summer of the Seventeenth Doll, The 34
Summit Conference 175–7, 178, 181
Sunday, Bloody Sunday 100–3, 117, 125
Sunday Express 216

Sunday Night Theatre 29
Sunday Telegraph 14, 120, 240
Sunday Times, The 43, 211
Suzman, Janet 66, 67, 68, 69
Sweeney Todd 191
Swift, Clive 190

Tamburlaine the Great 18
Tandy, Jessica 169
Taste of Honey, A 47
Taylor, Elizabeth 112, 116, 117, 200
Taylor, Paul 204
Taylor, Steve 197, 198
Tchaikovsky, Piotr Ilyich 94, 96–7
Tell me Lies 83
Tempest, The 84, 85, 157
Tempter, The 122
Terence Higgins Trust 205
Thames Polytechnic 192
Thatcher, Margaret 163, 166, 183,
    192–4, 200, 205, 221, 237–8
theatre, British
    censorship 47, 49, 58, 60, 64–5, 80
    experimental 48–65, 75–86, 119
    impresarios 46
    sixties 'new' 46–50
    West End 44–6, 86, 175
Théâtre des Nations 84
Theatre of Cruelty, The 55–9, 57, 61, 62,
    76, 87, 189
Theatre Quarterly 82
Theatre Royal, Stratford East 47
Theatre Workshop 47
Thomas, Michael 111
Three Sisters, The 83, 148
Thwarting of Baron Bollingrew, The
    81
Time 99, 142
Times, The 82, 160, 194, 211, 246
Tinker, Jack 179, 180
Titanic 68
Titus Andronicus 48
To Kill a Cat 21
Today 240, 246
Tony Awards 72, 169
Tora! Tora! Tora! 143
Touch of Class, A 109–10, 112–16, 122,
    126, 131, 151, 156, 189
Townsend, Deborah 201, 216
Townsley, Colin 216
Toy Libraries Association 164
Trades Union Council (TUC) 166

Tree, Sir Herbert Beerbohm 24, 25
Triple Echo, The 110–12, 126, 174, 191
Trog 217
Trollope and Colls 34
Tudor Cinema, West Kirby 19
Turner, Clifford 28
Turtle Diary 183, 184
Tutin, Dorothy 103
Twenty Thousand Leagues Under the Sea
    143
Tynan, Kenneth 61, 81–2, 189, 190,
    222

UNICEF 164
Union of Jewish Students 221
United Artists 101, 184
United British Artists 184
United Nations Organisation 193
Unity Theatre, Glasgow 33, 34, 47
Universal Pictures 155
Upstairs, Downstairs 143
US 75–84

Vaccaro, Brenda 73, 101, 128, 129,
    138–9, 149, 153, 154, 155, 186, 234
Van Dyke, Dick 191
Vanbrugh, Dame Irene 24
Vanbrugh, Violet 25
Vanbrugh Theatre 25, 28
Variety 72, 99
Vaudeville Theatre, London 150, 178
Venice Film Festival 103
Vietnam War (1954–75) 75–82, 84
Villiers, James 148
Visconti, Luchino 124
Vogue 98
Voight, Jon 101
Voluntary Services Overseas (VSO) 192
Volvo 84
von Meck, Barbara 96

Wagner, Robert 173
Waiting for Godot 47
Waldegrave, William 243
Walker, Alexander 118, 163
Walker, Tim 202, 215, 222
Wall Street Journal 216
Wallis, Hal B. 99, 105, 116, 118
Walton, Tony 185
Wanamaker, Sam 32
War of the Roses, The 68
Wardle, Irving 82, 160

Warner, David 68–9
Washbourne, Mona 150
Watford, Gwen 31
Wax, Ruby 157
Weatherby, W.J. 185
Webster, John 148
Weigel, Helen 203
Weiss, Peter 60, 66, 70, 71
Weldon, Duncan 178, 179
Weldon, Huw 89
Welles, Orson 146
Welsh, Anna 33, 34–5, 37, 38, 41, 73
We're in the Money 1
Wesker, Arnold 42, 90
West Kirby 7, 8, 16, 19, 95
West Kirby Grammar School for Girls
    10–12, 15–16, 18, 26
West, Rebecca 173
West, Timothy 53, 61, 64, 65, 66, 69,
    87, 132, 133, 135, 136, 137, 139,
    152, 153, 154
Whately, Kevin 174
*Which of These Two Ladies is He Married
    To?* 178
Whistle Down the Wind 89
White Devil, The 148–9, 152
White Sheep of the Family, The 31
Whitemore, Hugh 28, 41, 149–50, 151
Whittaker, Ben 195, 216
Who's Afraid of Virginia Woolf? 112,
    178, 186–7, 188, 189, 191, 192,
    196, 201
Wicks, Laura 'Dinkie' 17, 20
Wild One, The 24
Wilde, Oscar 183
Wilder, Billy 113
Wilding, Michael 193
Williams, Clifford 32, 61, 66, 67, 150,
    151, 159
Williams, Esther 19
Williams, Kenneth 30
Williams, Michael 61, 76, 79, 104
Williams, Simon 163
Williamson, Nicol 42
Williamson, Susan 51, 61
Wilson, Eric 5
Wilson, Harold 57, 65, 71, 75
Wilson, James Cameron 175
Winner, Michael 89, 90
Winter's Tale, The 28
Wirral, The 7, 10, 20, 21, 73, 117
Wise, Ernie 107–9, 116

Wolfit, Donald 18
Women Beware Women 49
Women in Love 89–93, 99–100, 102, 112, 113, 120, 128, 132, 138, 183, 191
Women in Skirts 112
Women's Playhouse Project 184
Women's Rights Campaign 165
Wood, John 121
Wood, Natalie 173
Woodward, Edward 203
Woodward, Ian 21, 110
Woolf, Henry 61, 64, 77–9
Woolworth 31

World War II (1939–1945) 6–9, 168
Worth, Irene 84
Wrede, David 224
Wynne, Norman 44

YMCA Players, Hoylake 17, 20–1, 36, 188
York, Susannah 122
Young, B.A. 69

Zieff, Howard 151, 154, 155

10 Rillington Place 143